A PEDESTRIAN'S RECENT HISTORY OF DALLAS

A Pedestrian's Recent History of Dallas

Zac Crain

La Reunion
DALLAS, TEXAS

La Reunion

La Reunion Publishing, an imprint of Deep Vellum
3000 Commerce St., Dallas,Texas 75226
deepvellum.org · @deepvellum

Deep Vellum is a 501c3 nonprofit literary arts organization
founded in 2013 with the mission to bring
the world into conversation through literature.

FIRST EDITION, 2020

ISBN: 978-1-64605-006-2 (hardcover) | 978-1-64605-009-3 (ebook)

LIBRARY OF CONGRESS CONTROL NUMBER: 2020932580

Distributed by Consortium Book Sales & Distribution
Cover design by KGT
Interior layout by Kirby Gann

PRINTED IN THE UNITED STATES OF AMERICA

for Stefania

On sunny days like this one, a temporary, steeper escalator of daylight, formed by intersections of the lobby's towering volumes of marble and glass, met the real escalators just above their middle point, spreading into a needly area of shine where it fell against their brushed-steel side-panels, and adding long glossy highlights to each of the black rubber handrails which wavered slightly as the handrails slid on their tracks, like the radians of black luster that ride on the undulating outer edge of an LP.

—The Mezzanine, *Nicholson Baker*

When facing a writing deadline, I usually opt for a walk instead. That invariable delay usually takes me to a wooded area outside of the city, following a crude path in solitude. Hopefully, at some point during the process, I'm thought-riffing and making some loose connections tauter so as to be assumed worthy of actually scribbling them down later.

Given that diversion, I don't attempt to write at my day job and I almost never walk in the city on purpose, especially in a freedom-seeking manner. Nearby in the 'burbs—where we all grew up—walking as an adult is commonly seen as visual warning alarm: homeless, flat tire, tourist, mental illness, pay phone, danger! However, downtown is a fair-to-medium buffer zone for perambulating about in a large metropolitan city like Dallas, Texas.

A middle-aged man is employed as a writer for the city's name-checked magazine. He writes in a building downtown (with the titular "D" hung on its façade) and not-so-quietly obsesses over our recently retired sports franchise savior. He leaves his medium-sized screen at his desk for the blurry edges of the sidewalks in the lightly folded grid of the city, looking for quietly revealed details while using the timely constraint of his lunch break as a stopwatch.

•

The city consists of architecture, weather, light, signage, occasional flora, and debris while its inhabitants pivot their day from one location to another as schedules require. An expanded routine is tantamount to winning; small screen in hand while waiting for the light to change.

Zac Crain put down his phone in order to see. Every day at lunch (weather permitting) he walked as far as he could amid the civic expanse, seeking out details of a slowly revealed conversation between its environs: rhythm, reflection, contrast, repetition, color, repeat. Once the moment of recognition occurs, Crain pulls out his phone to document such an occasion.

Our magazine writer didn't set out to take these photographs initially, but after a while of establishing his self-imposed ritual of discovery, some visual evidence was required to perhaps convince him of what he'd found—and maybe others—or at least document his thorough mapping. As with most fleeting newness issued these days, awareness was spread via social media.

Crain employs a deft but quizzical touch to these excised details of what could be a commercial photographer's weekend test shots. Slightly off-kilter views with a squared-up frame, marrying the mundane with the patience of one anxiously awaiting the lifting of the veil. Crain's daily forays break up his workaday hours, charting a Beckettian course over many months from his initial elevator ride down and through his building's lobby, stretching into the retracing of steps, dialoguing with past conversations or expanding into uncharted newness altogether.

With about four years of psychographic drifting under his belt, this pedestrian's recent history continues on, both as a daily practice and as an expansive documentation on Instagram. Much like the narrators of Nicholson Baker's *The Mezzanine*, he ventures quietly into the everyday, noticing all that slowly reveals itself: the changes in light, the subtleties that only come with repeated viewings and an eye attuned to understanding a city's downtown and all of the angles and juxtapositions that usually go unnoticed by the steady stream of his lunch-faring companions.

Brandon Kennedy

A Pedestrian's Recent History of Dallas

I think I figured out how to take pretty good photos mostly because I didn't set out to take photos, good or otherwise. The point of what I was doing wasn't clear at first, but it in time it revealed itself. And it wasn't photographing things but merely looking at them. Trying to see them, really see them, often for the first time. Eventually I began trying to reproduce what I saw. I made mistakes. Early on, I used Instagram filters and frames, not confident in what I had, trying to force a good photo. But it already was. I learned, not easily, that I didn't have to do much other than keep my eyes open. It really is all about showing up.

That is how this began.

I started walking around downtown Dallas, usually at lunchtime, one day in January 2016. Despite the timing, it wasn't part of a New Year's resolution. I honestly don't remember exactly why I started going for walks, but I do know it wasn't that.

To completely rule out any sort of "fresh start" narrative, I am almost certain that the first one didn't even happen at the beginning of a week. Just one day, maybe it was a Tuesday, instead of going down the block for my usual dumb lunch, which wasn't healthy or satisfying or even strictly speaking a real lunch, I took a walk. Like any number of things that I've done—like most things that I've done, actually—it started on a whim and kept going on its own momentum.

I don't remember those early walks very well, because they weren't the point yet. I needed a break from the office, and I decided to walk instead of sit on a bench, staring into the middle distance, lost in non-thought. So, yes, OK, I was walking, but I wasn't going anywhere. I was meandering, wandering in lazy concentric circles around the building where I work, at the corner of Ross and St. Paul, retracing steps I'd taken probably 200 times since my job moved downtown—outside, in real life, but essentially on a treadmill. I was probably staring at my phone, because I hadn't realized there was anything else to see yet, because I thought I had already seen it all, because I'd lived in Dallas since college and I'd worked in and around downtown for most of that time. What else was there to see?

Only everything.

Soon enough, I got bored and curious. I escaped the shadow of my office and began exploring. My phone stayed in my back pocket, only coming out when I wanted to take a photo. Which began happening more and more.

Three years later, I've seen every building from every angle. I know why it persistently smells like cookies near City Hall. I've watched graffiti appear and seen it be whitewashed out of existence and then seen that be used as another canvas, sometimes by the same artist. I recognize photos on Instagram by a crack in the sidewalk. I can make a topographic map of the central business district from memory.

What I mean is: I know the core of my city intimately, am well familiar with each flaw and idiosyncrasy and unappreciated flourish, the endearing mistakes and overlooked beauty, the parts that make it Dallas and not anywhere else.

•

As I started walking more and more, I came to understand that most places—all places—were much closer than I thought. Freed from one-way signs and every other restriction one traffic engineer or another had placed on me, I found I could get from anywhere to anywhere else in about 20 minutes. If I wanted to. I didn't always want to: the more I walked, the less I felt like hurrying. And, again, there wasn't much need. Everything, I swear to you, is so much closer than you realize.

But what struck me the most was just how far away everything is when you're inside a car. Not destinations, OK, but everything else in between.

Here is what I can tell you: when you drive anywhere, a few inches of steel and glass and a few feet of concrete might be all that separates you from a door or window or an alley or a sign or a man or woman or cat, but it might as well be on the other side of a river, be buried underground, be hidden behind a mountain, never have existed to begin with.

You pass so much without seeing even a glimpse—not a single frame, a flash, nothing. In a car, especially if you're a passenger, you engage when you want to, or when you are forced to, and even if you think you're vigilant and observant, you'd be stunned at what you don't notice on a five-minute drive. The difference between what you see in a car and what is actually there would make you feel dumb if it was pointed out to you.

Here is what I can tell you: you don't know what you're missing and you don't know that you don't know.

•

After I had walked every block of downtown Dallas, and all of the alleys and cut-throughs and parking garages and tunnels and sky bridges and everywhere else my feet could take me, I told a friend of mine that I had nothing else left to shoot. He gave me—accidentally, I'm almost positive—perfect advice. "Just go shoot it all again," he said, and so I did. And what I realized is that I still wasn't seeing because I still wasn't looking. You can't ever stop looking if you want to see. Nothing is ever the same. Maybe you stumbled onto the ideal composition. OK. But the sun has yet to shine in the exact same way on the exact same thing. I doubt it ever will. If it does, then maybe OK yes you can finally stop.

Now I'm walking.

I'm writing this on my phone. I used this phone—three of them, actually, but you know—for the rest, so why not the words? I'm walking around, revisiting some of my favorite places, trying to remember why I started doing this. Or how.

I never visited a place the first time solely to take a photo. But there are a few places I go back to, every few weeks or months. Now I'm at one—the triple underpass made famous by *JFK*. Above it there is a narrow pedestrian bridge that leads to a locked gate. I like to go halfway across and look at the city from there, the Old Red Courthouse dead center, the Bank of America tower looming over its stooped shoulders. I have probably come here the most of any other location, forming a sort of time-lapse image in my mind as the seasons and sun and shadows change.

Now I'm walking.

Now I'm at I.M. Pei's upside-down-cake City Hall building. Taking a good photo of something designed by a legendary architect is not exactly difficult. And yet. I didn't take my best photo of it—since revisited many times—for months, long after I'd taken lots of others. I think, again, I was trying to force it.

Then one day I stumbled upon the exact right scene. I don't remember the first photo I took while walking around downtown Dallas, the first one I took with intention, the first one I meant to be *something*, even if I wasn't sure what that something was. But I do remember the first photo I took that I actually thought was good and it was this one. I was walking past City Hall, on my way back to my office, and I glanced over and there it was: a pair of city workers on break, tiny and almost unnoticed as they sat on the edge of a planter, dwarfed by the audacity of Pei's design and framed by a cutout in the foreground. A tiny bit of sky peeked in from one corner, reflected by the windows. The rest of it, most of it: angles and shadows everywhere, the colors natural but sort of out of place, belonging to a canyon instead of a municipal building. I didn't really have to do anything other than lift my camera. The whole process took maybe 30 seconds. It was there, waiting, for me or someone to see.

Now I'm walking again.

All the way around the east side of downtown and up to where I've taken the image I associate the most with all of this. I could take it every week and still love it and still think I could do it better, that I will do it better, that everything will come together at some point and it will be perfect.

There is a sculpture—I won't tell you exactly where; go find it—and it is fine enough as a piece of public art. It's a bit like a mini downtown on the edge of the actual downtown, a cluster of small towers. But there is a trick to this sculpture, and I don't know if it was intended and I don't know if I want to know, feeling maybe better that I discovered it. You have to go into it, stand surrounded by it, and look up. Together with the building it stands sentry in front of, the crown of the sculpture creates this beautiful shape and, if the sun is out, on the right day, at the right time, a full spectrum of blues, like a Sherwin Williams display in the wild.

As good as I've gotten at capturing this image, as many times as I've taken it, it still doesn't completely match what I see when I look up.

So I'll keep trying. Keep walking. Keep looking.

Zac Crain
Dallas, 2020

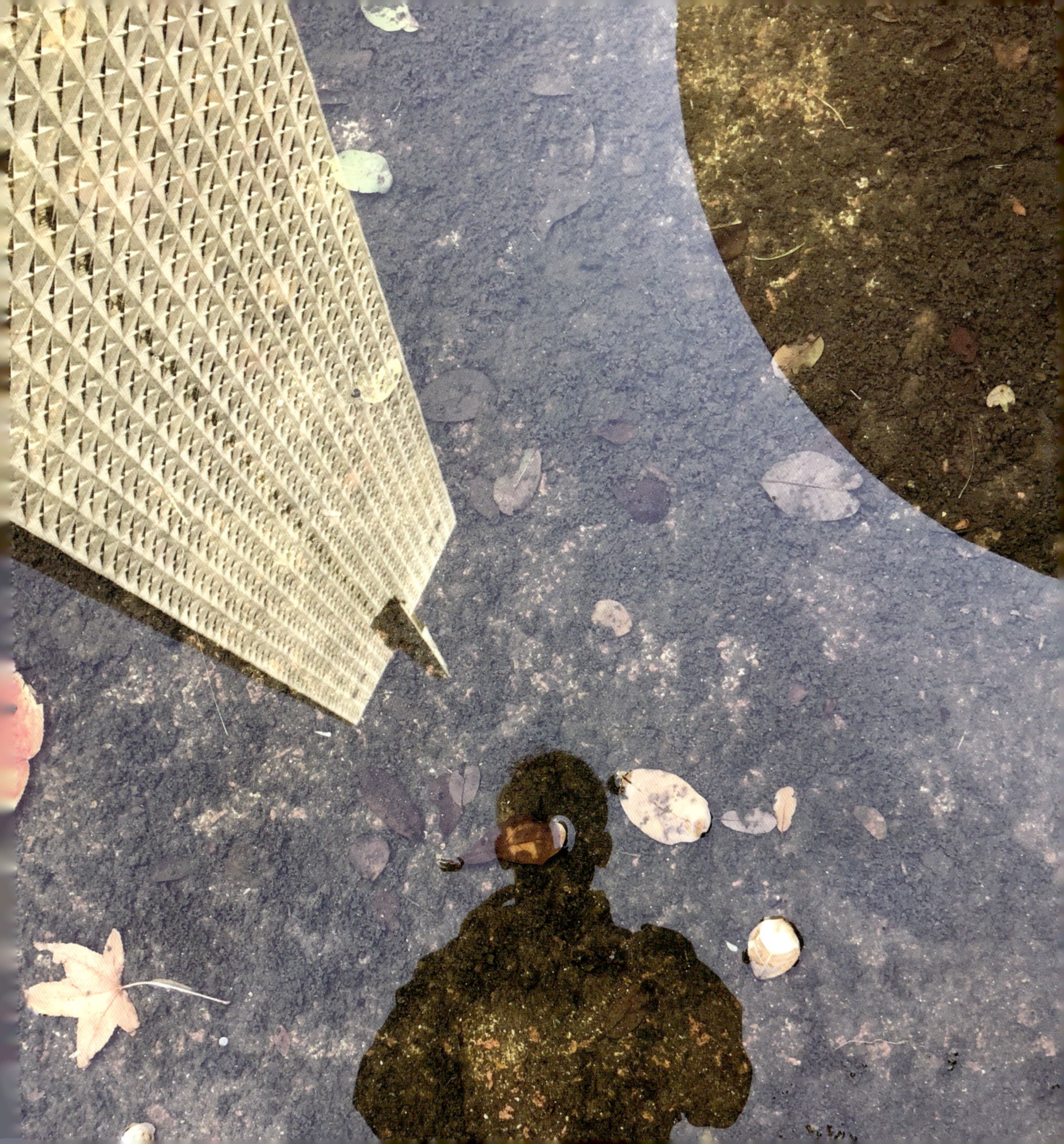

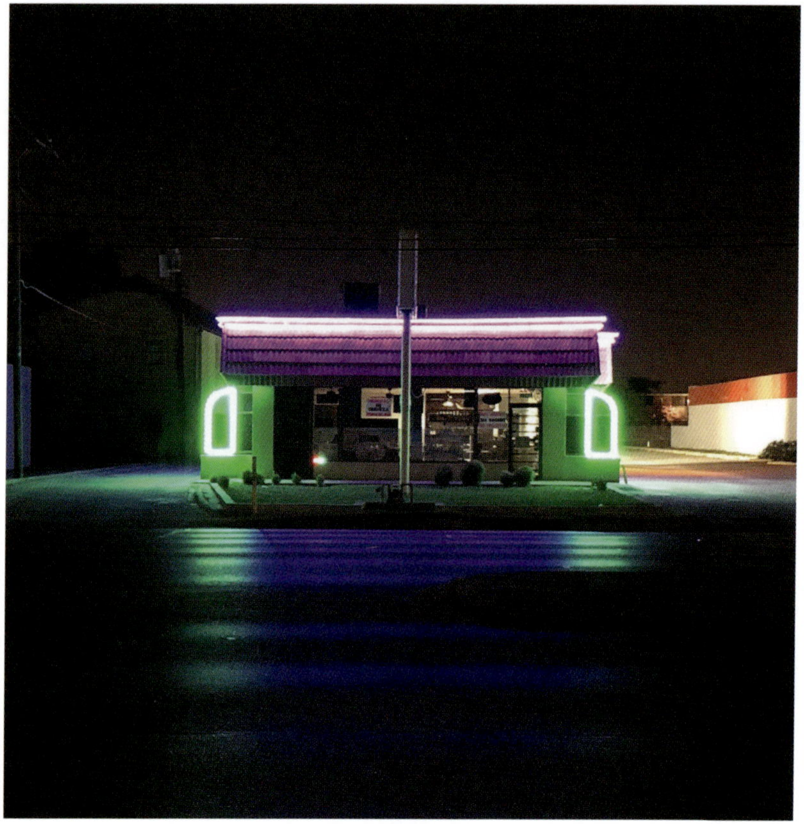

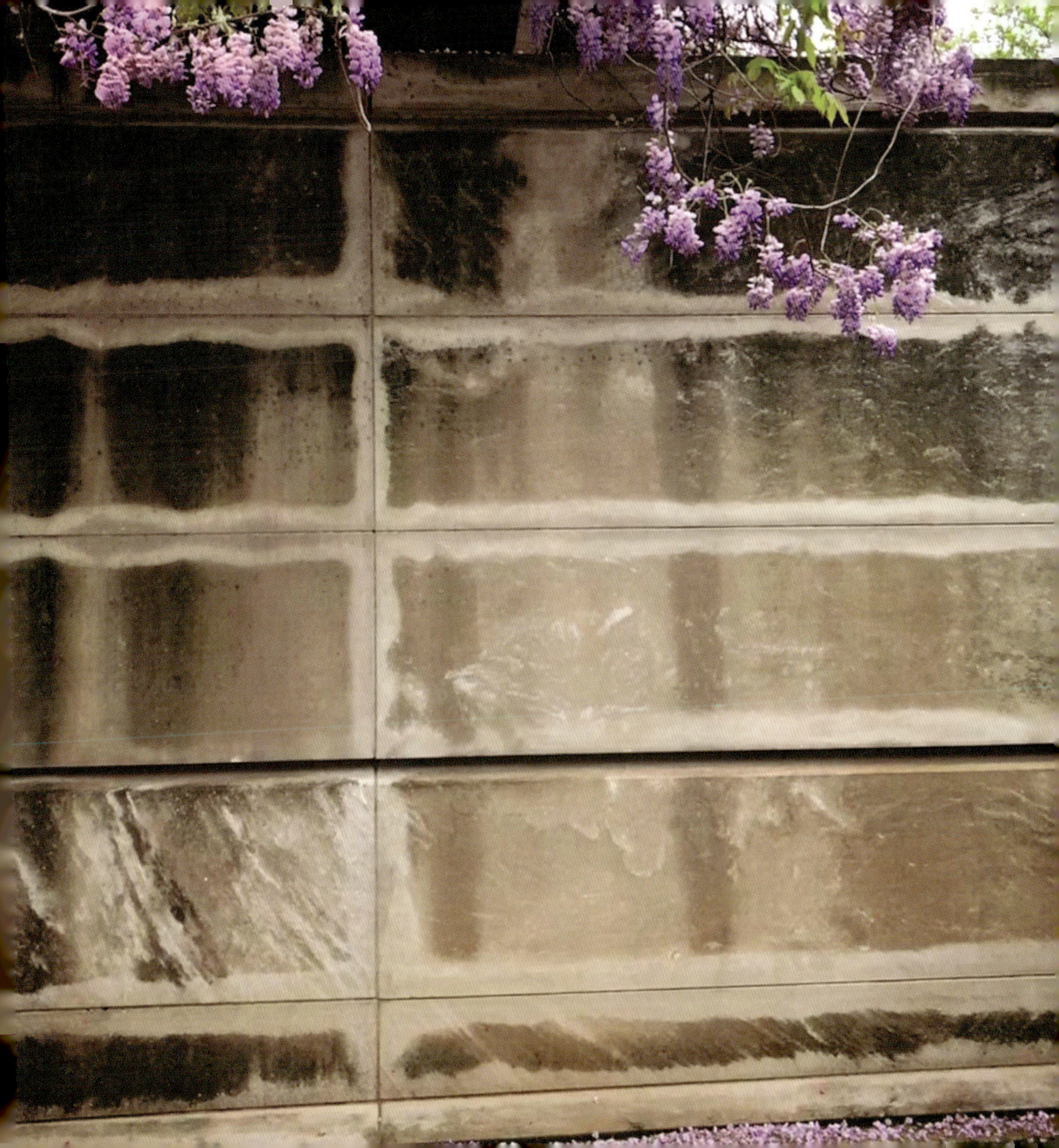

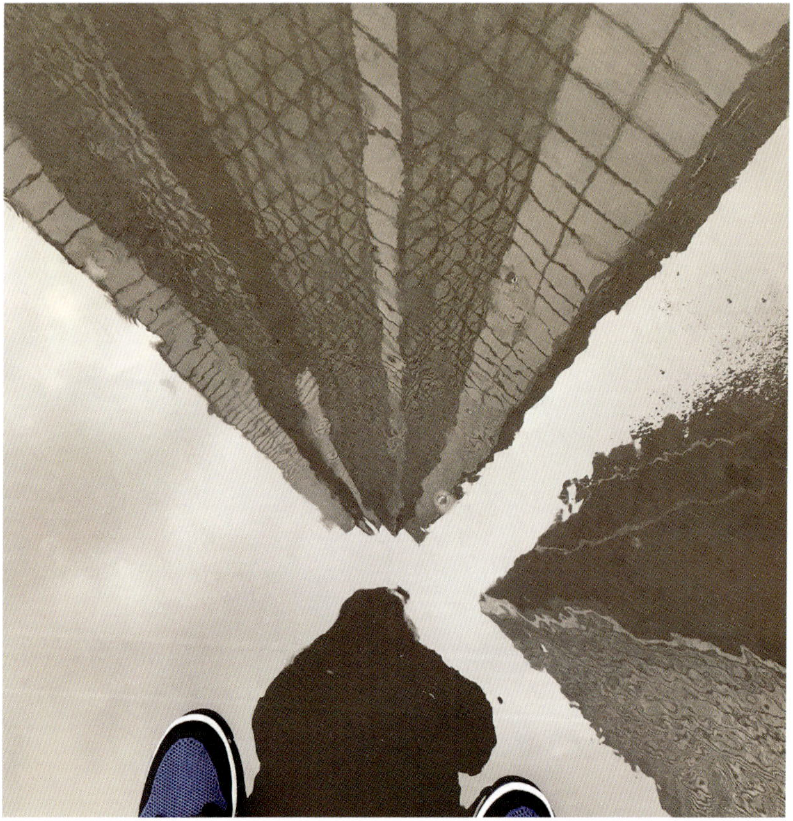

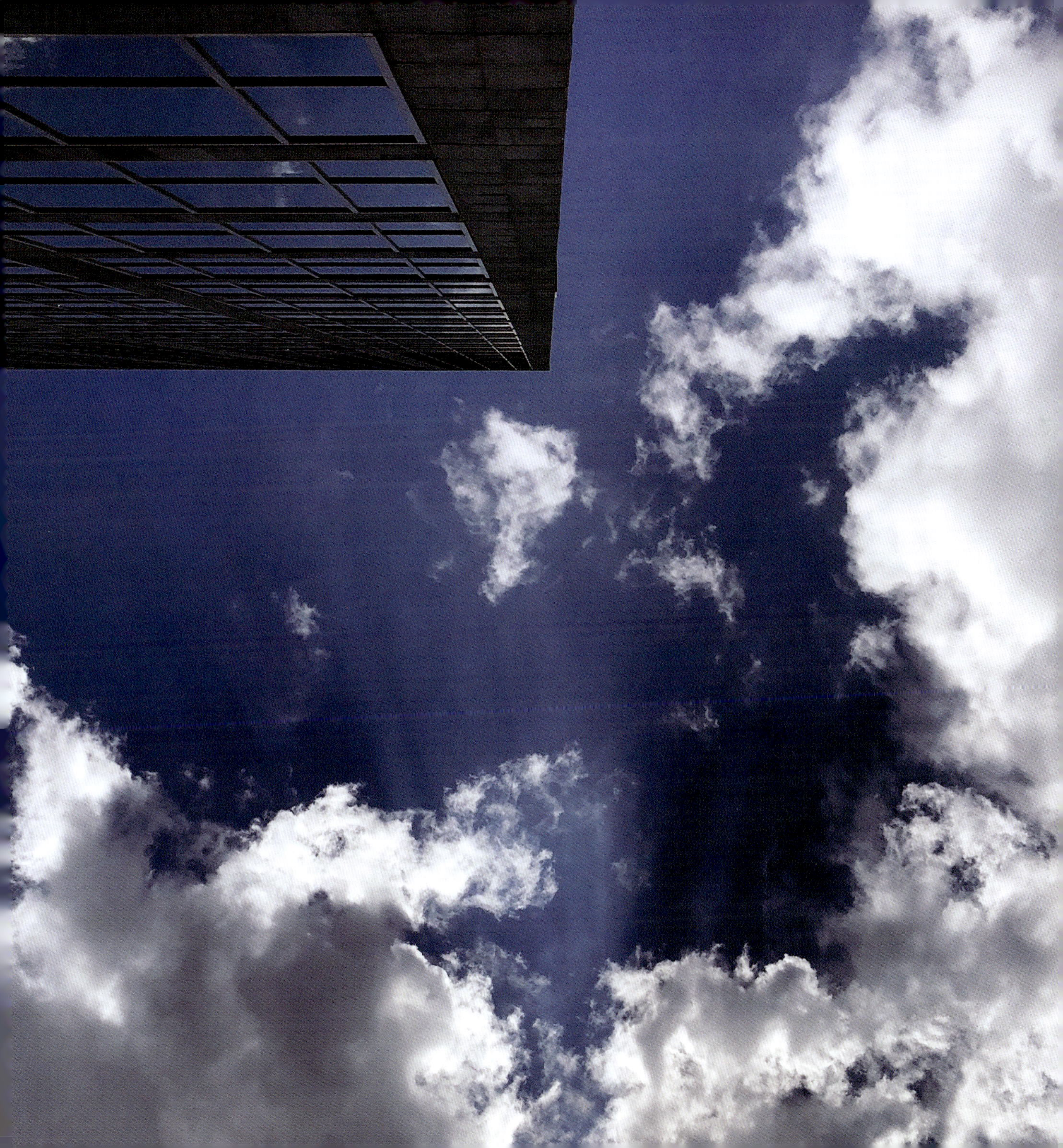

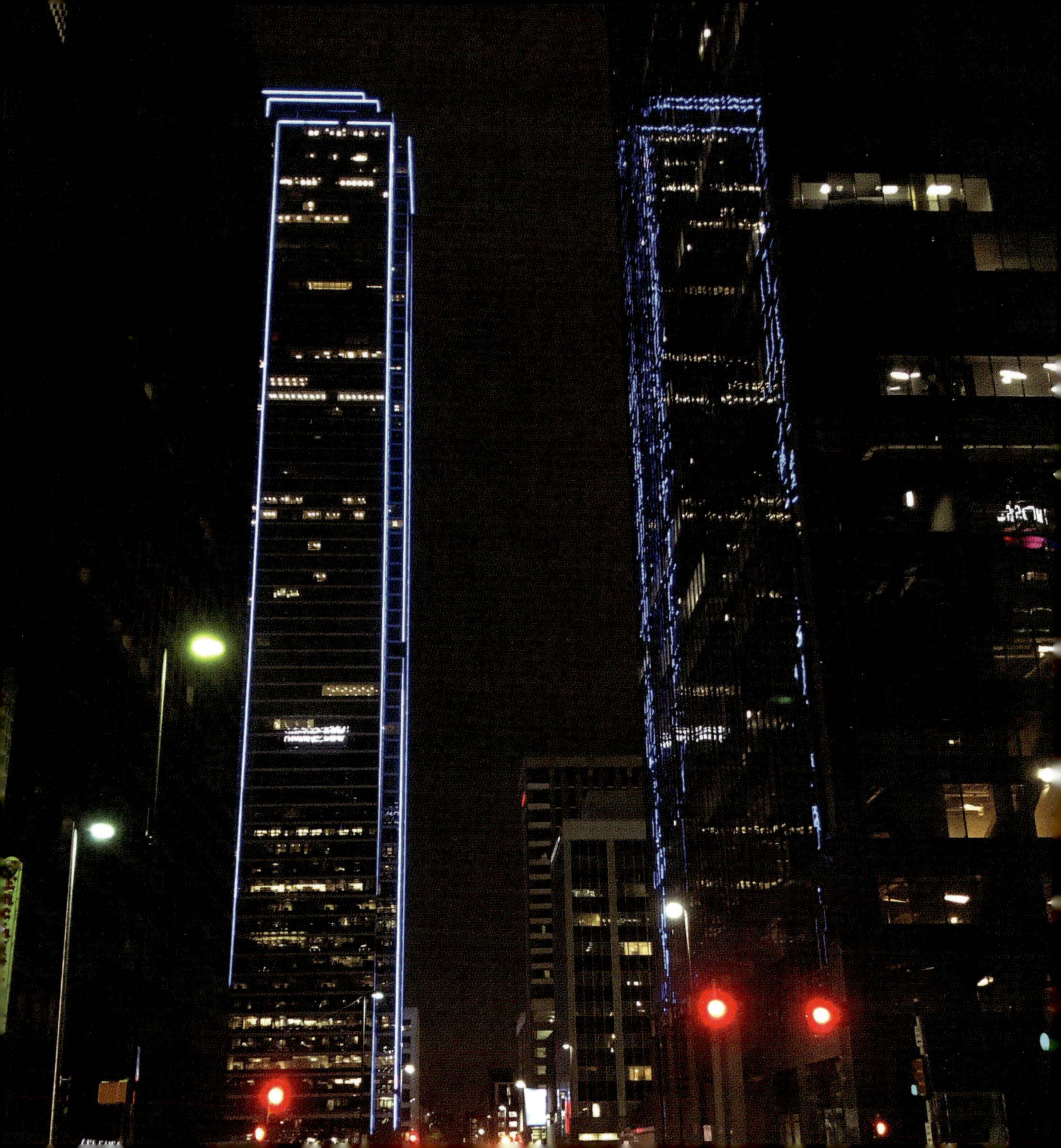

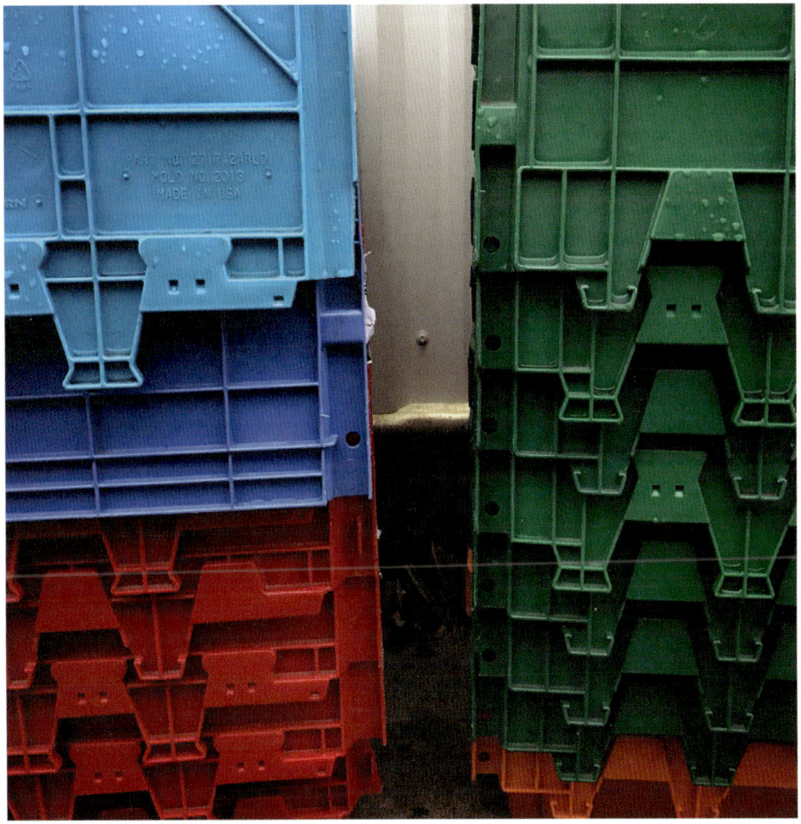
MADE IN USA

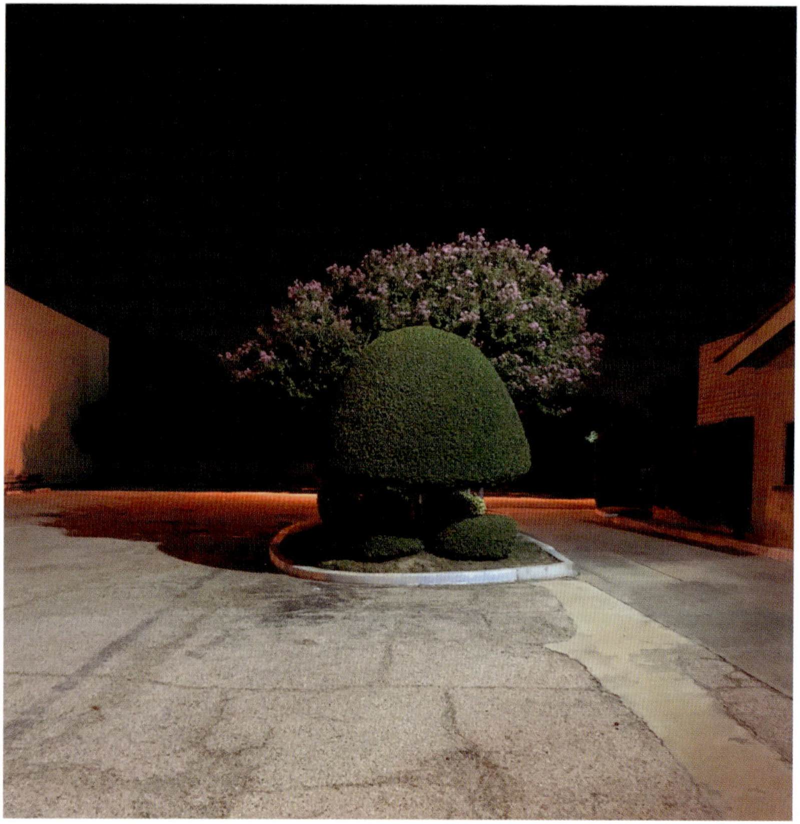

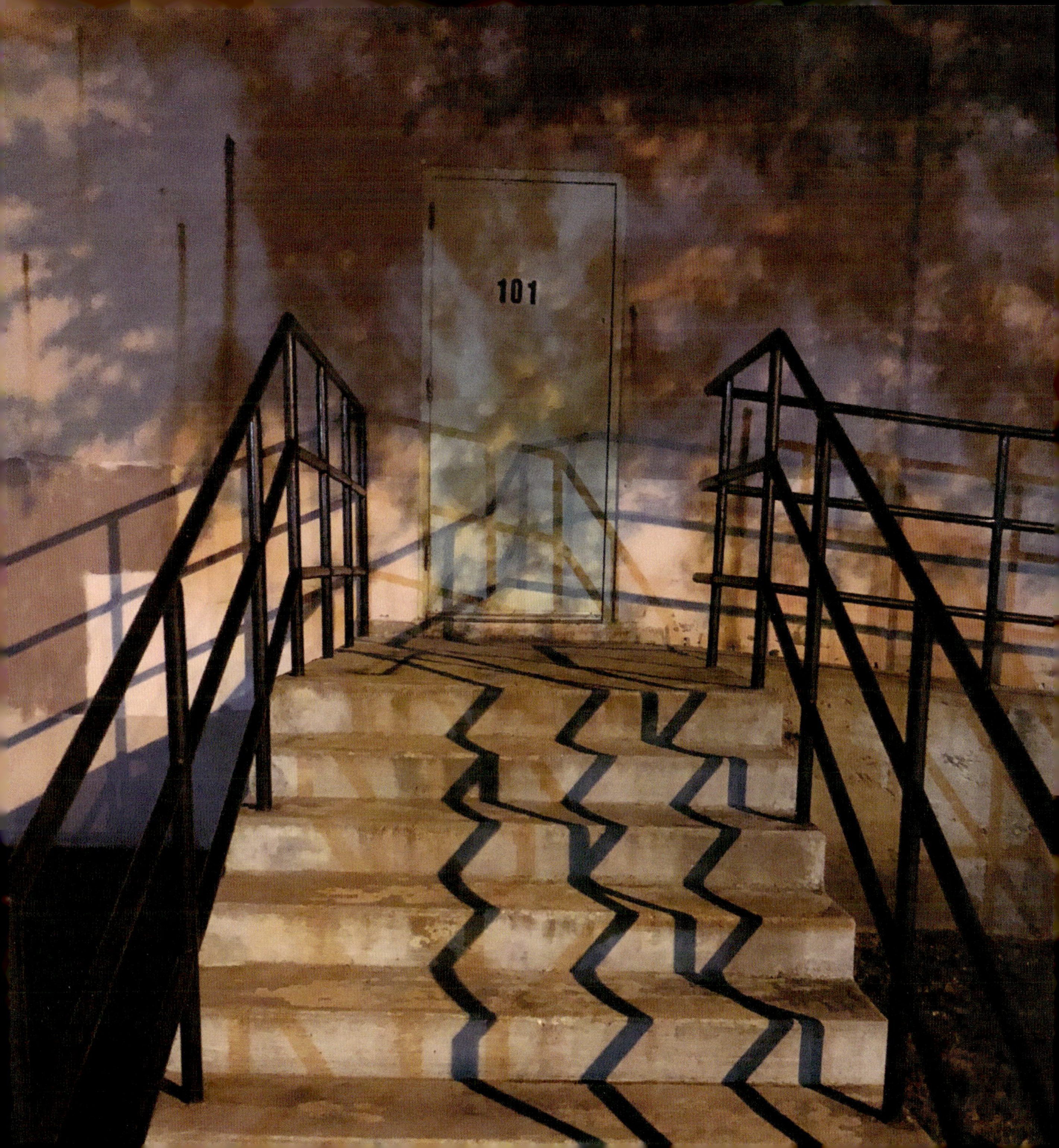
101

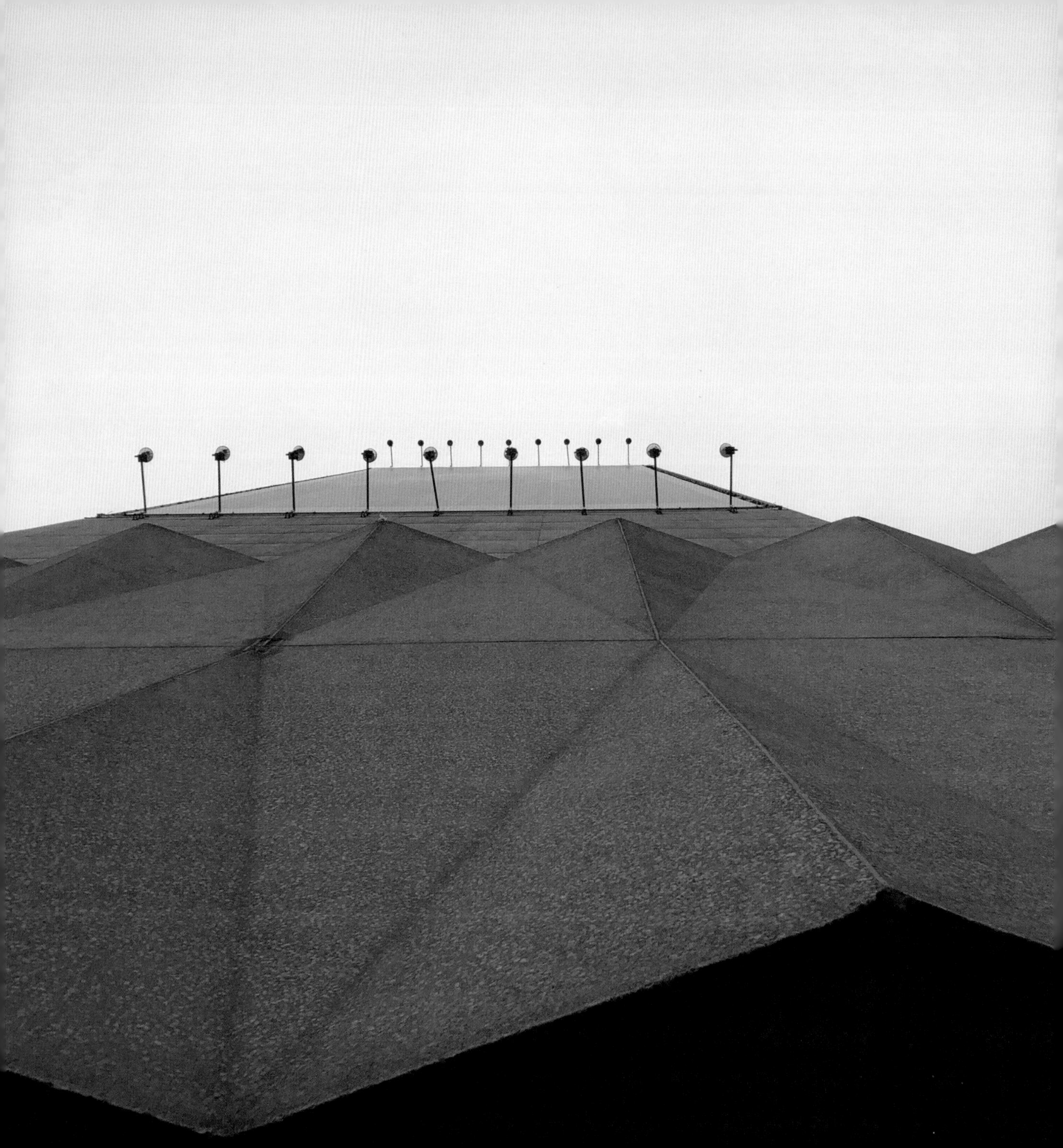

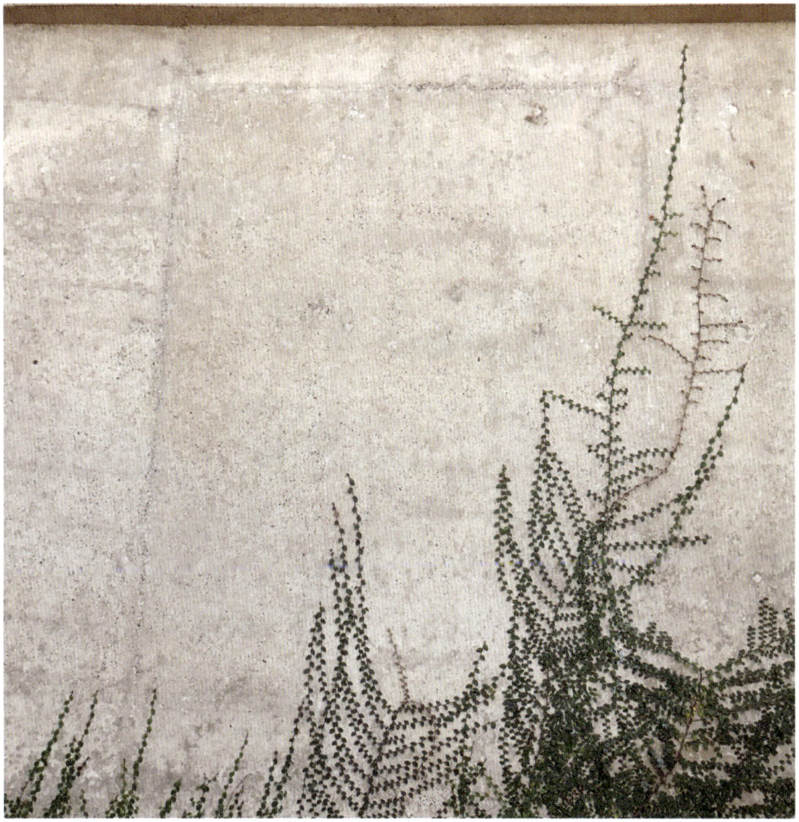

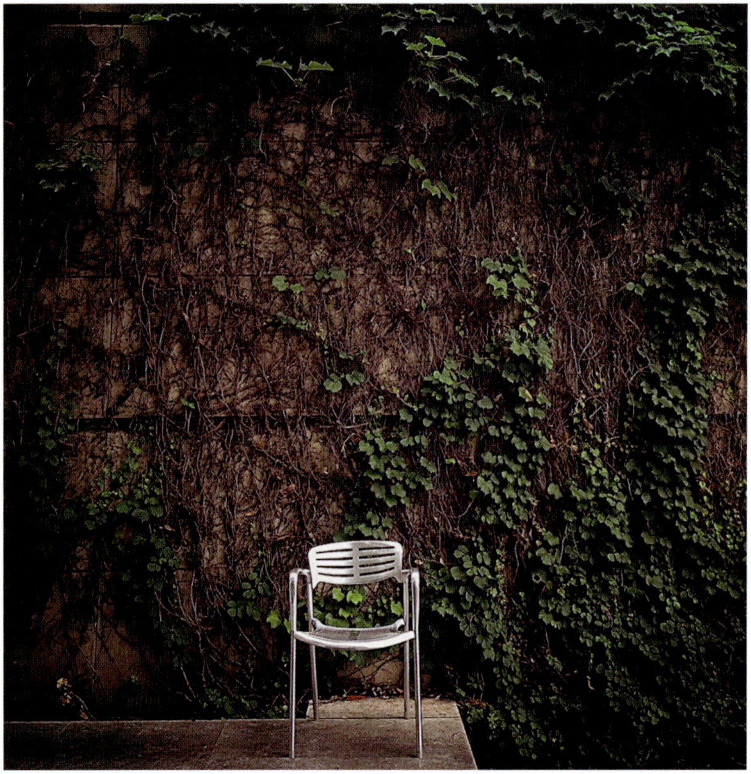

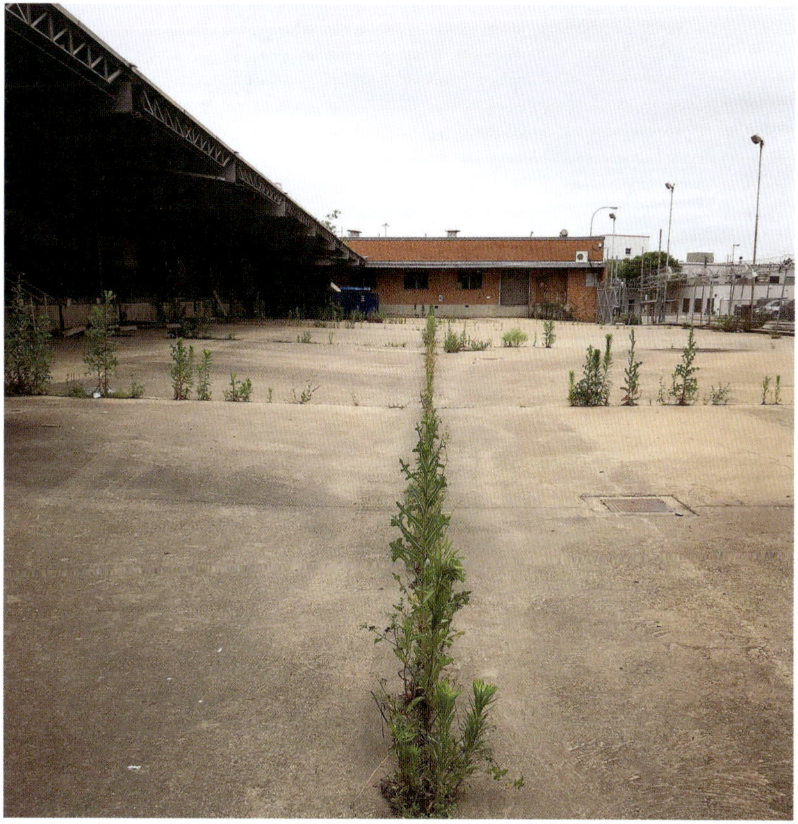

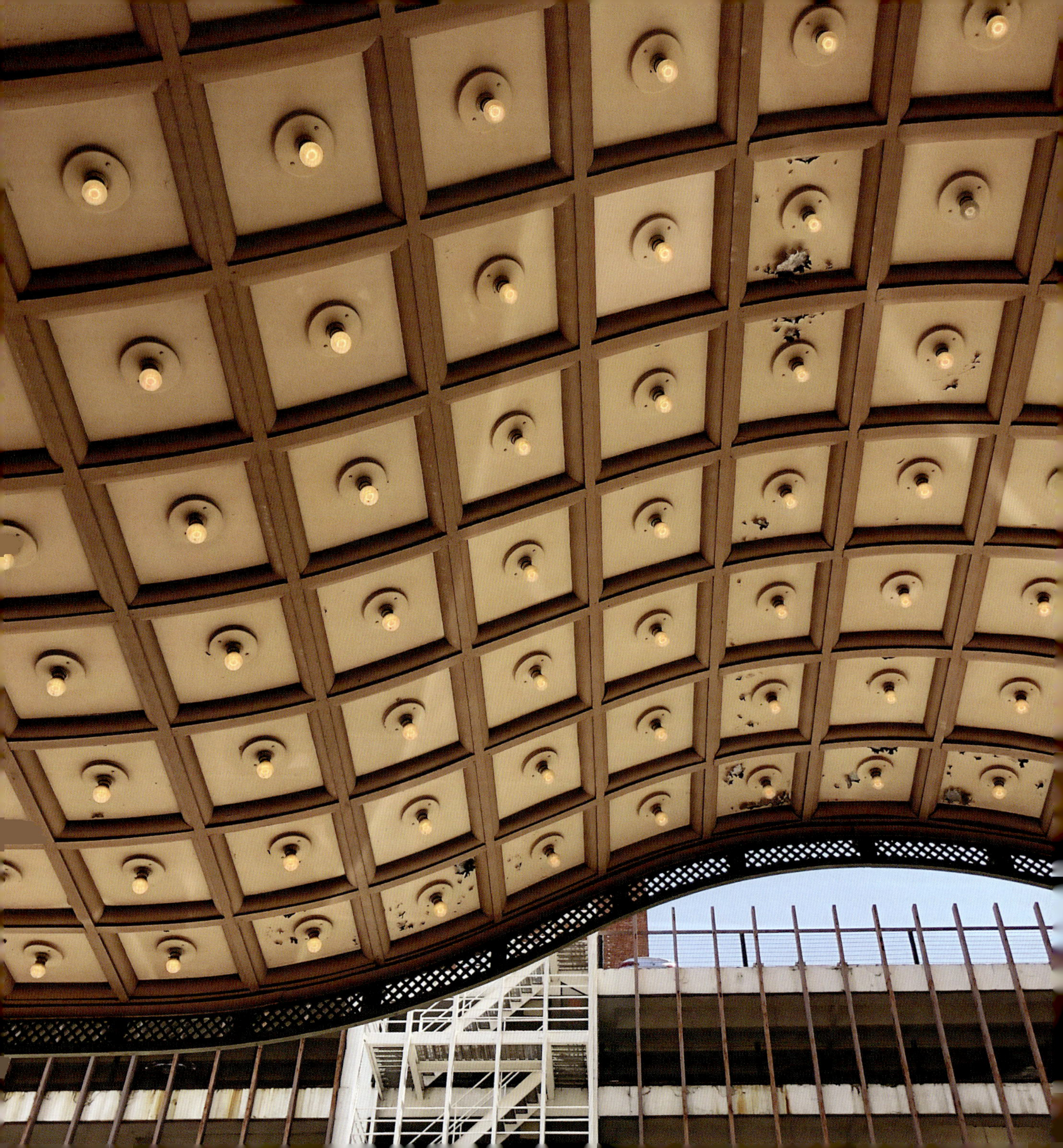

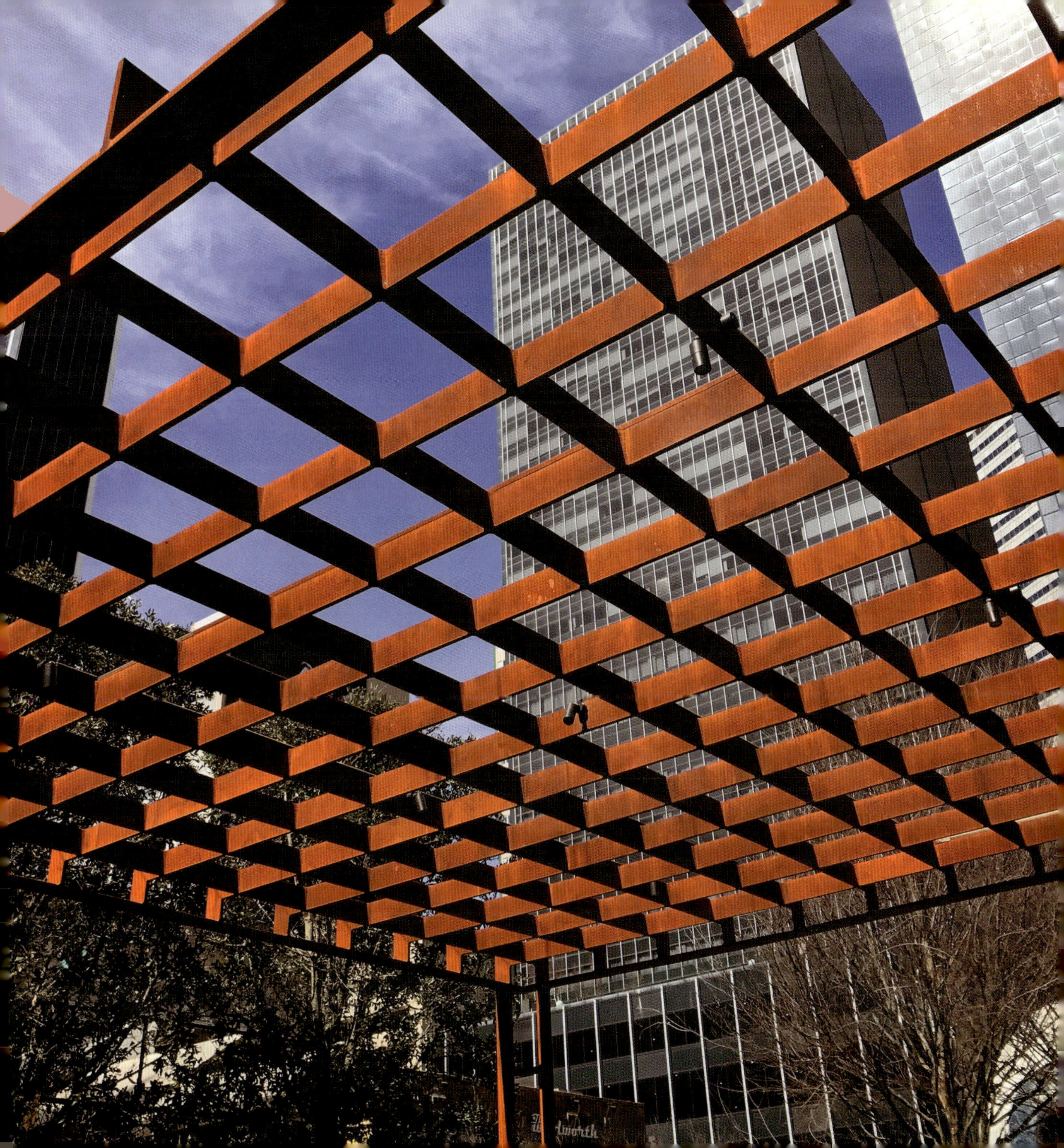

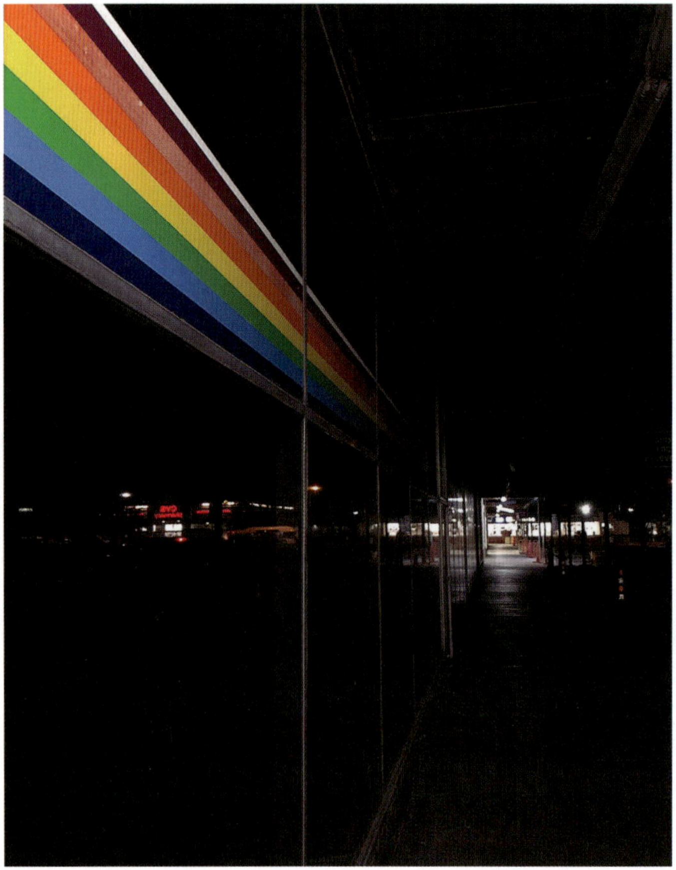

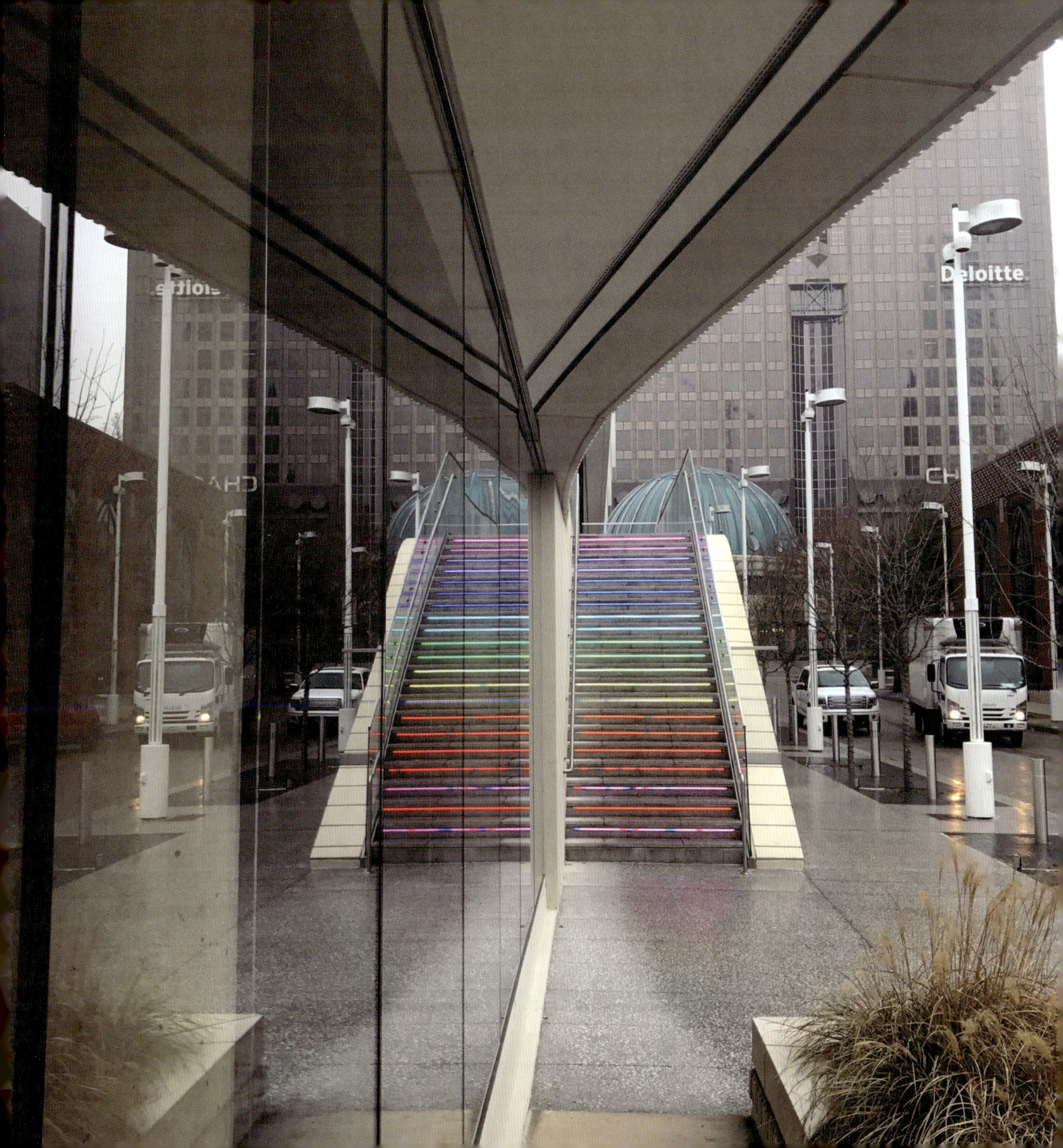
Deloitte.

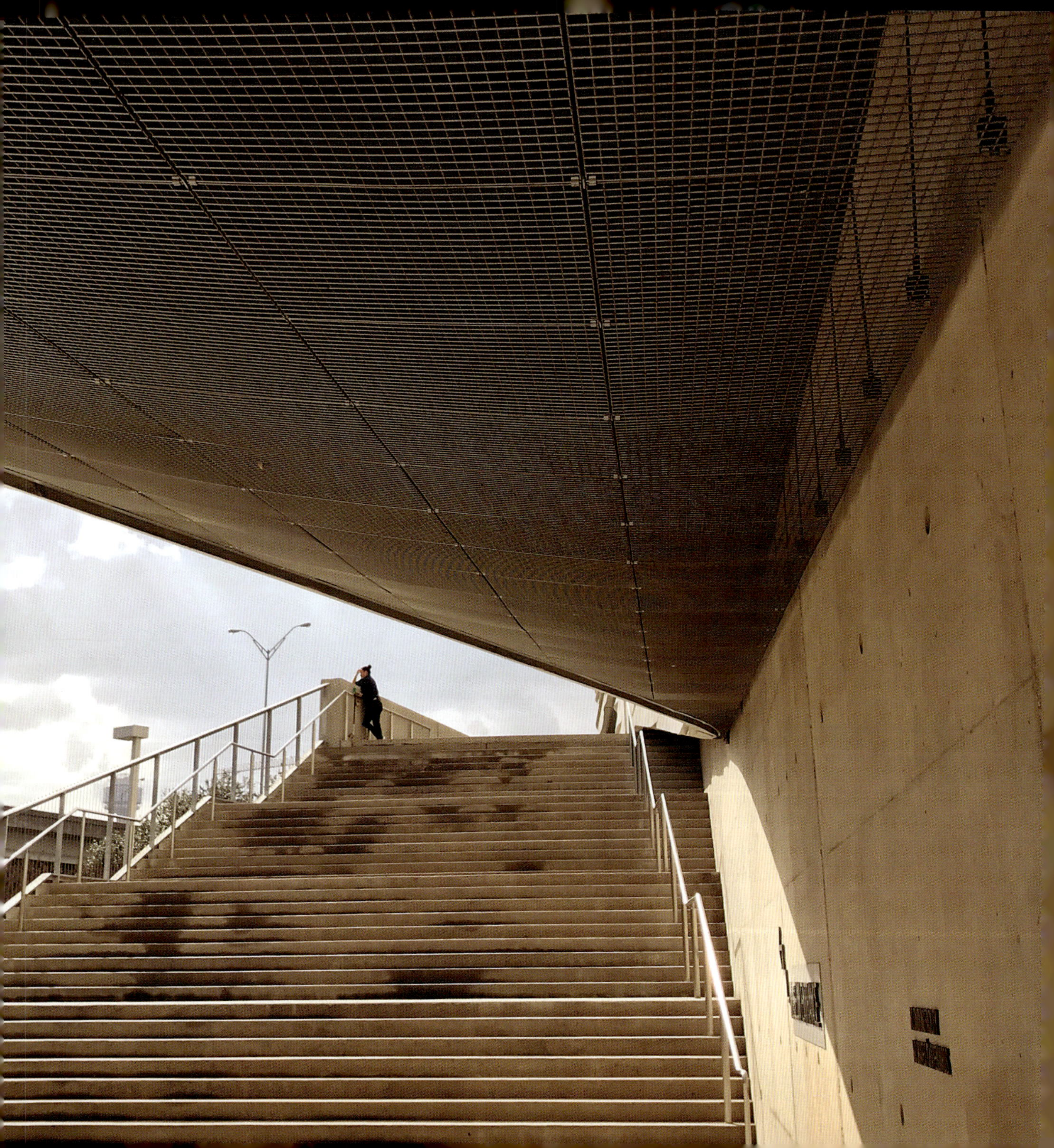

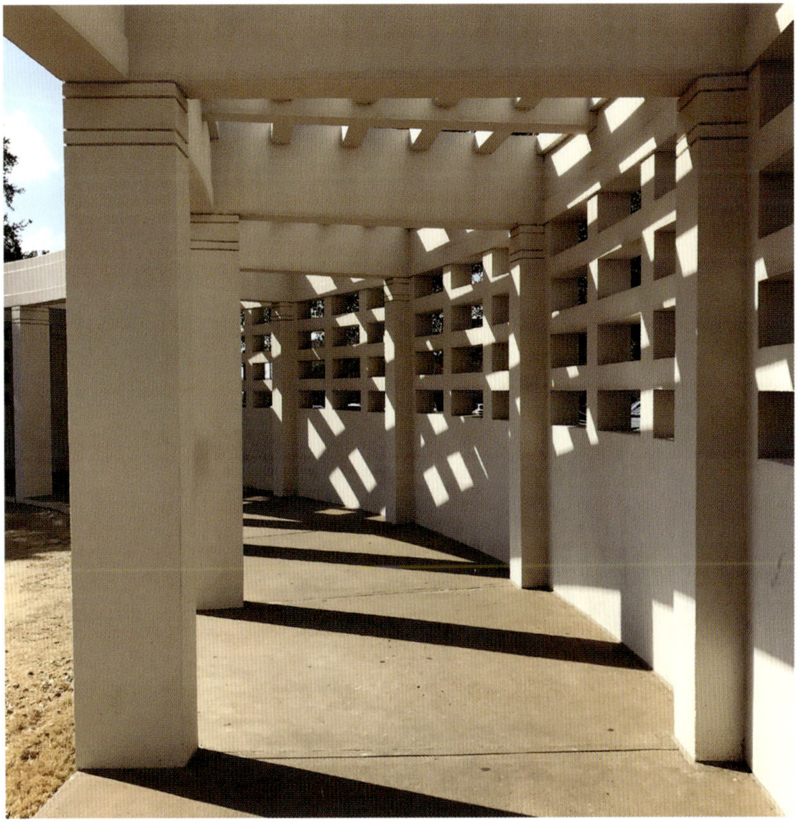

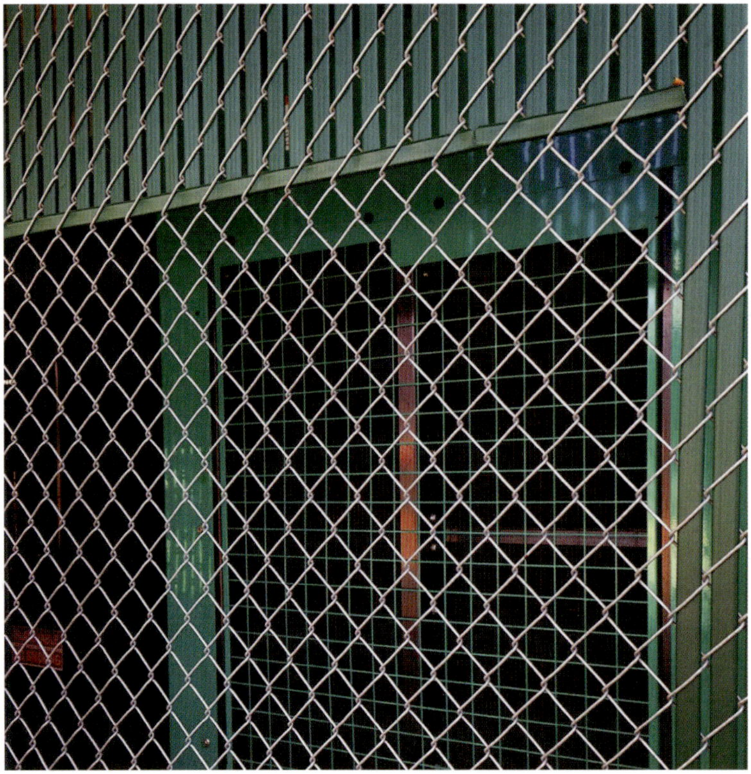

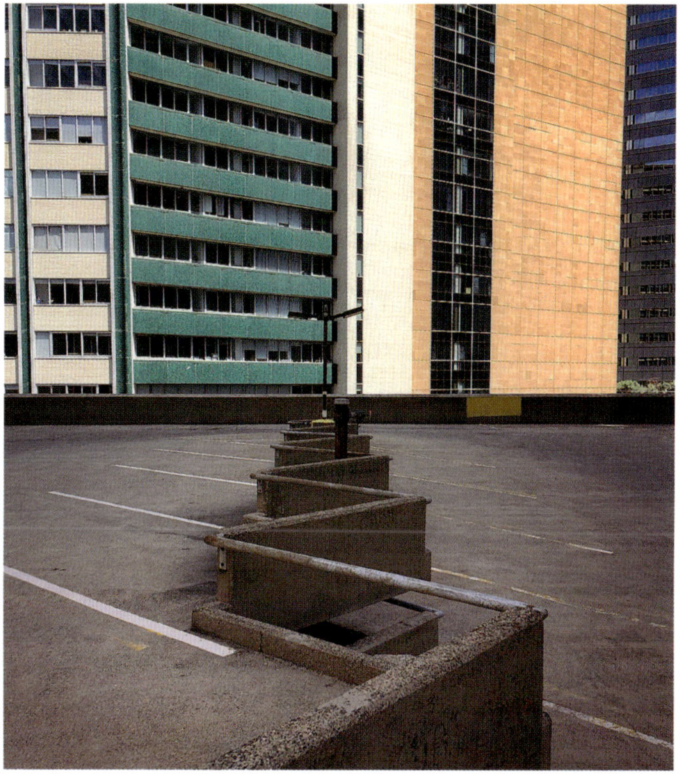

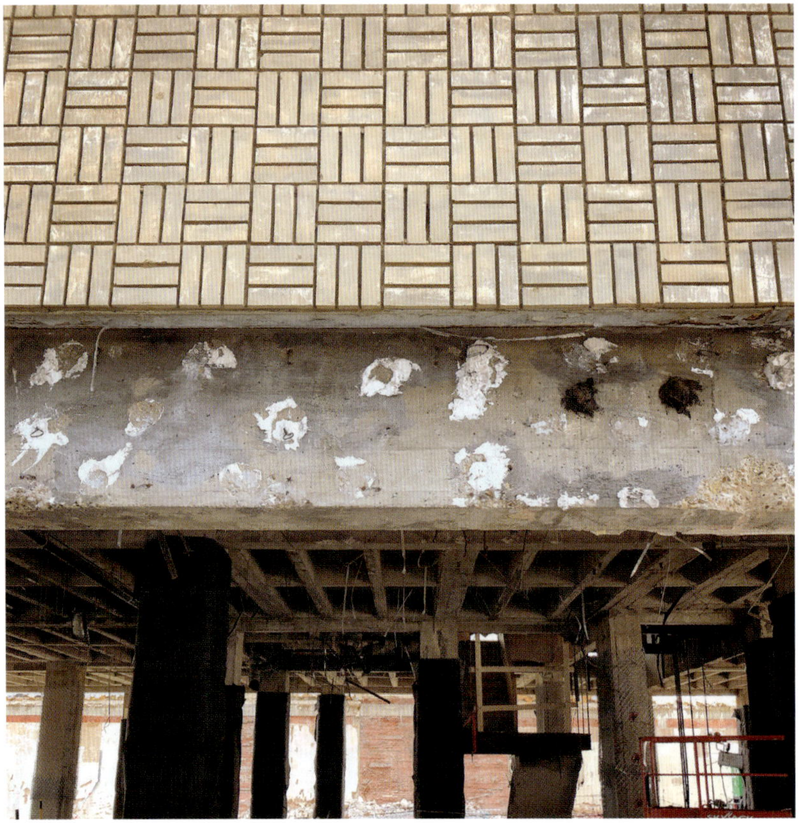

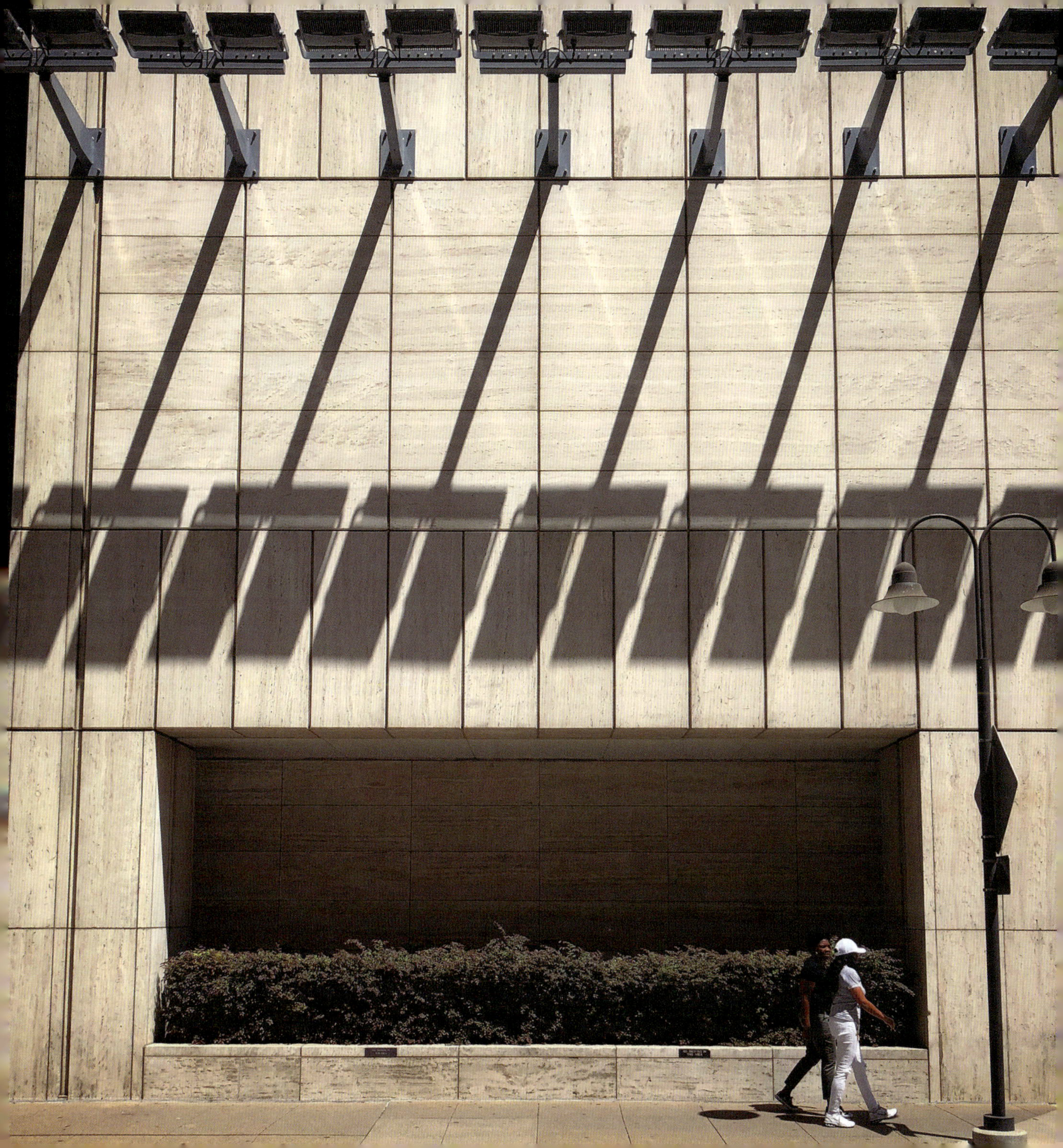

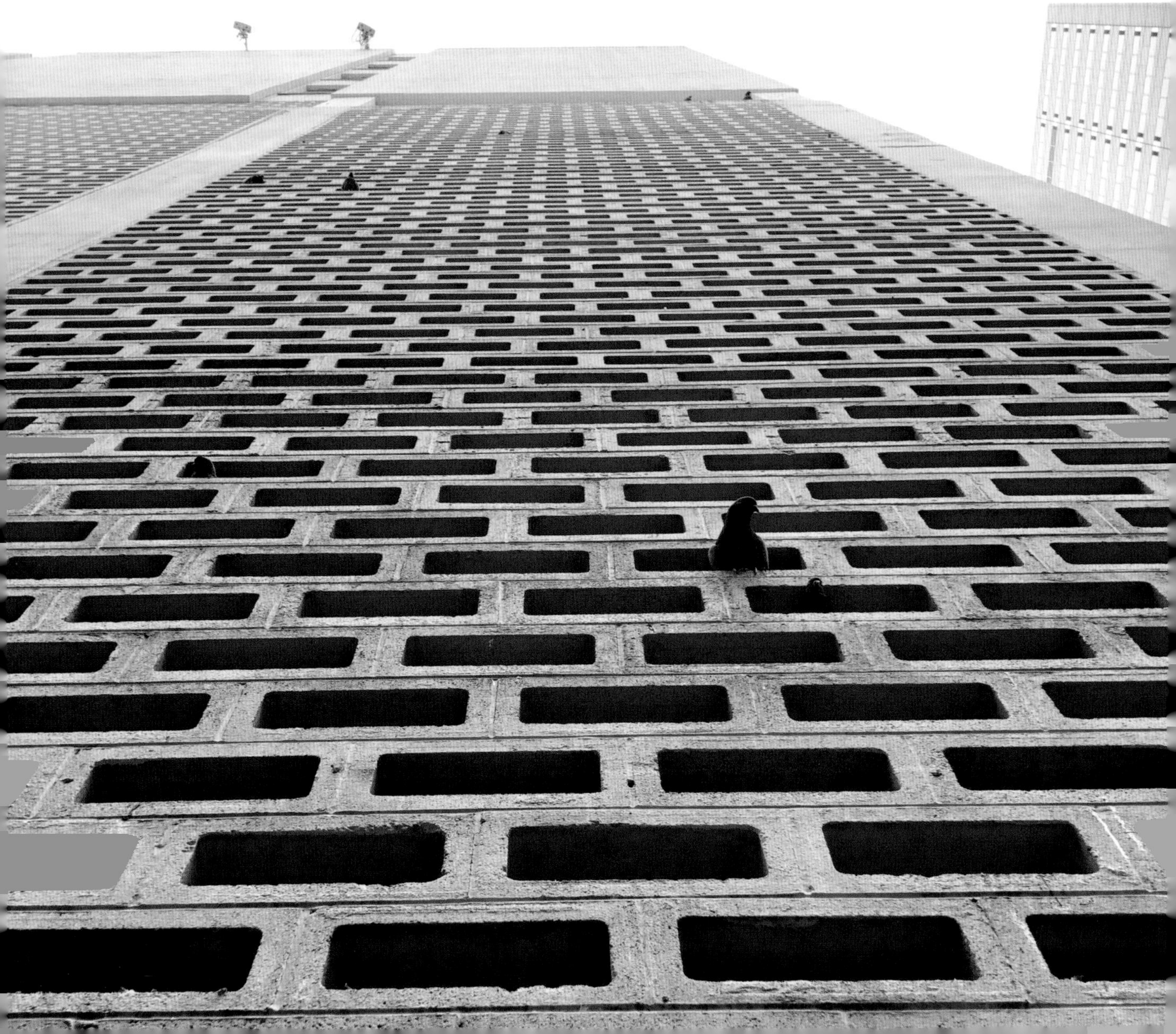

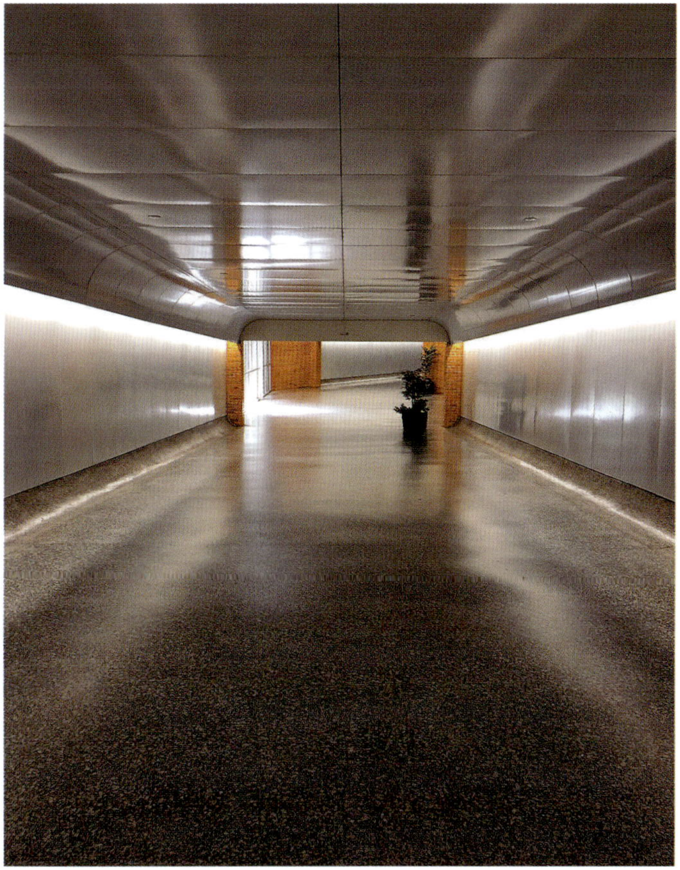

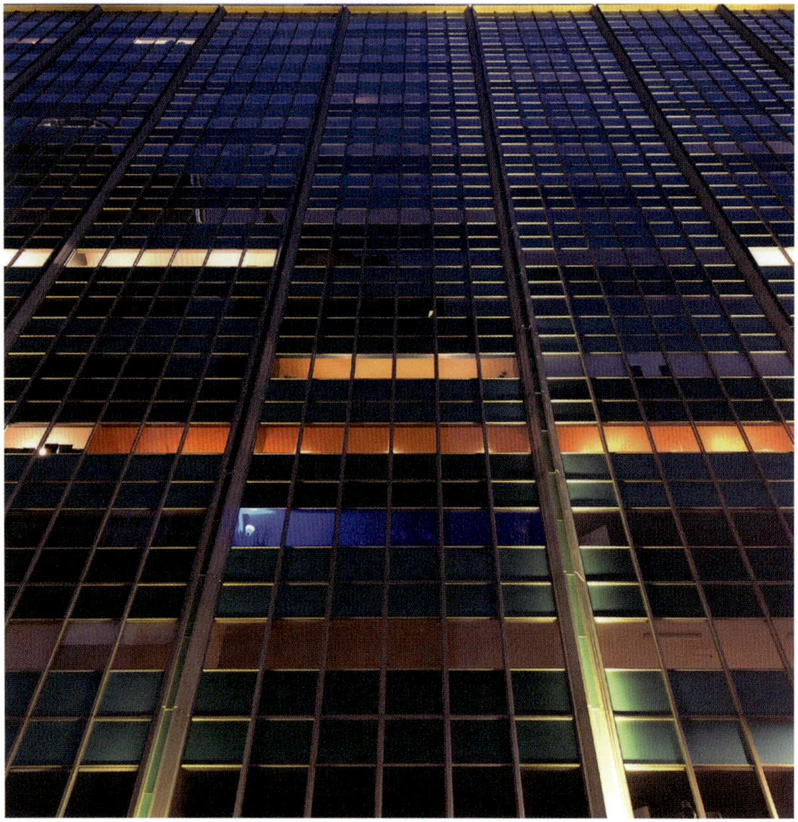

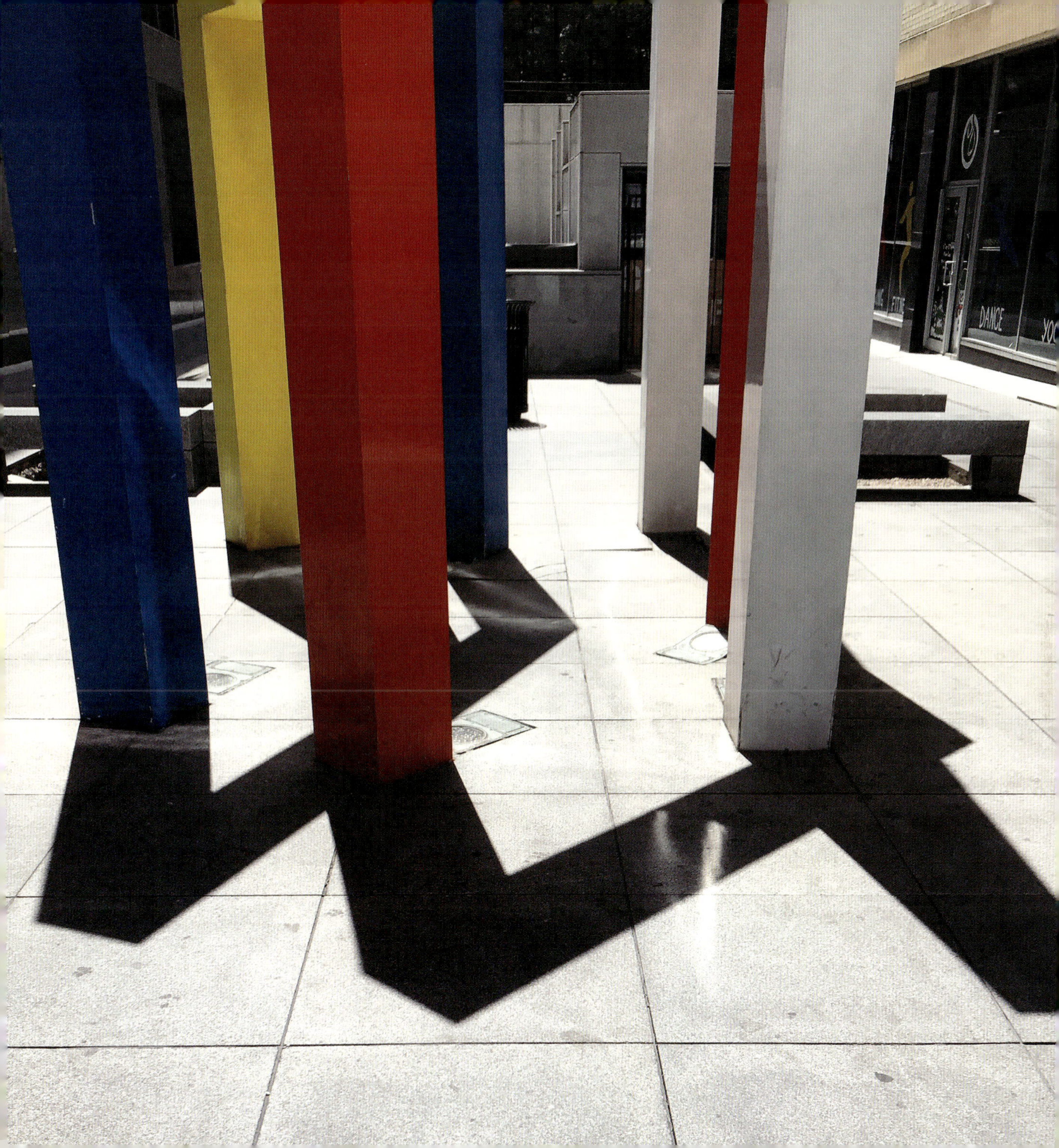
DANCE

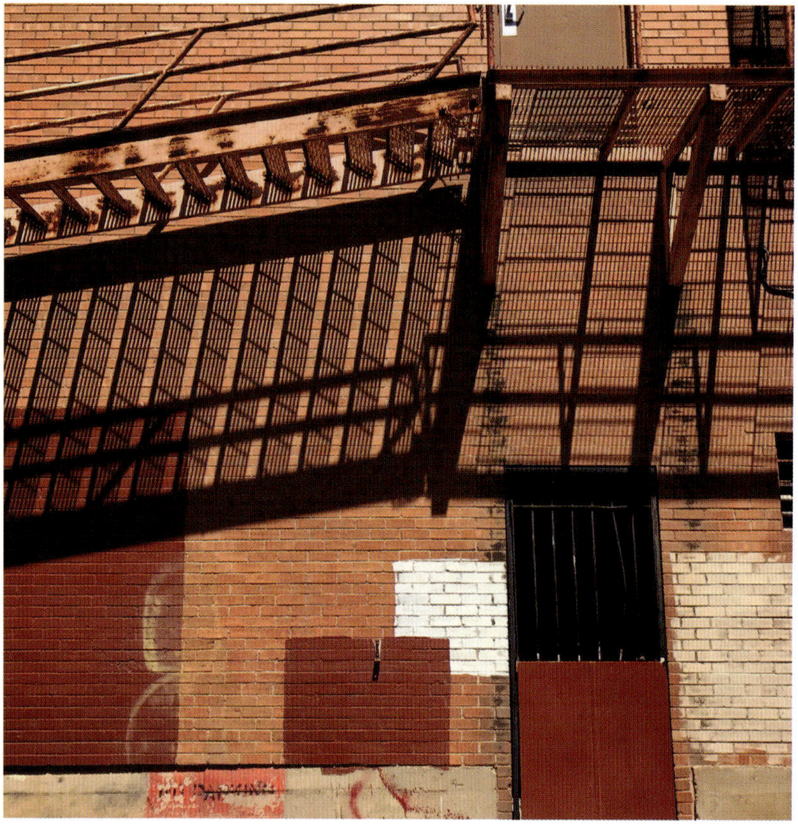

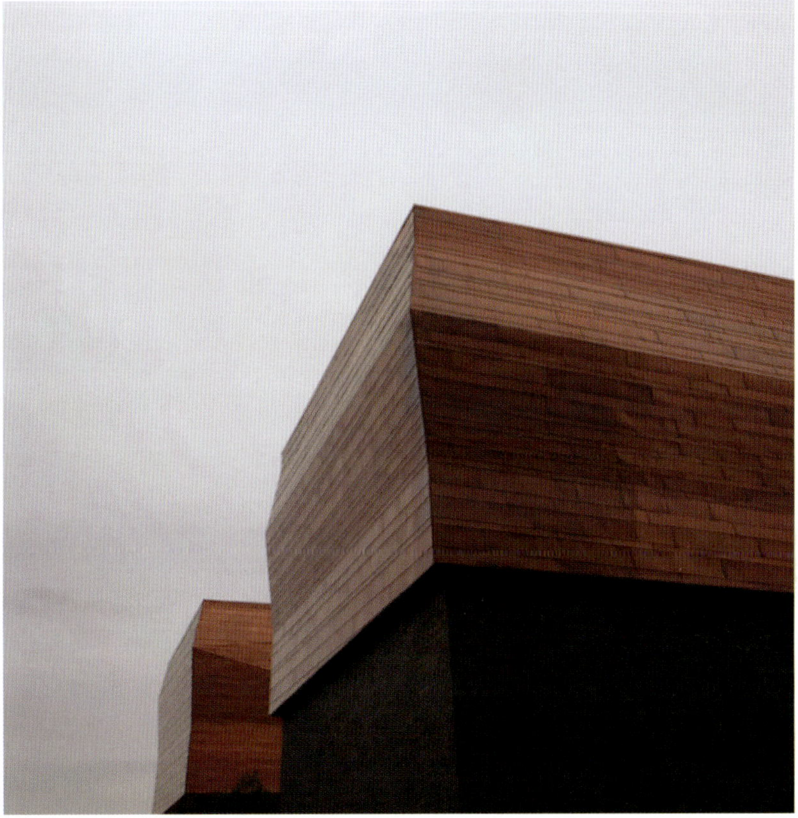

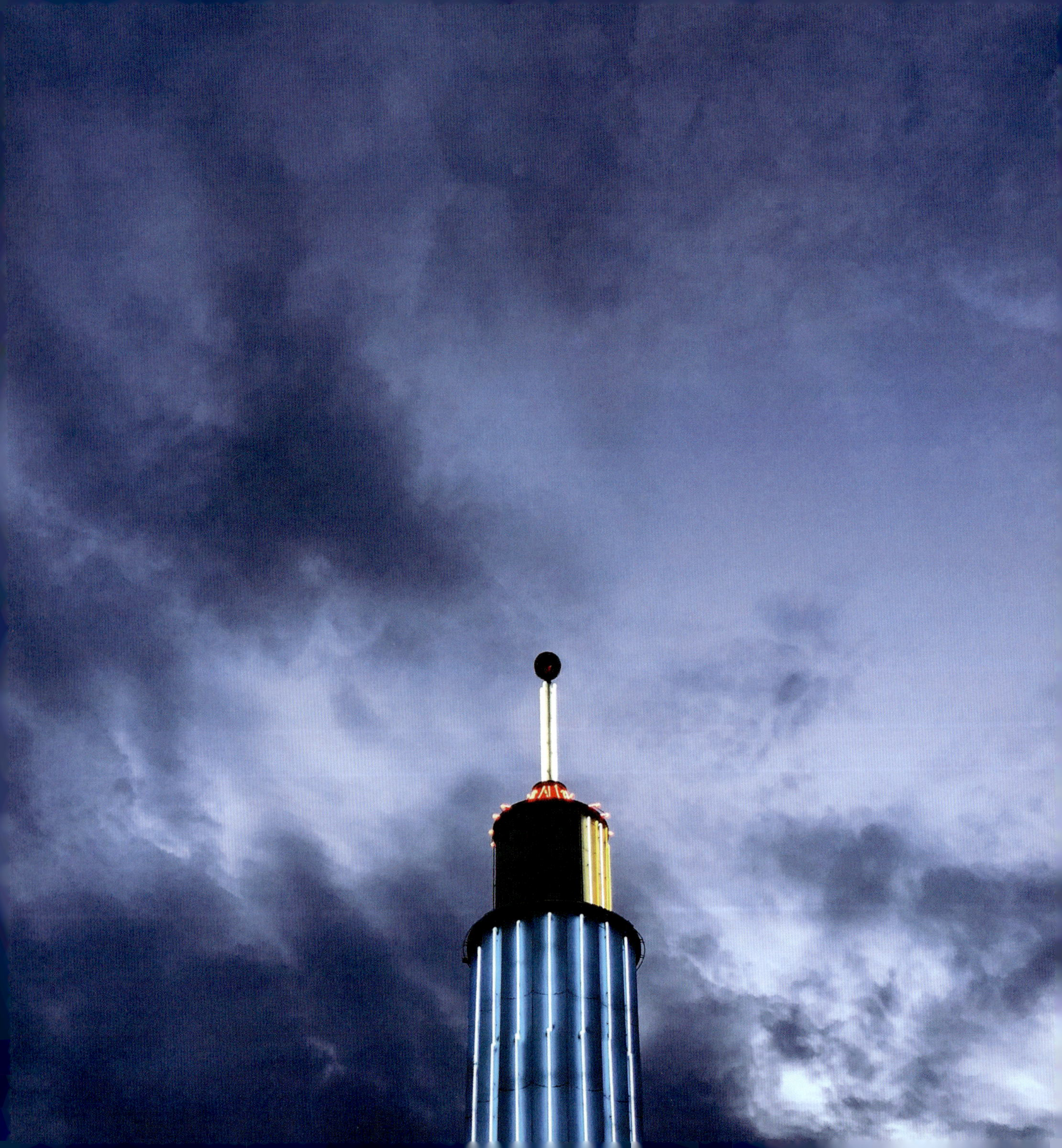

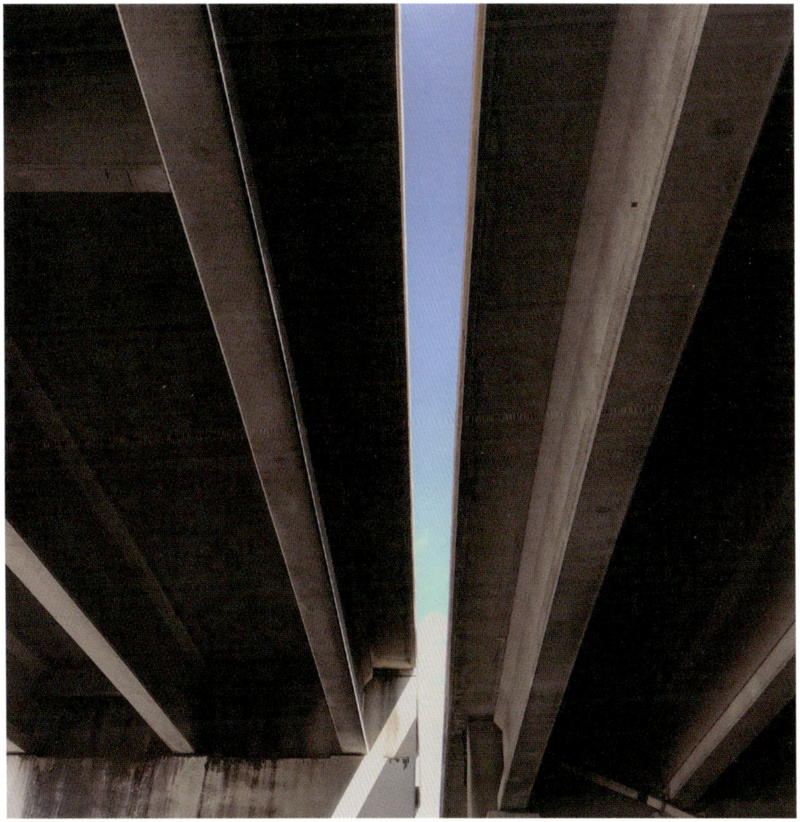

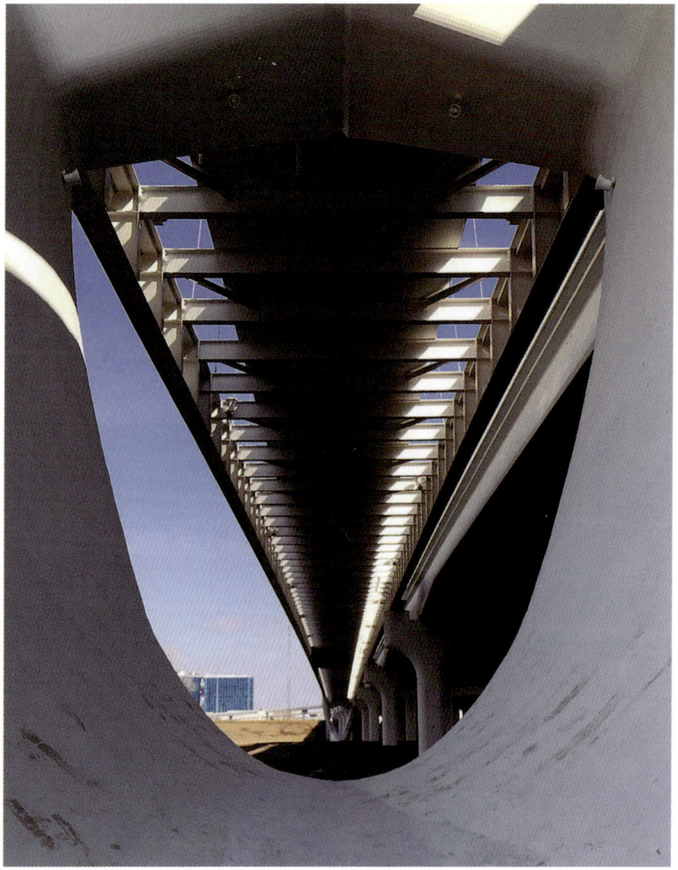

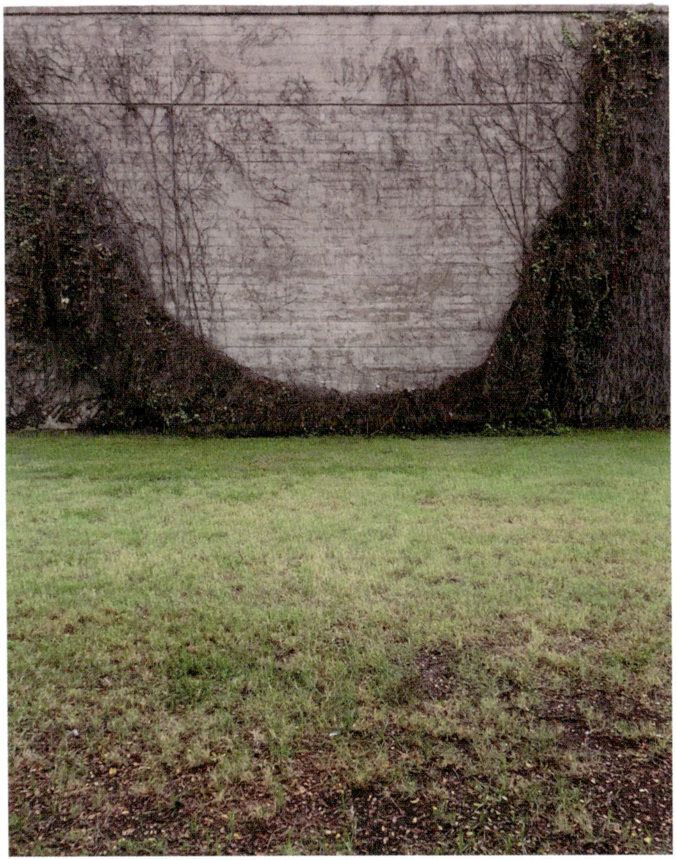

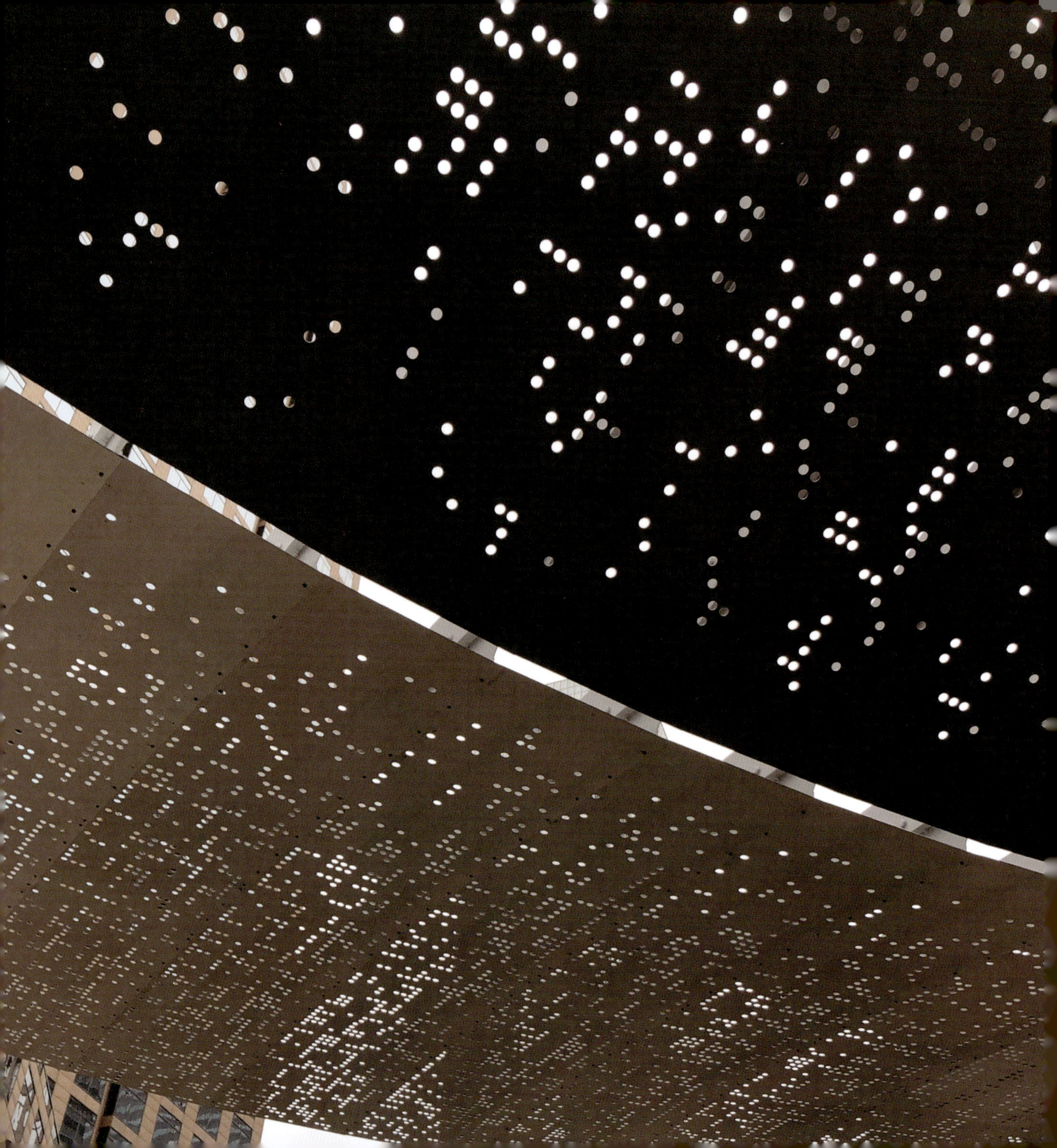

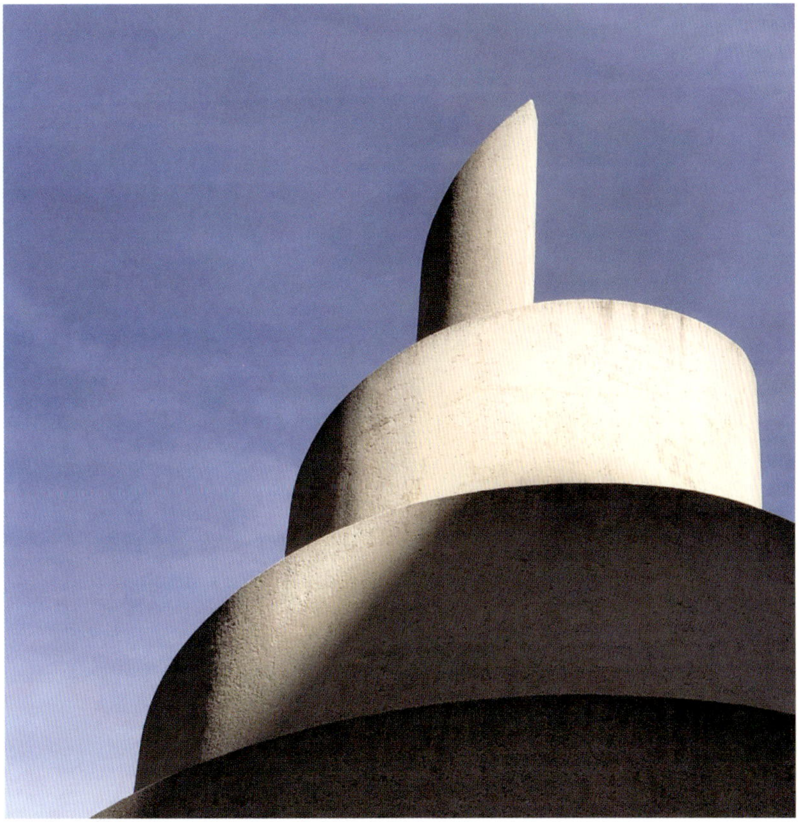

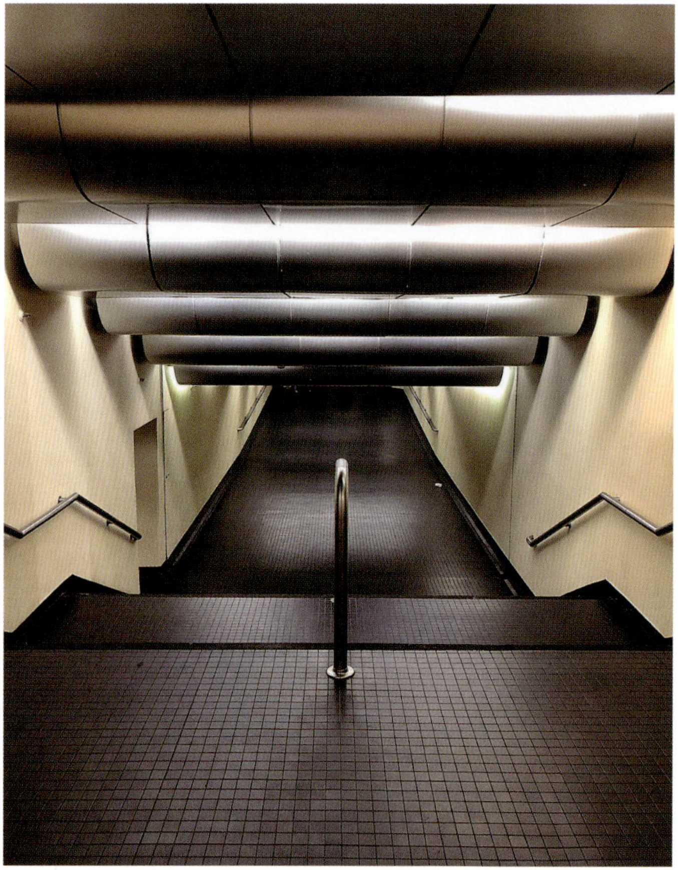

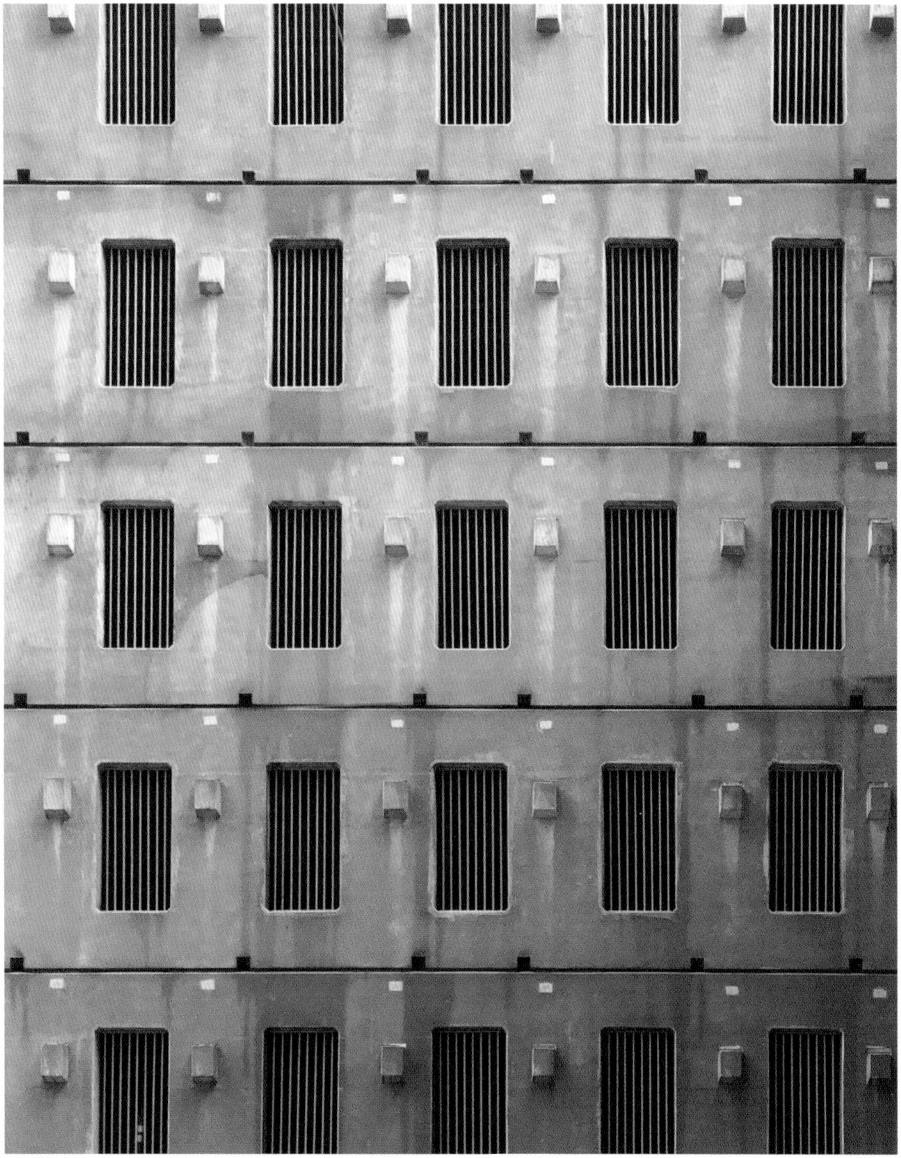

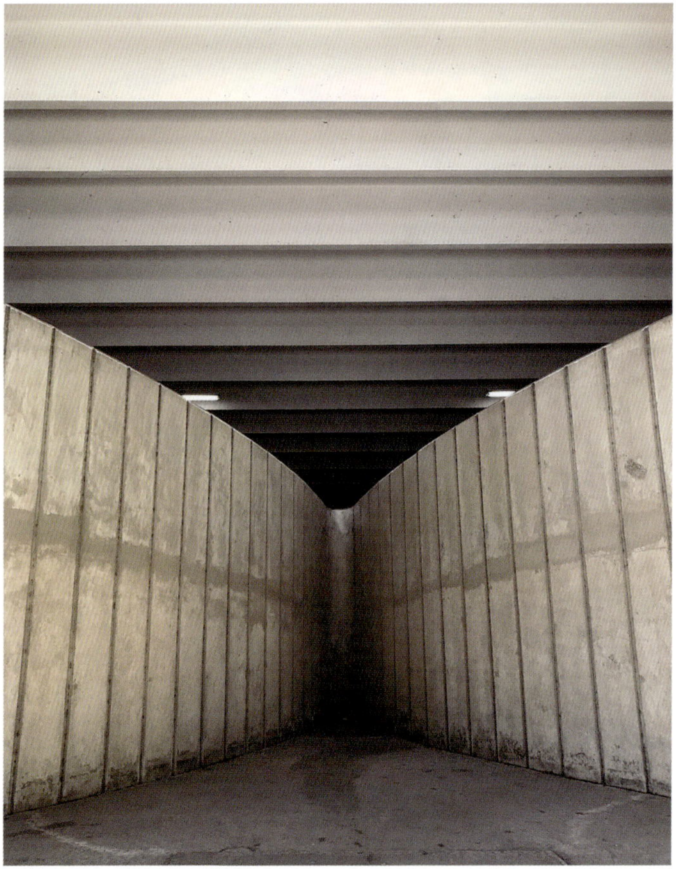

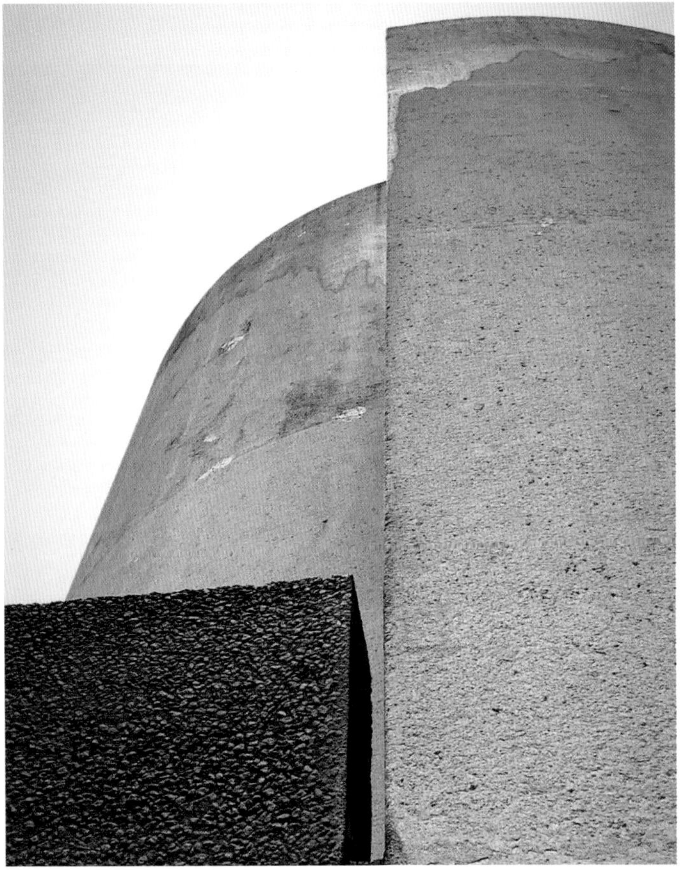

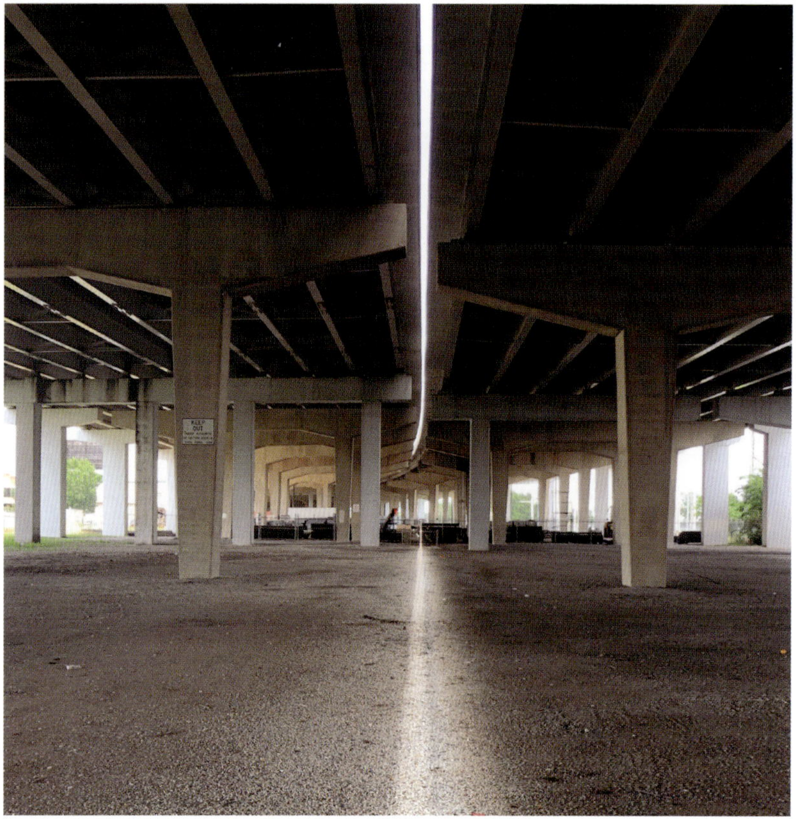
OUT

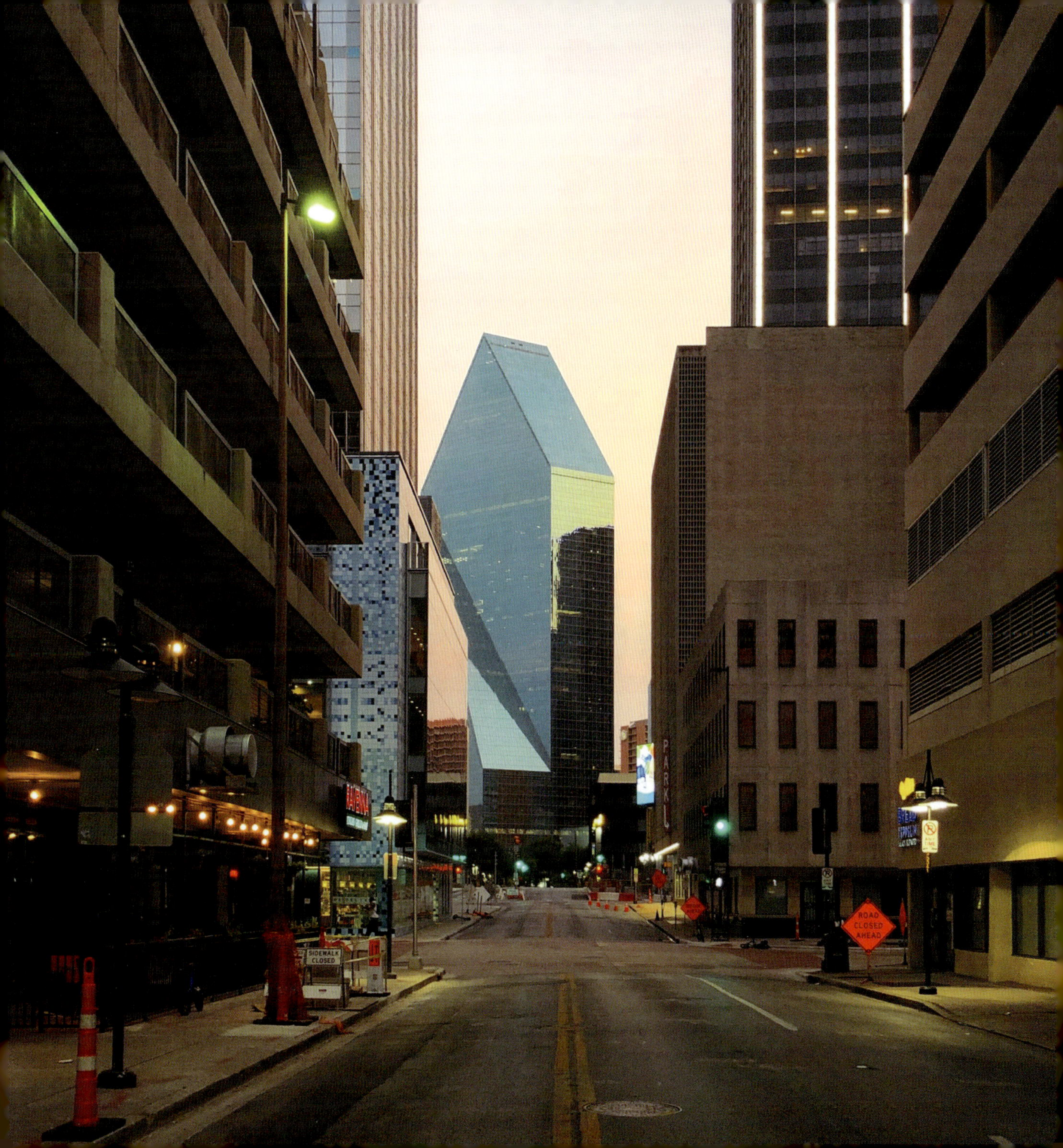
SIDEWALK
CLOSED
ROAD
CLOSED
AHEAD

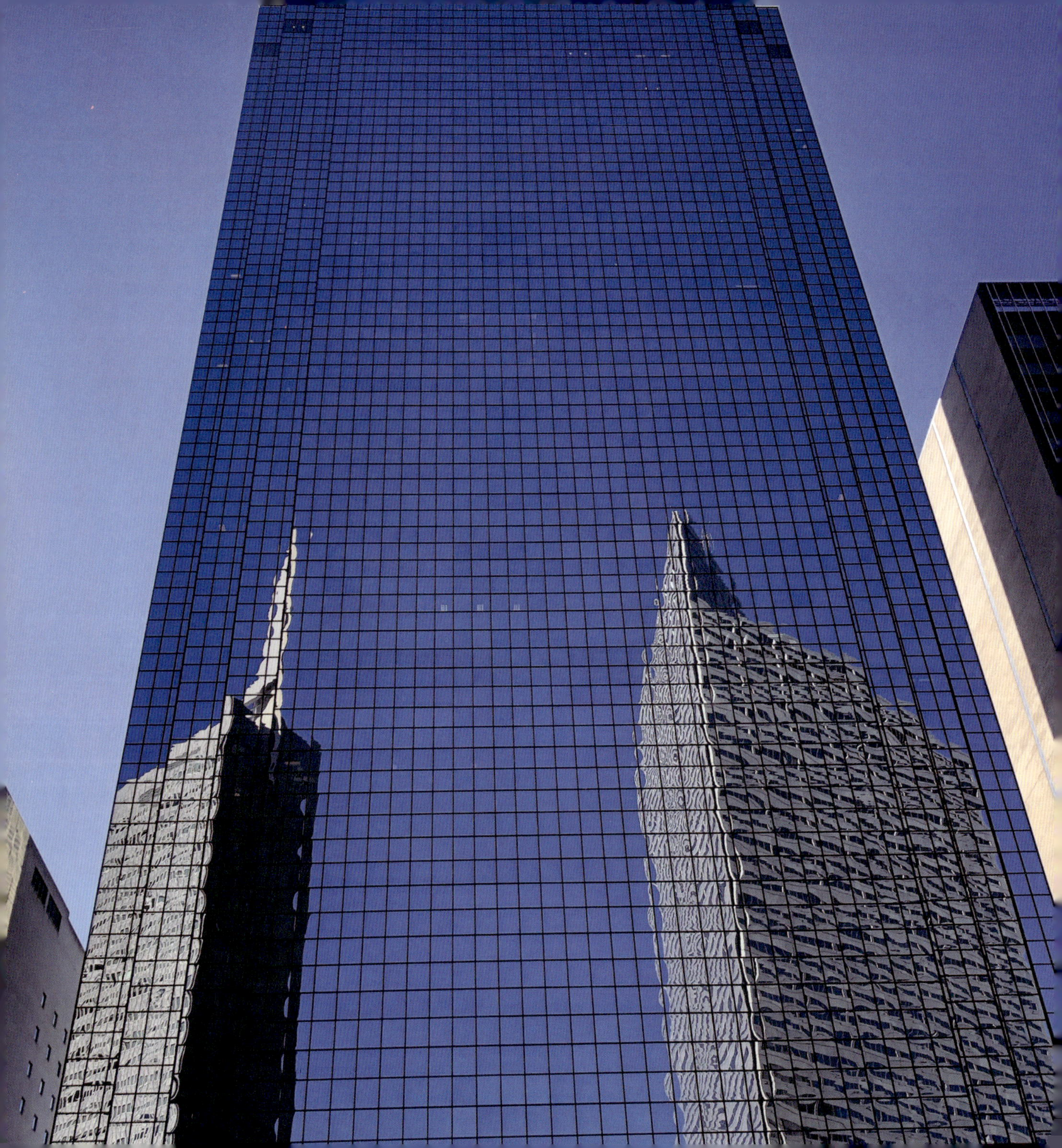

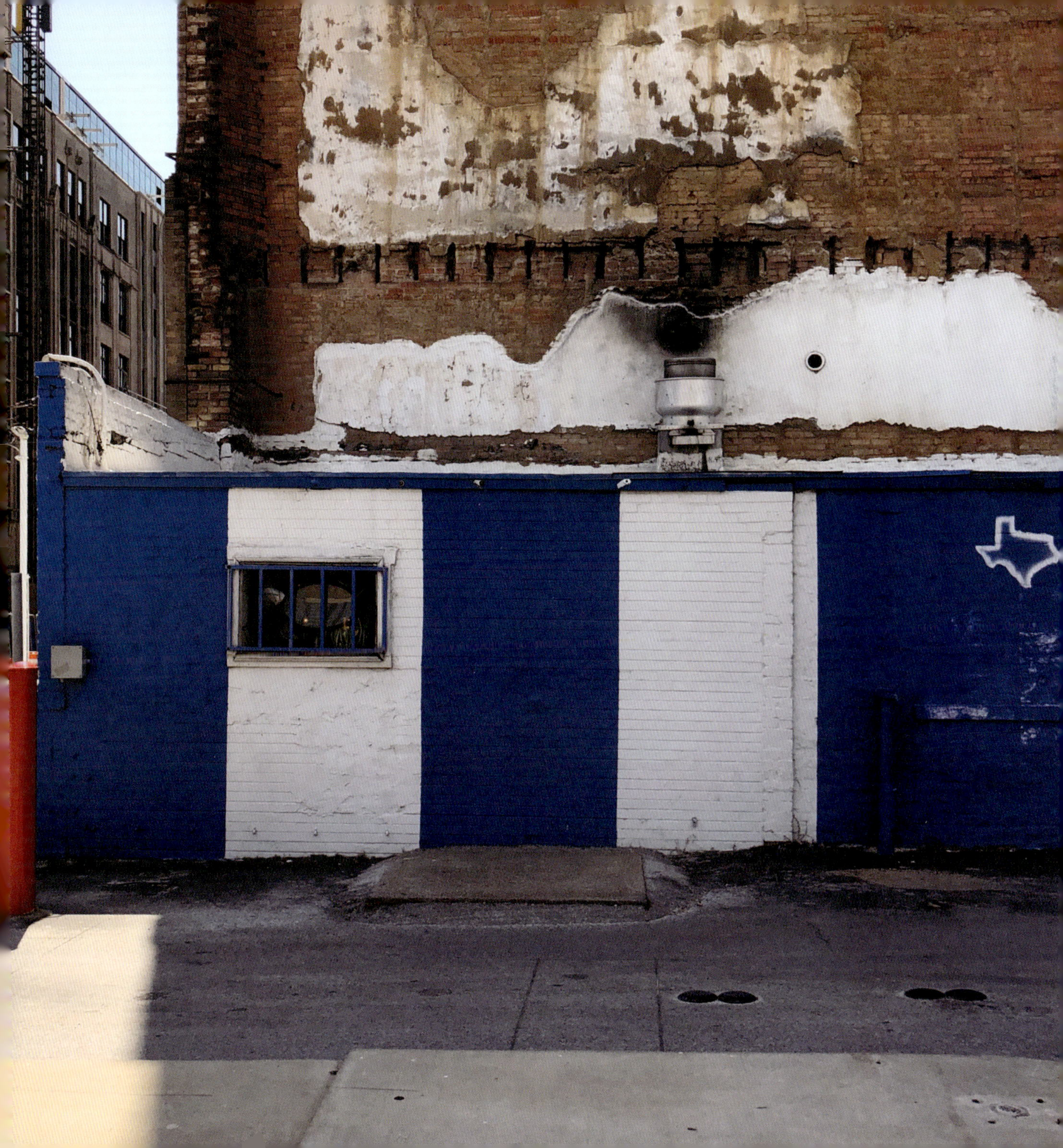

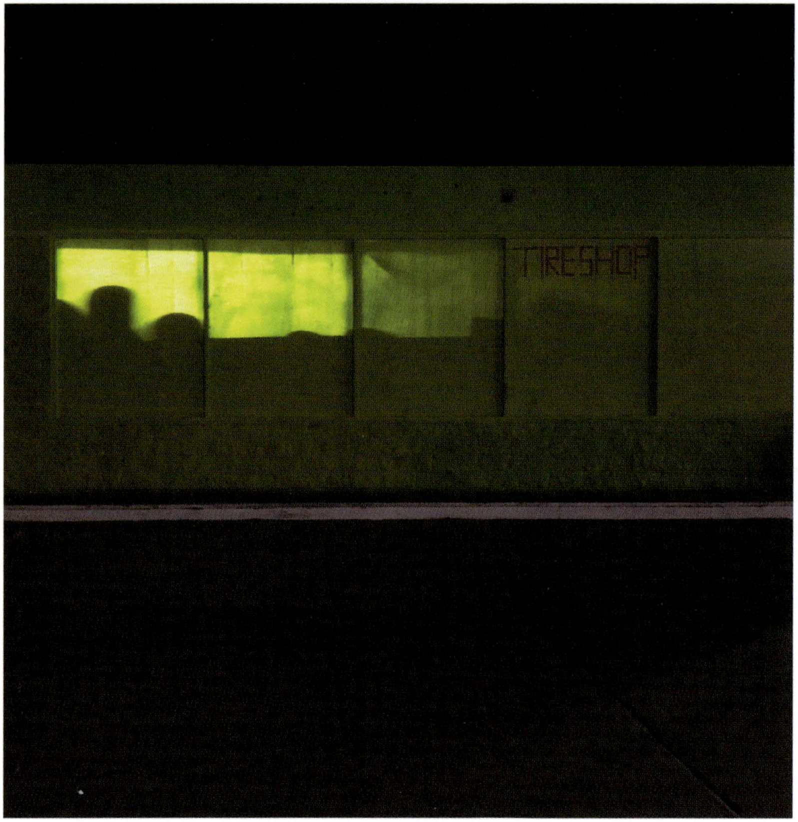
TIRESHOP

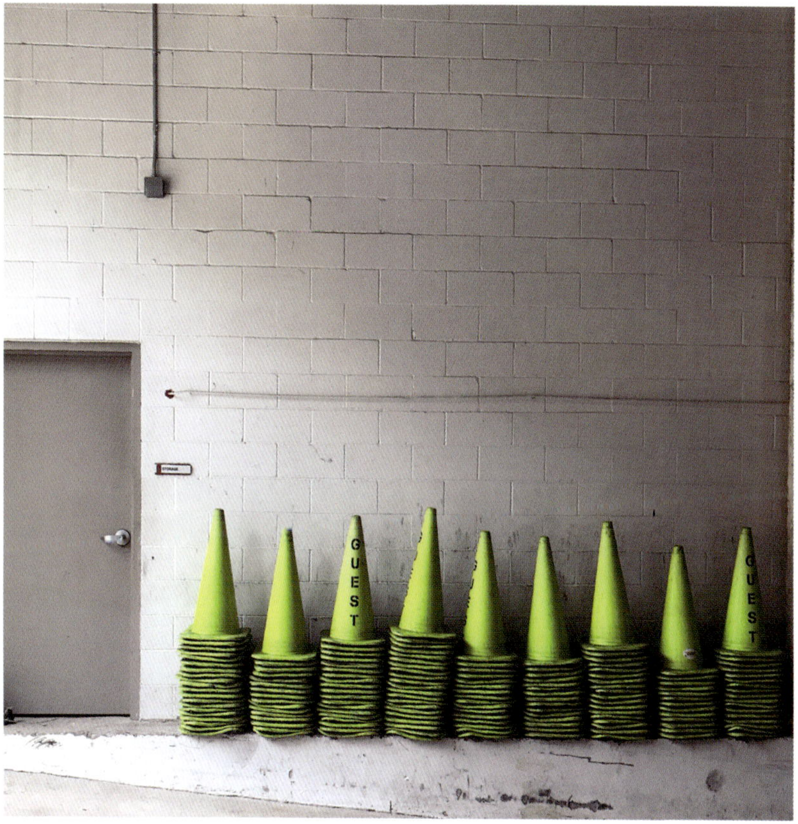
GUEST
GUEST

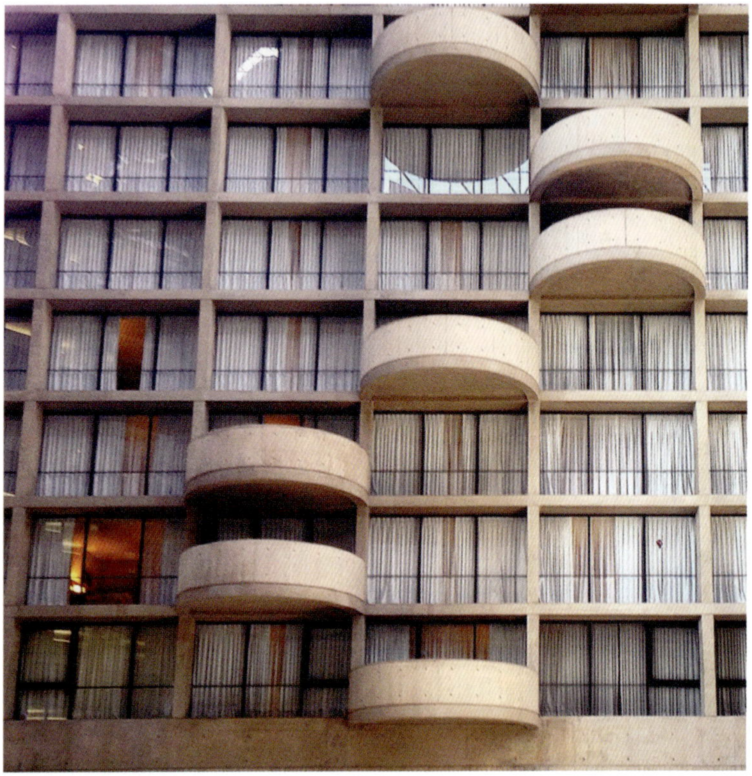

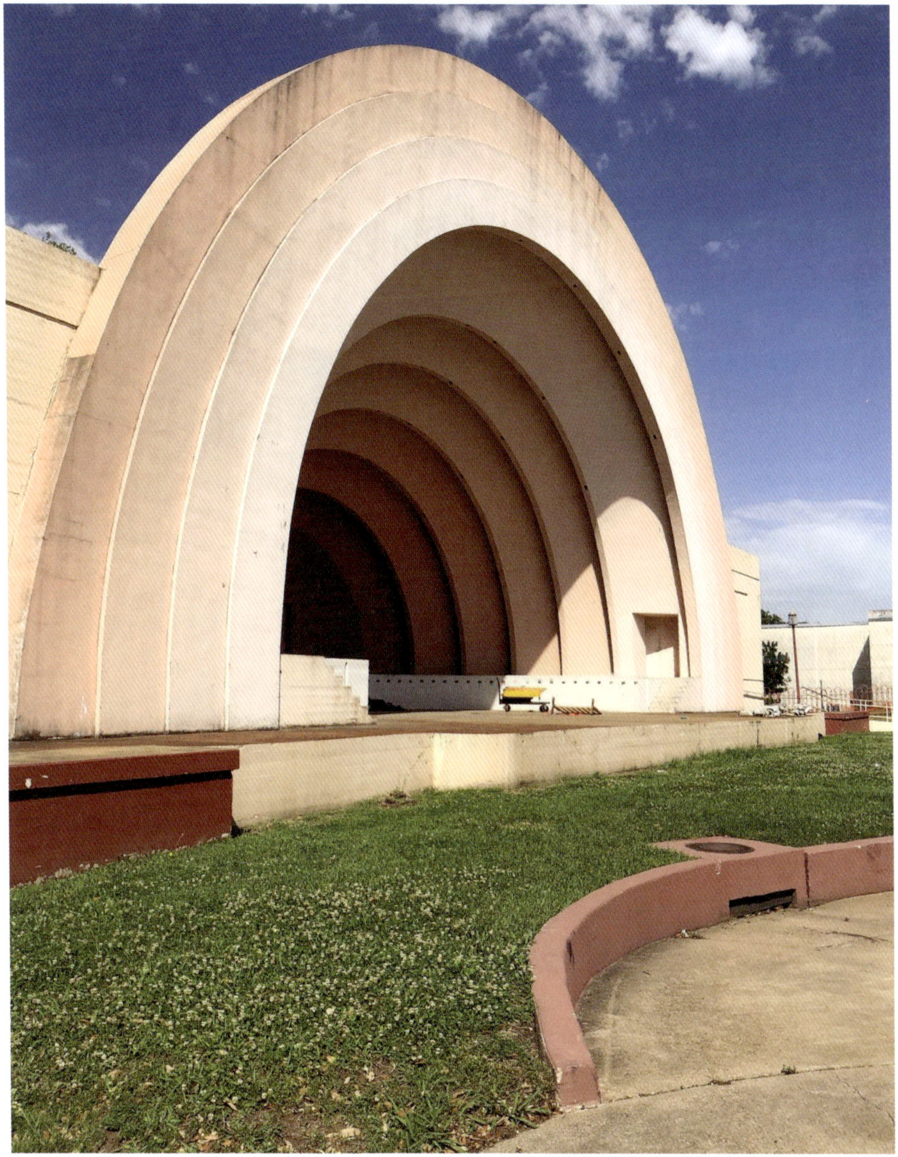

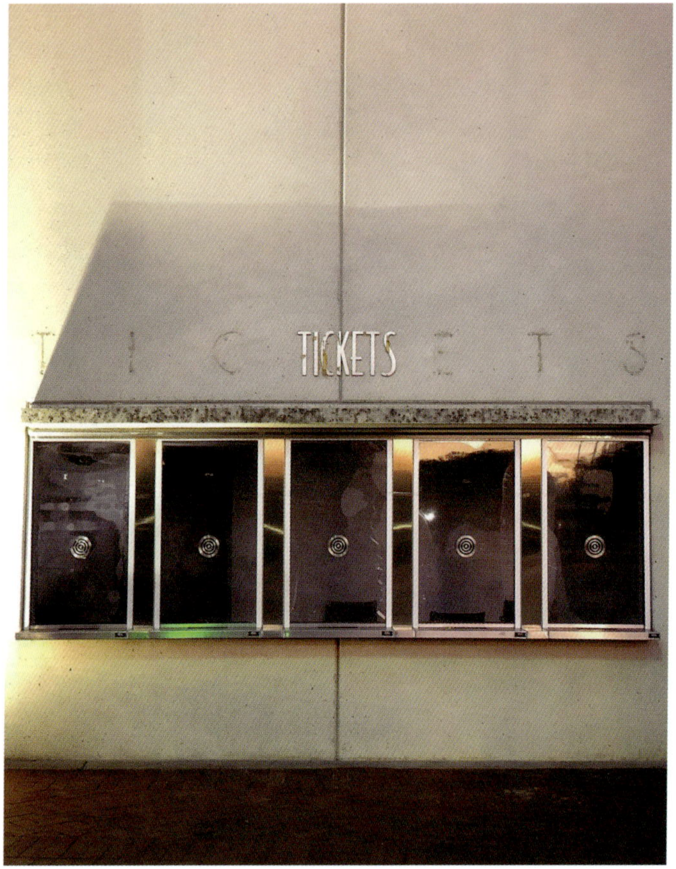
TICKETS

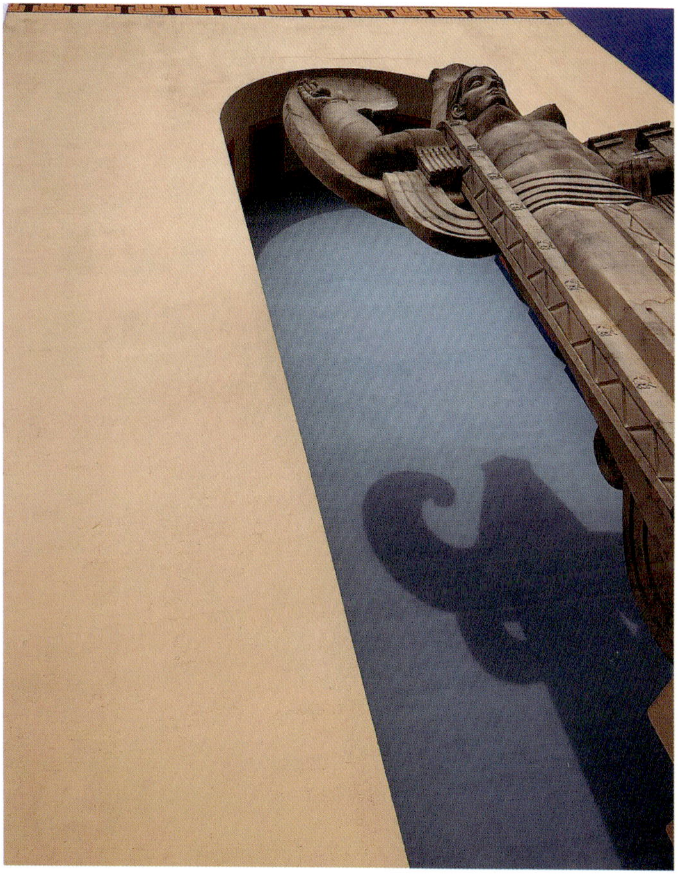

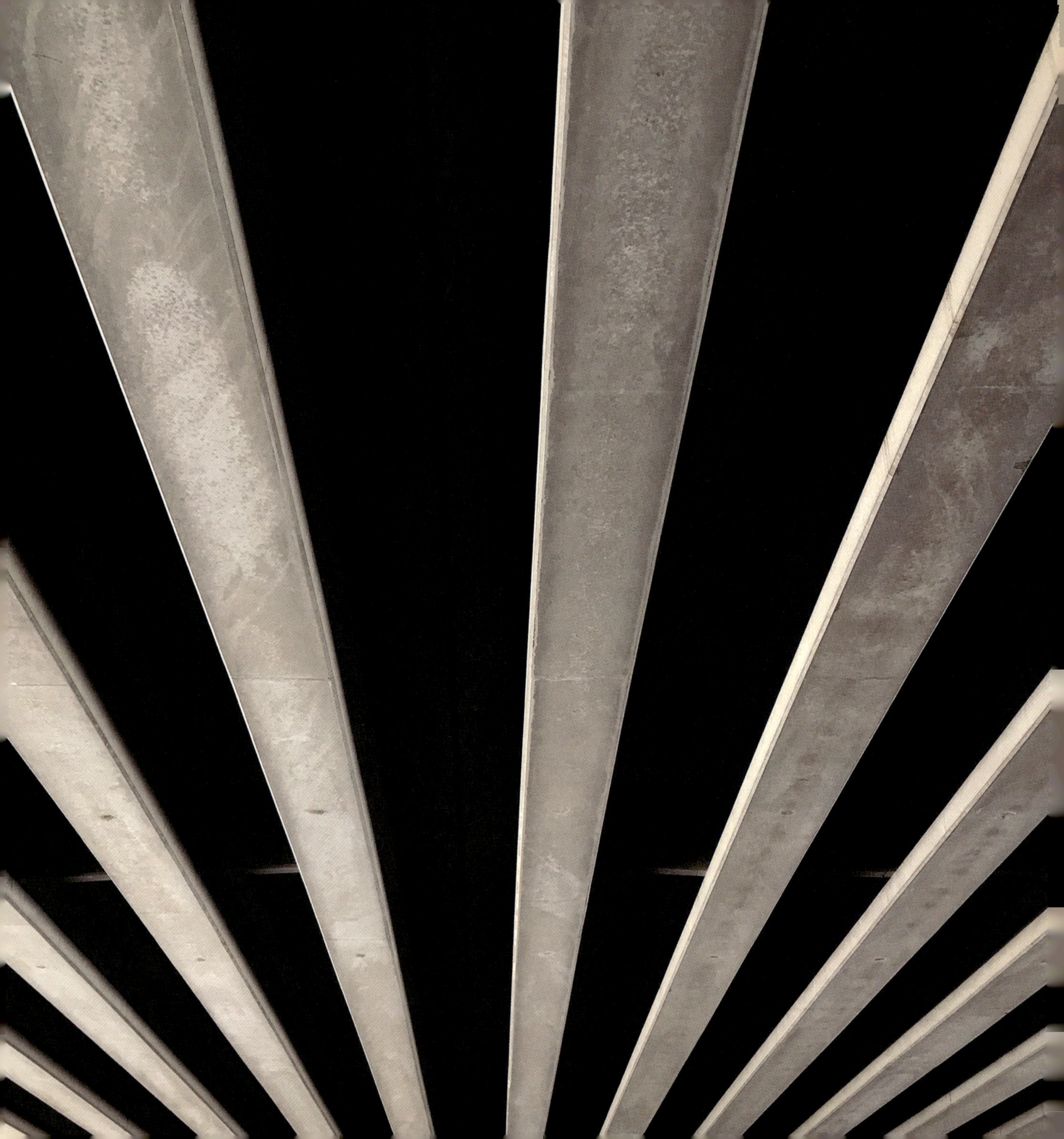

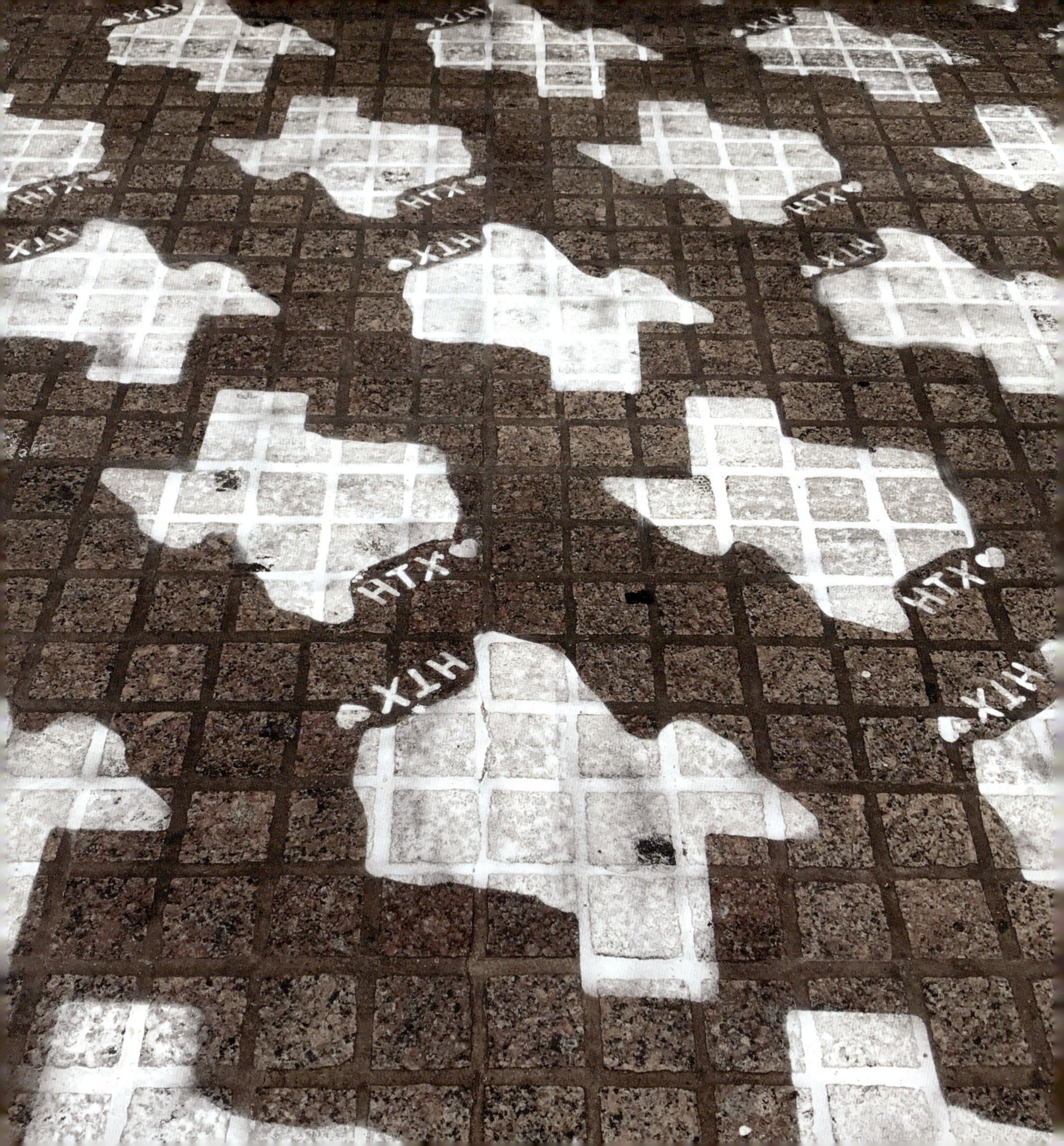
HTX

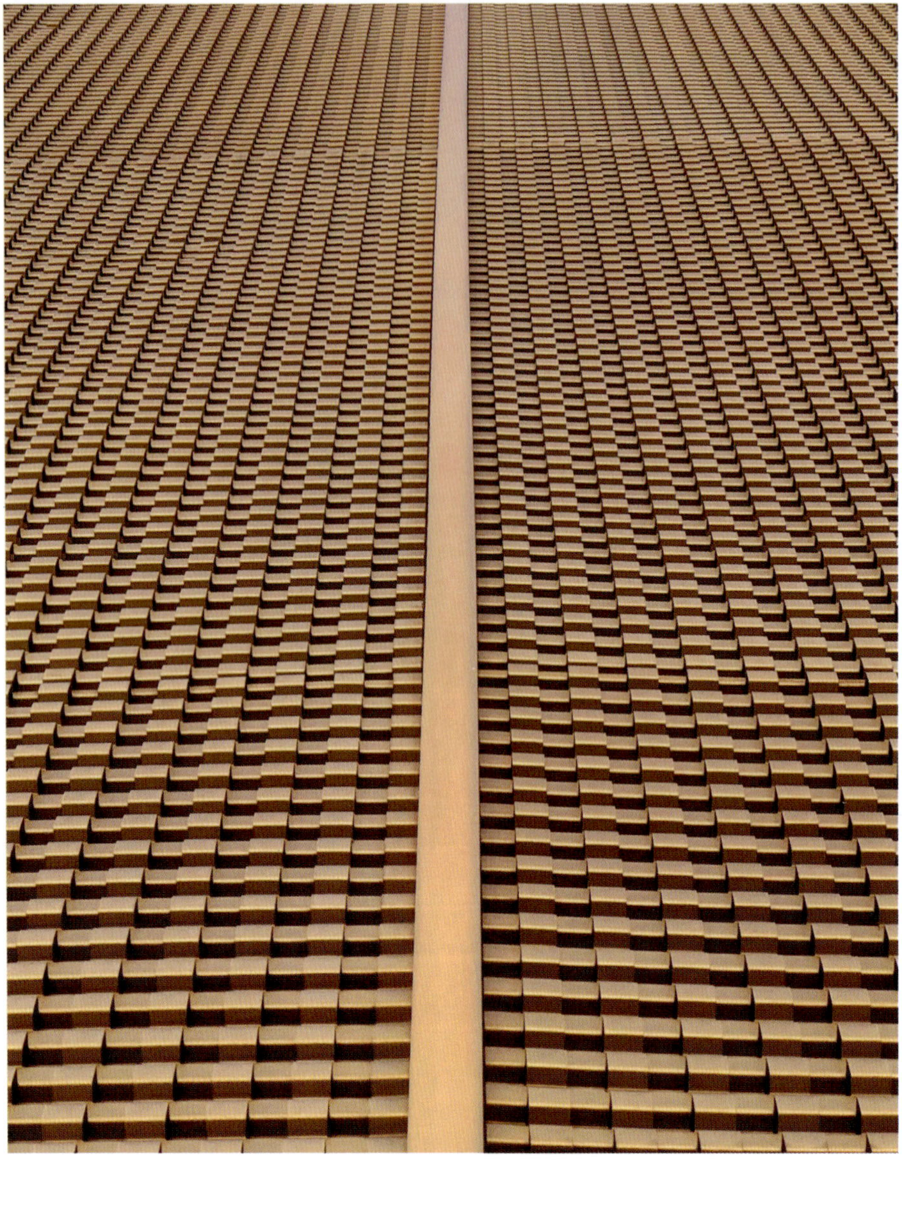

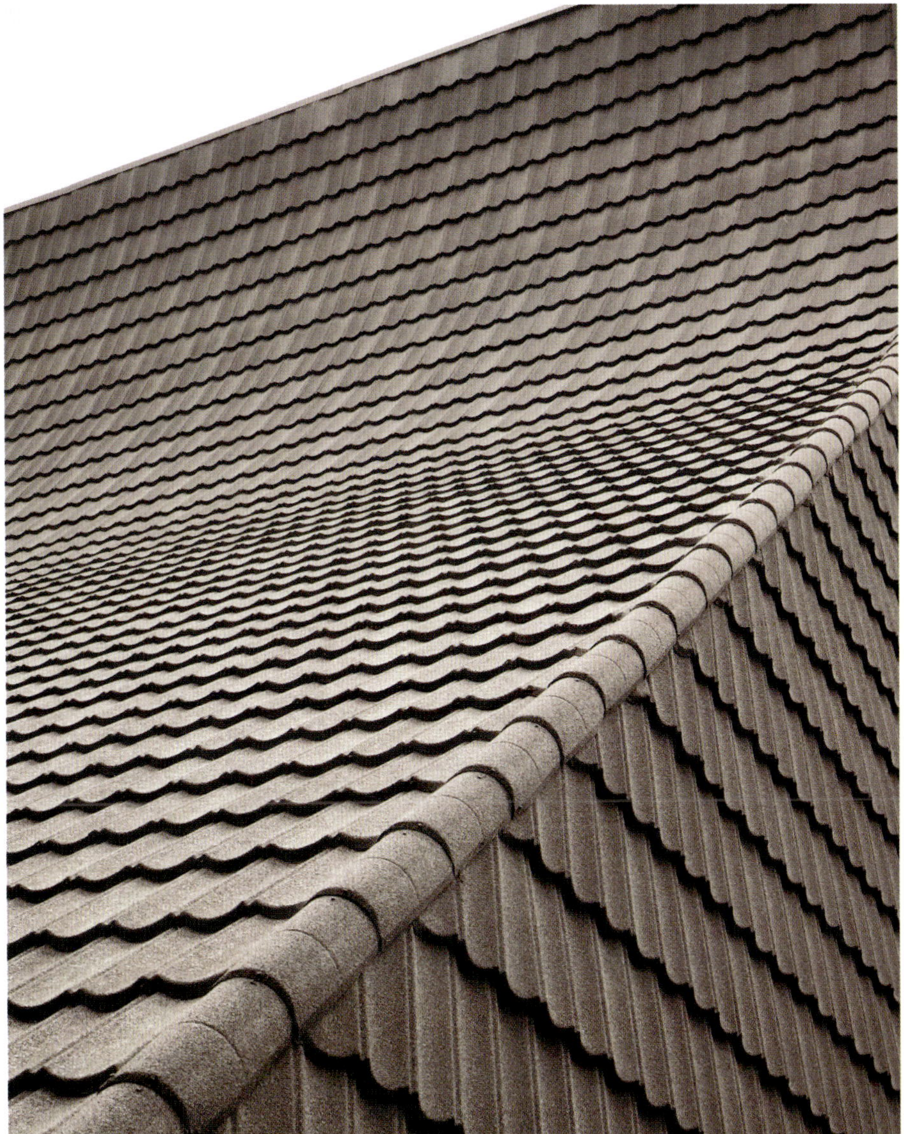

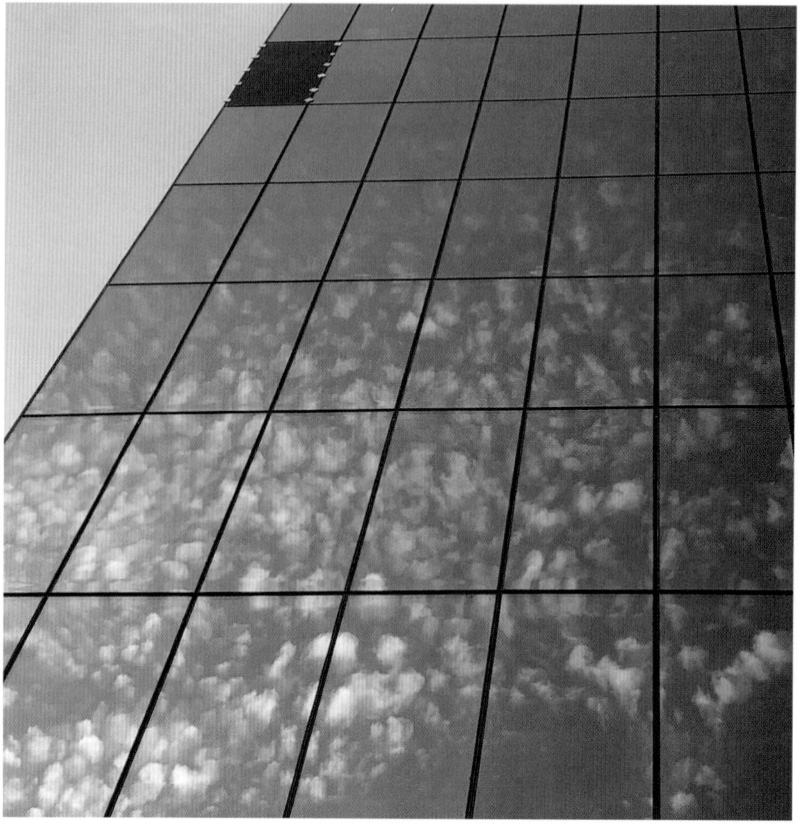

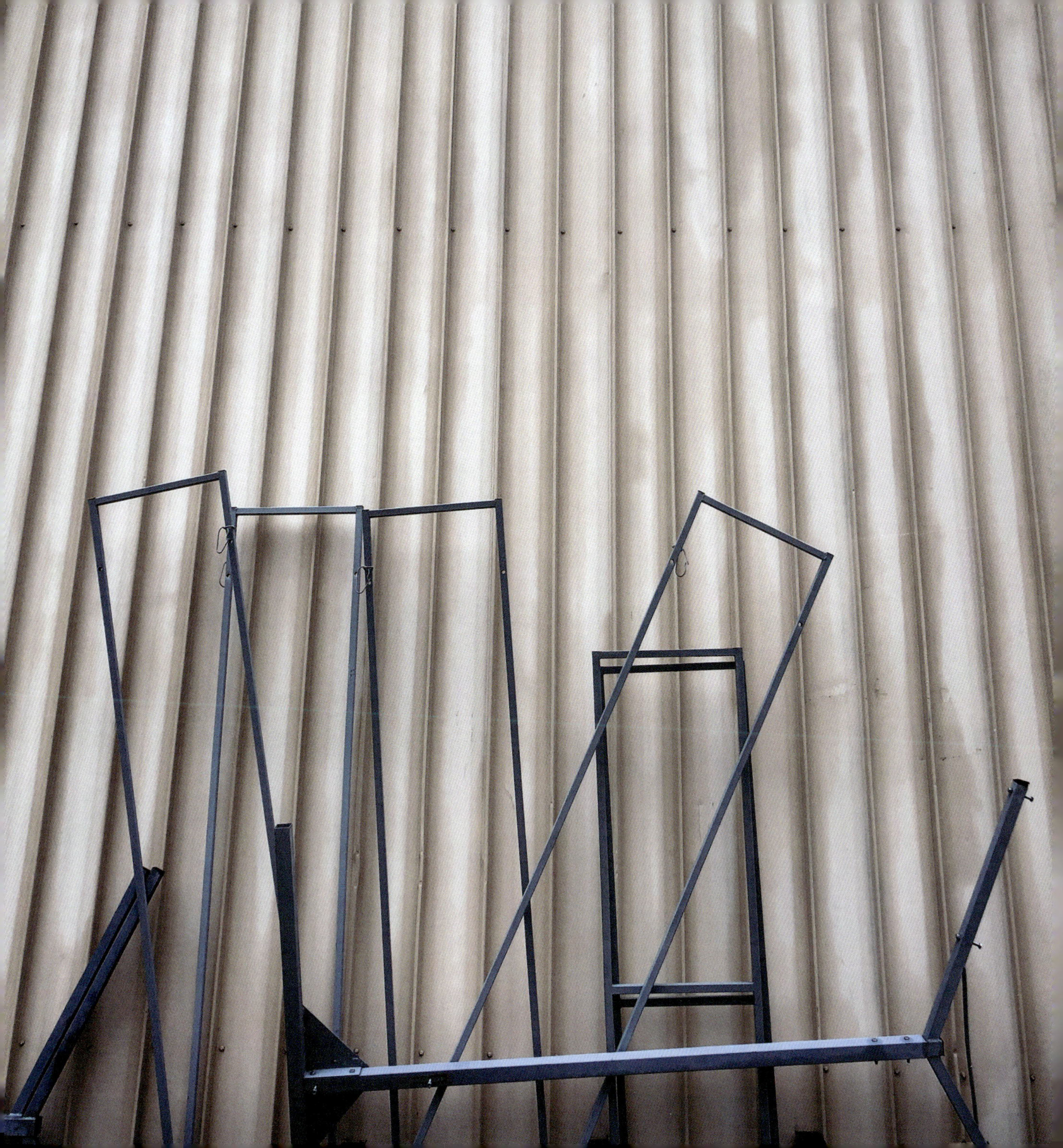

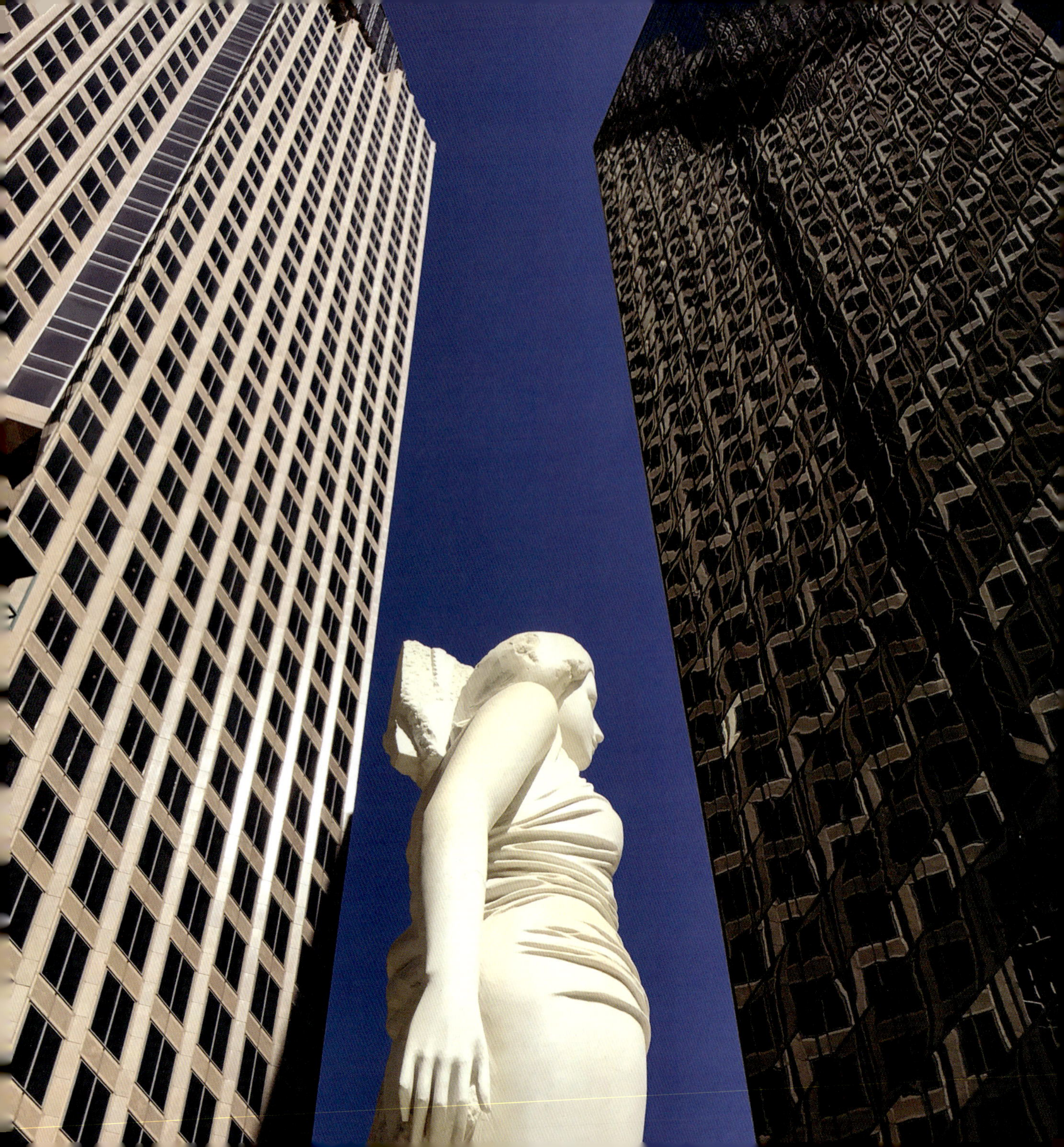

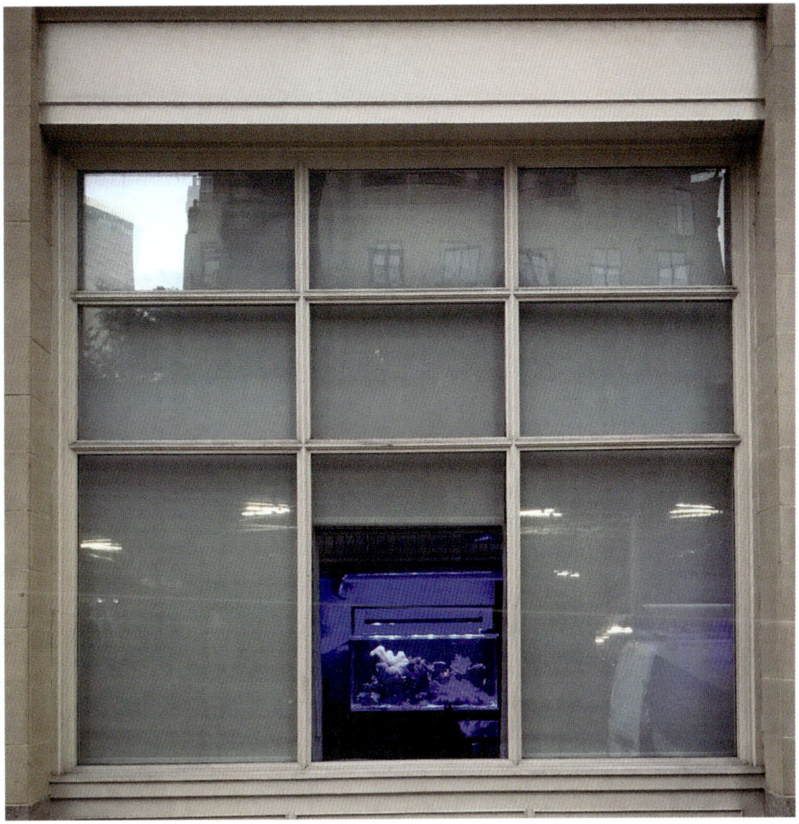

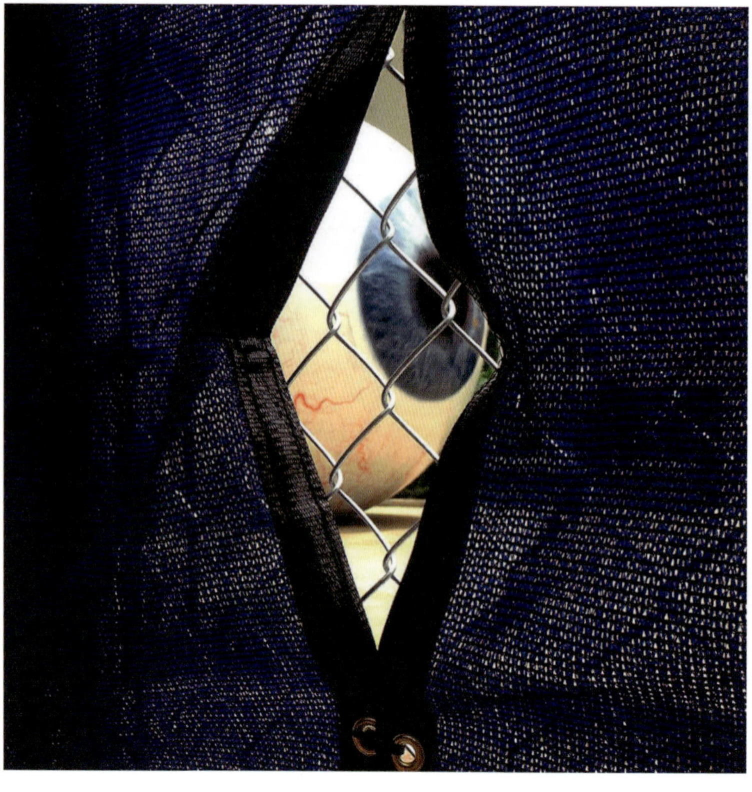

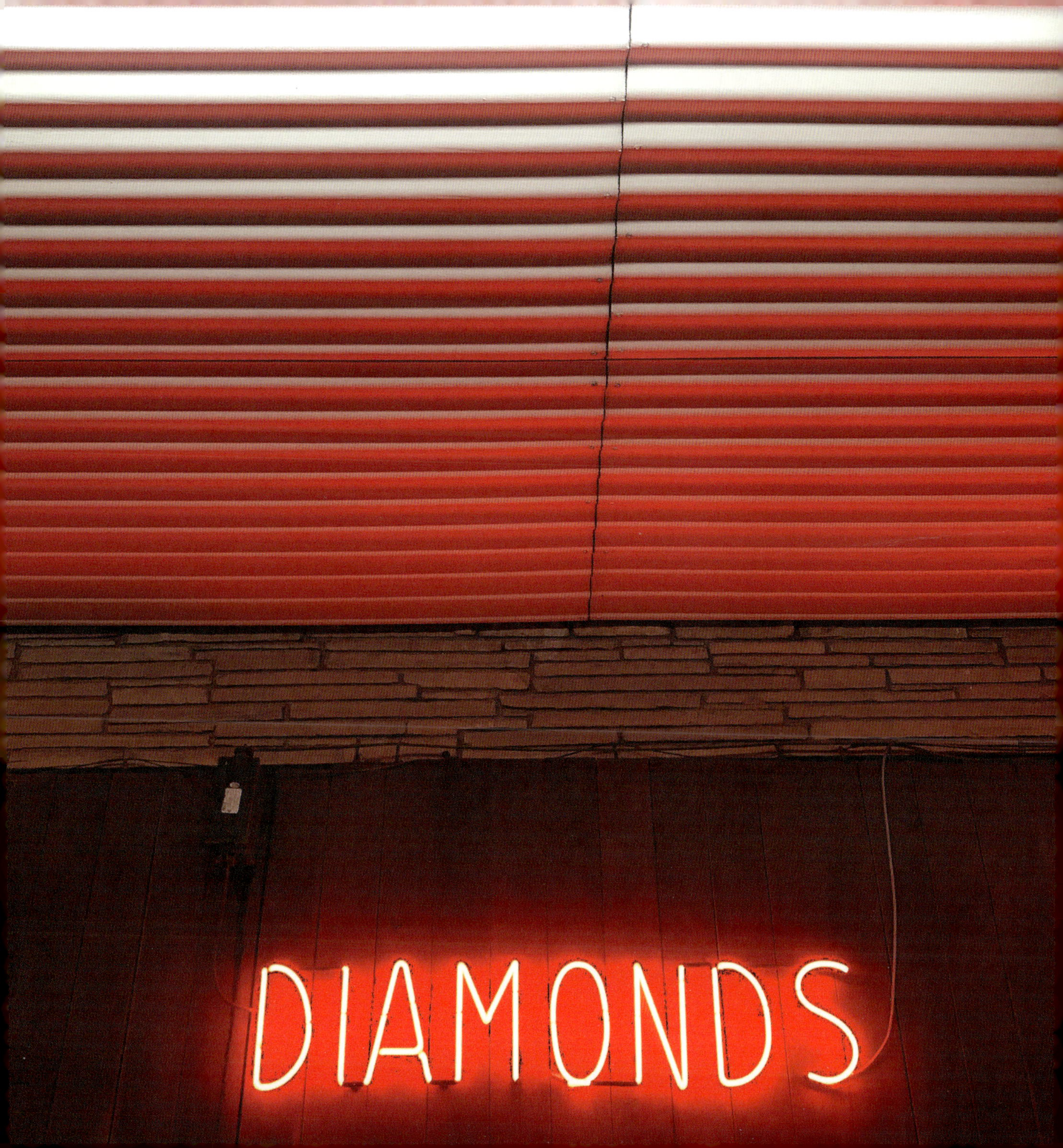
DIAMONDS

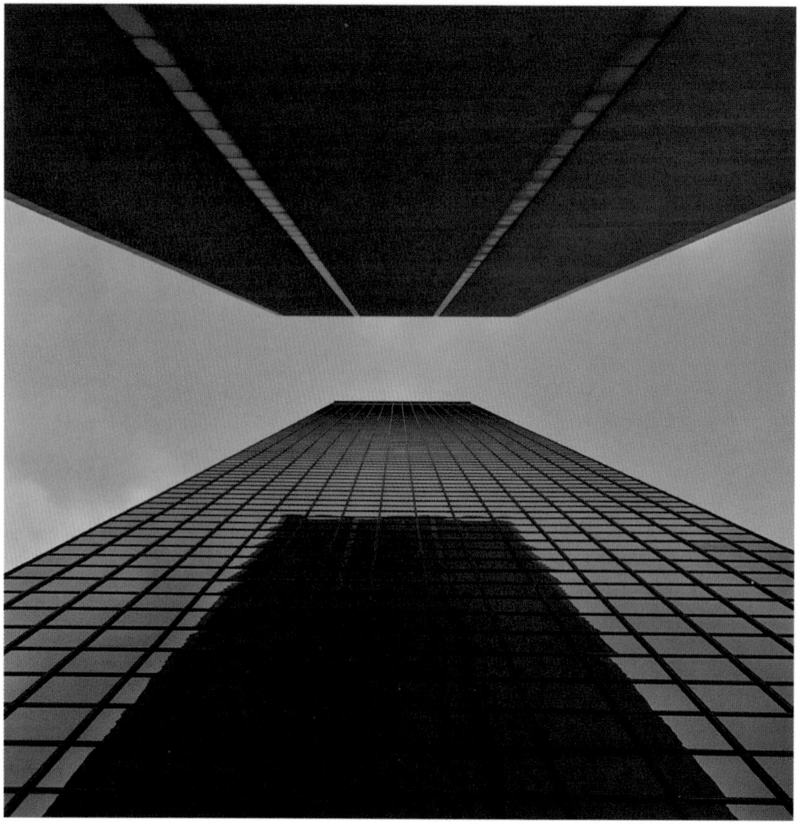

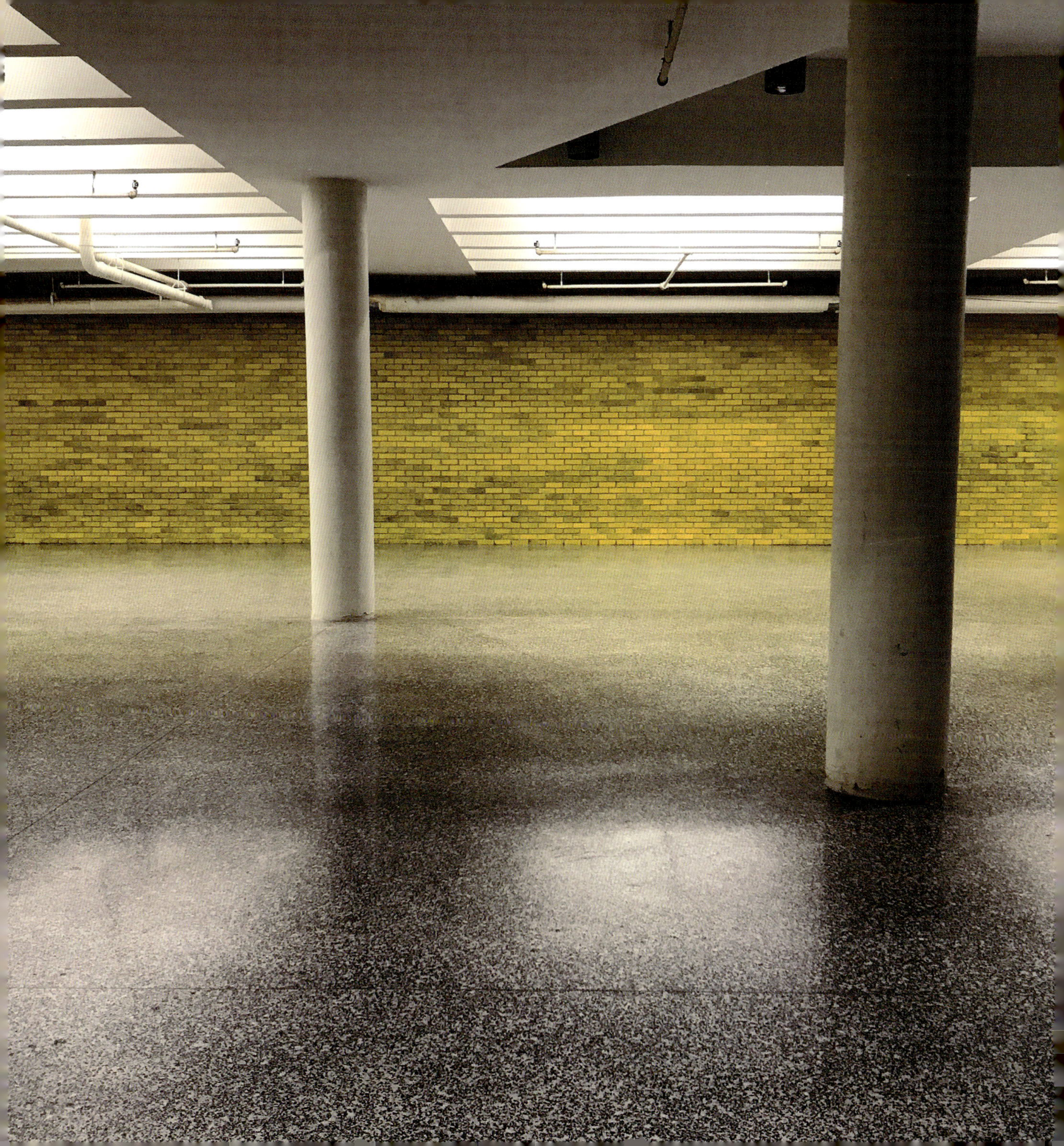

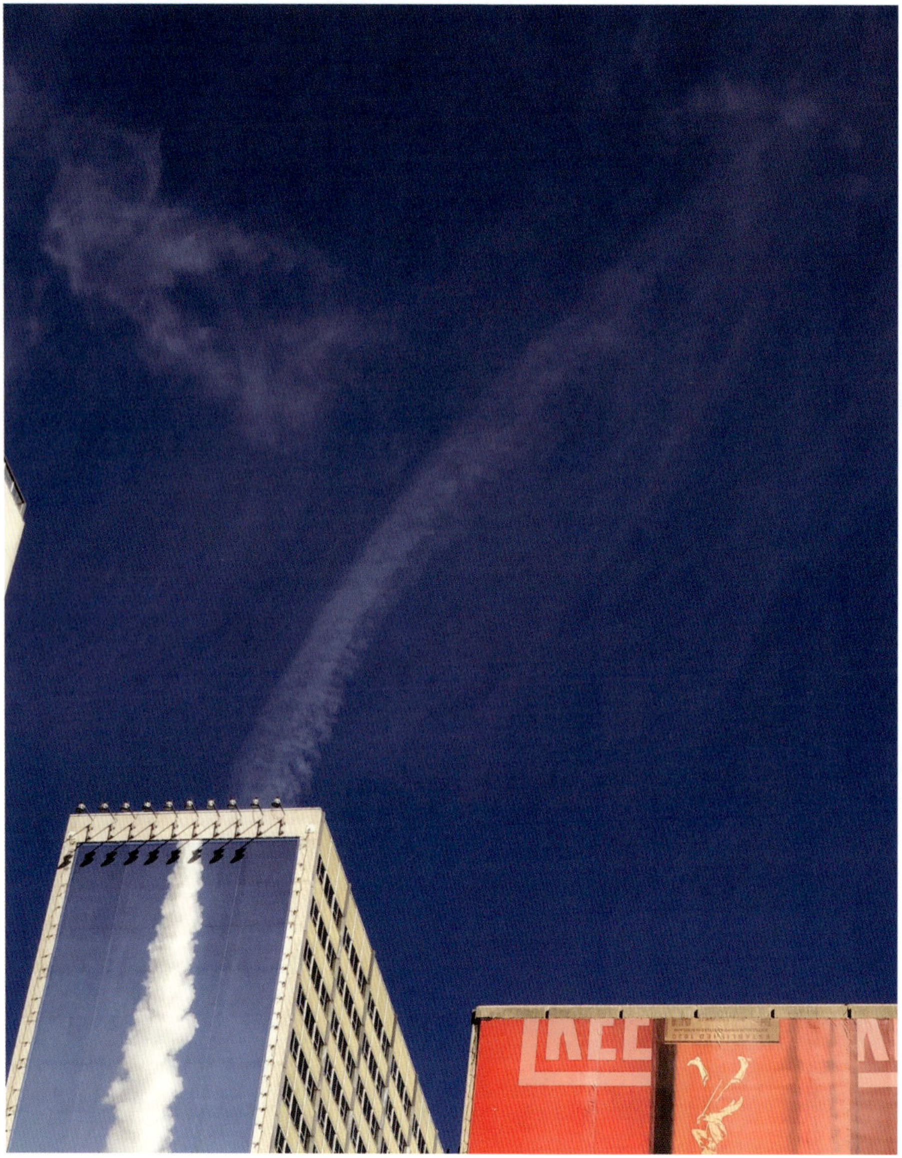

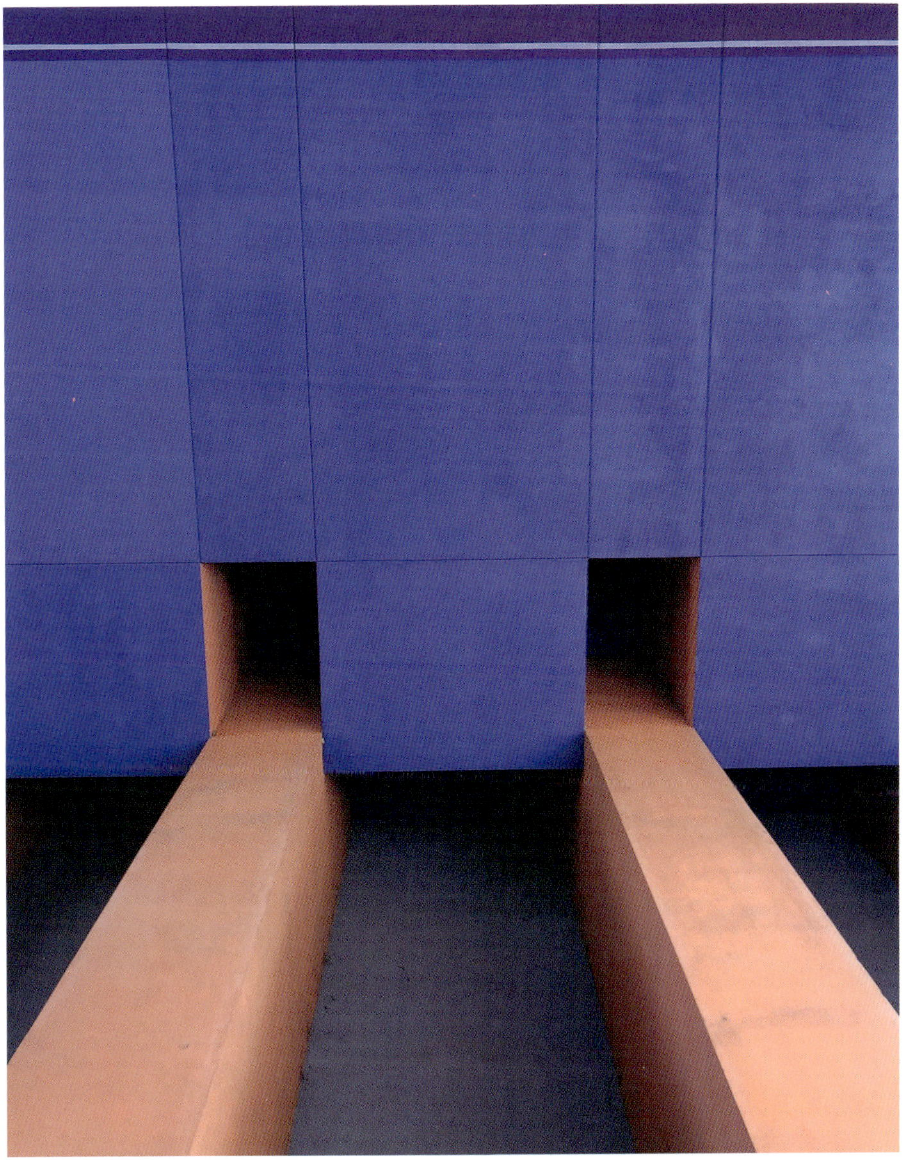

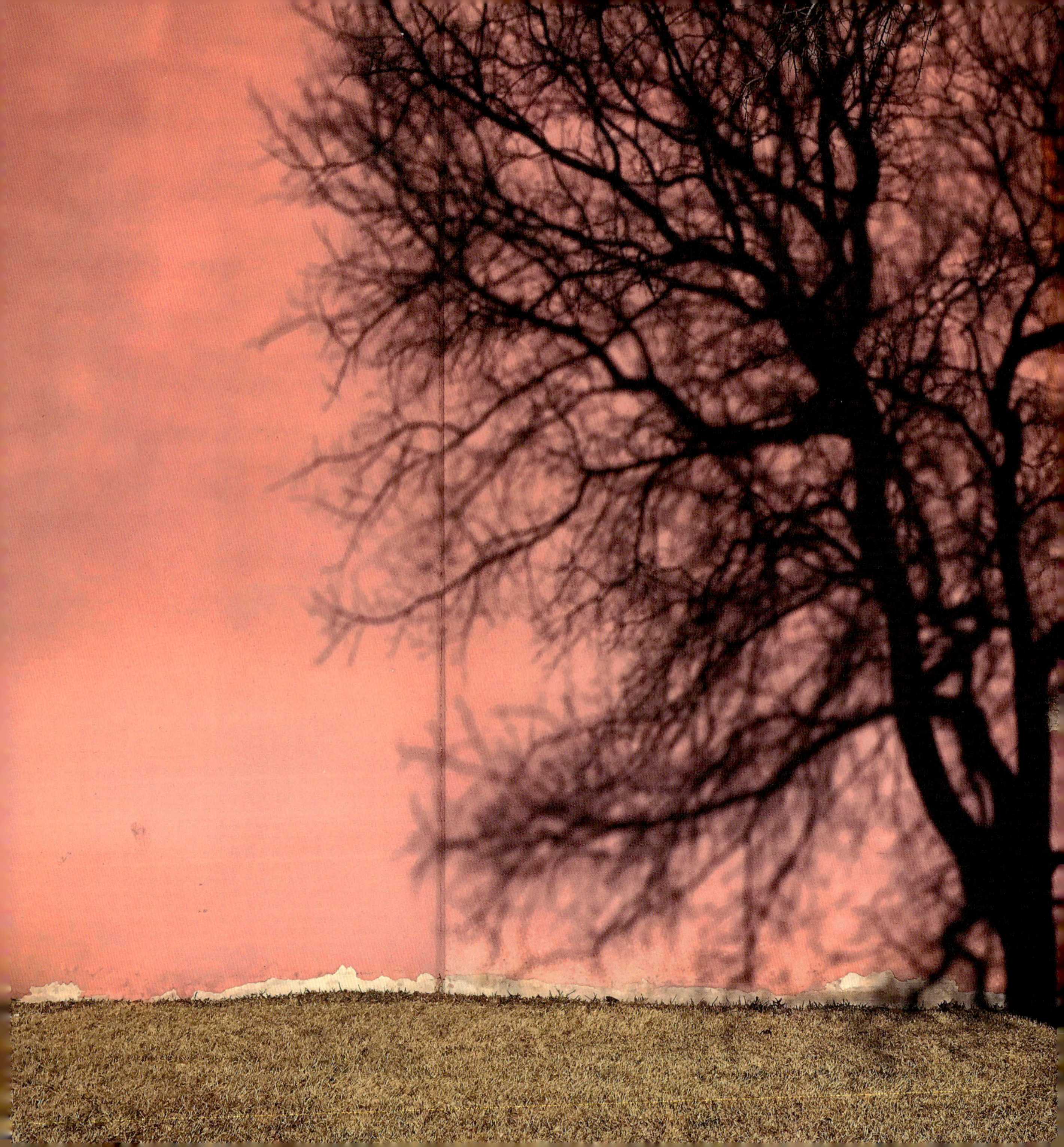

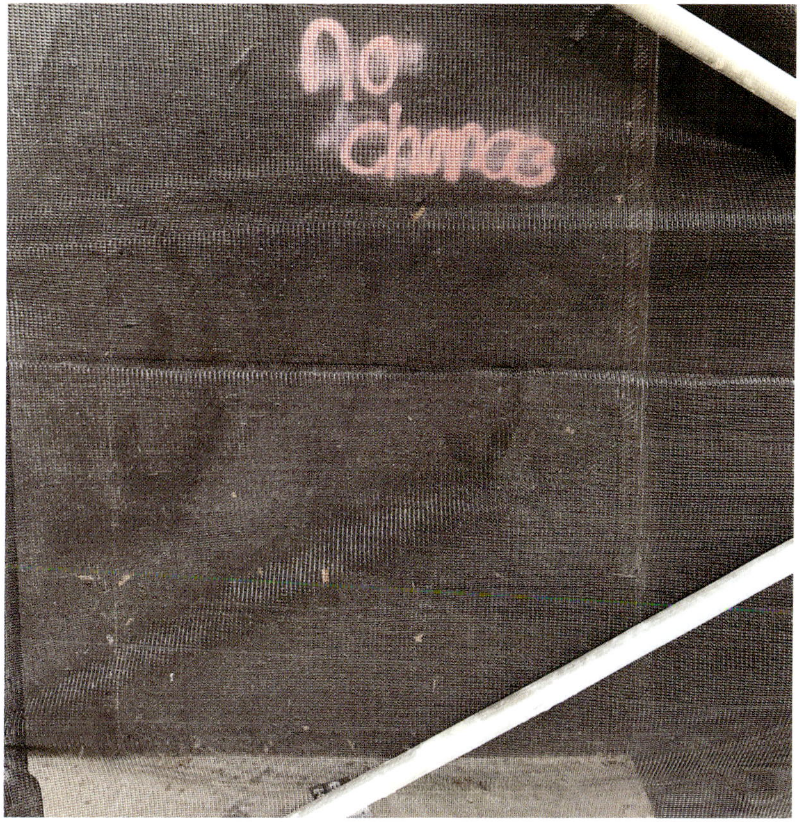

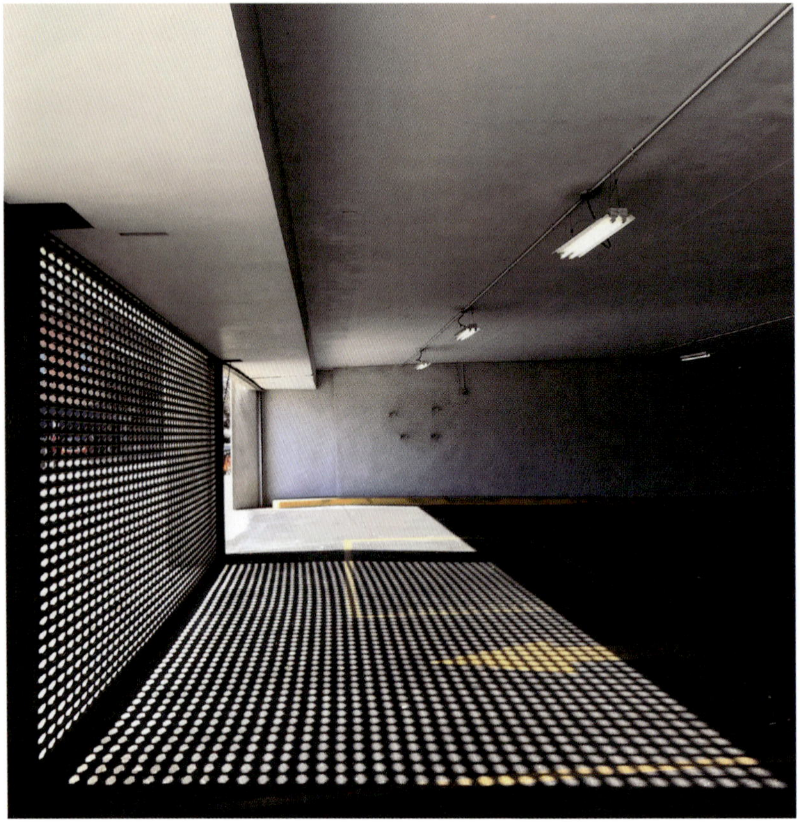

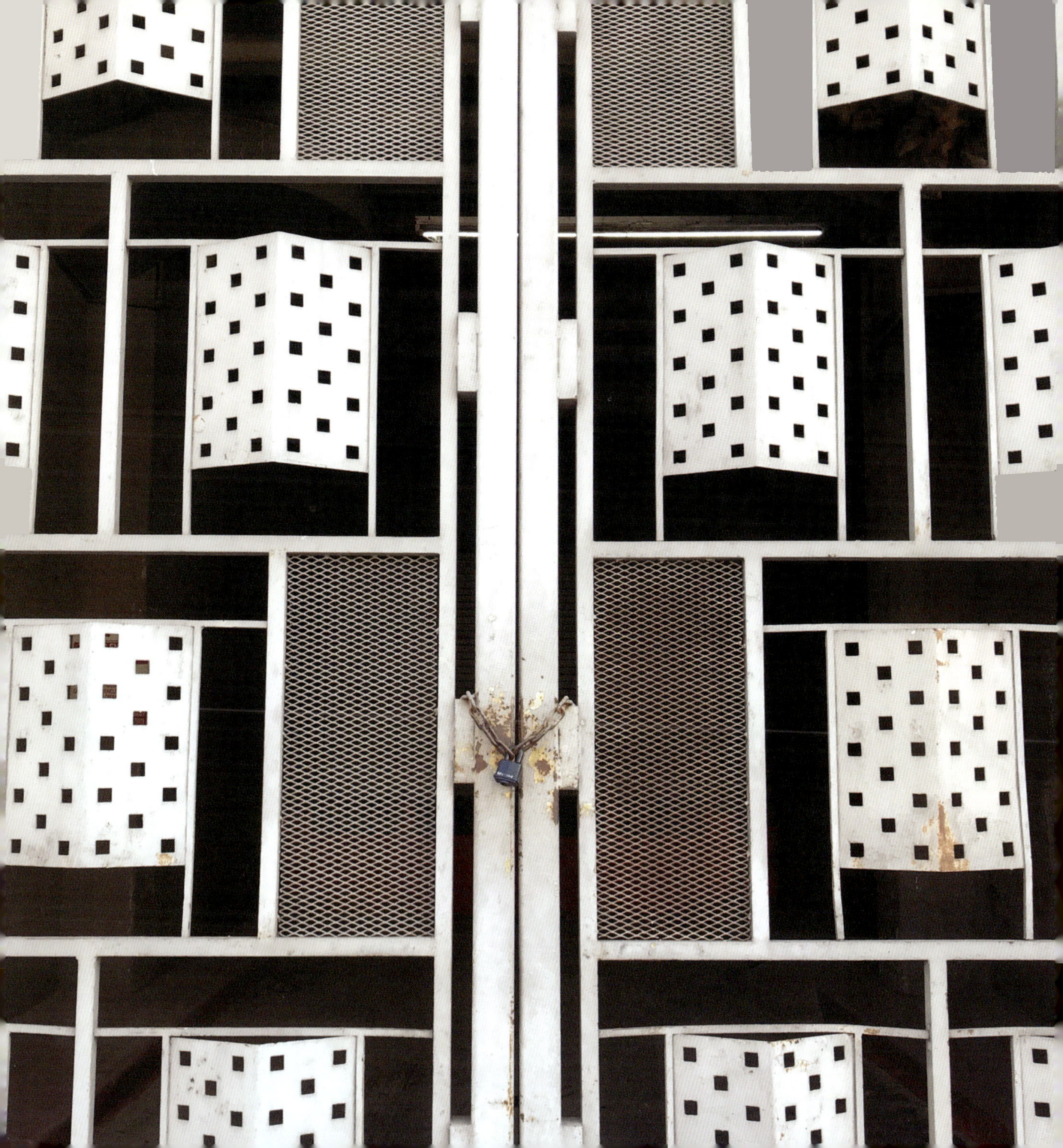

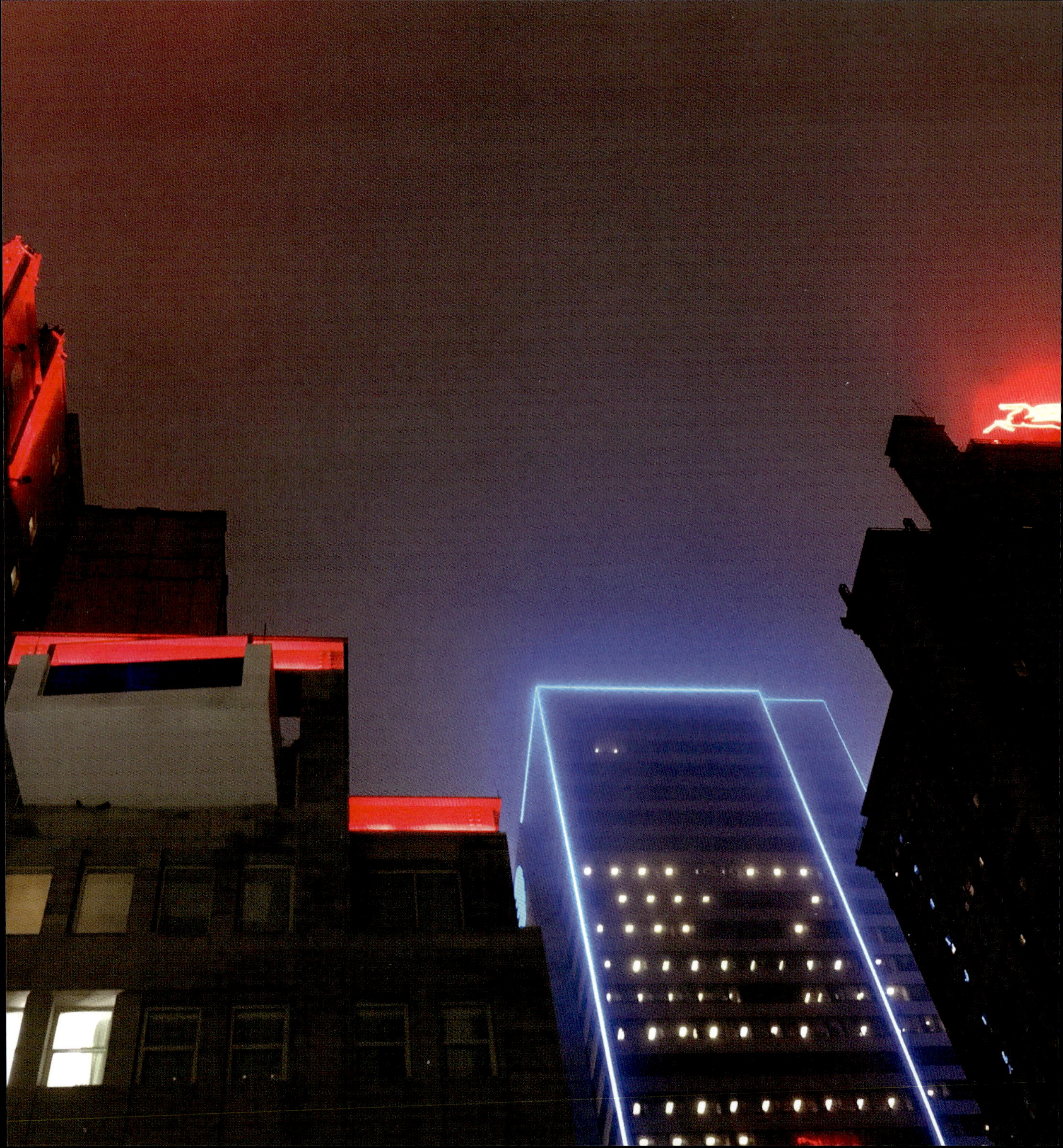

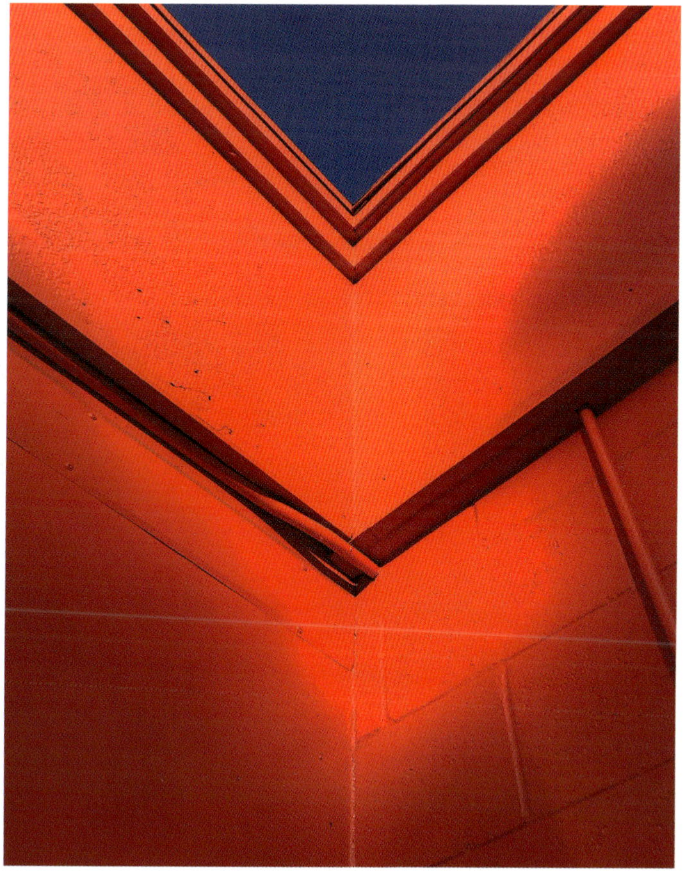

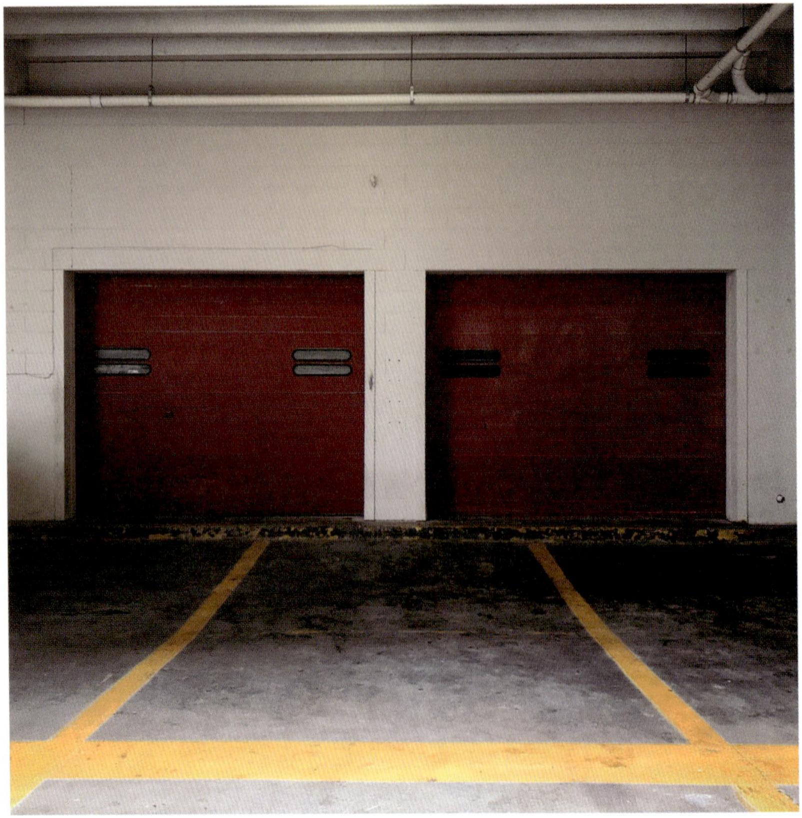

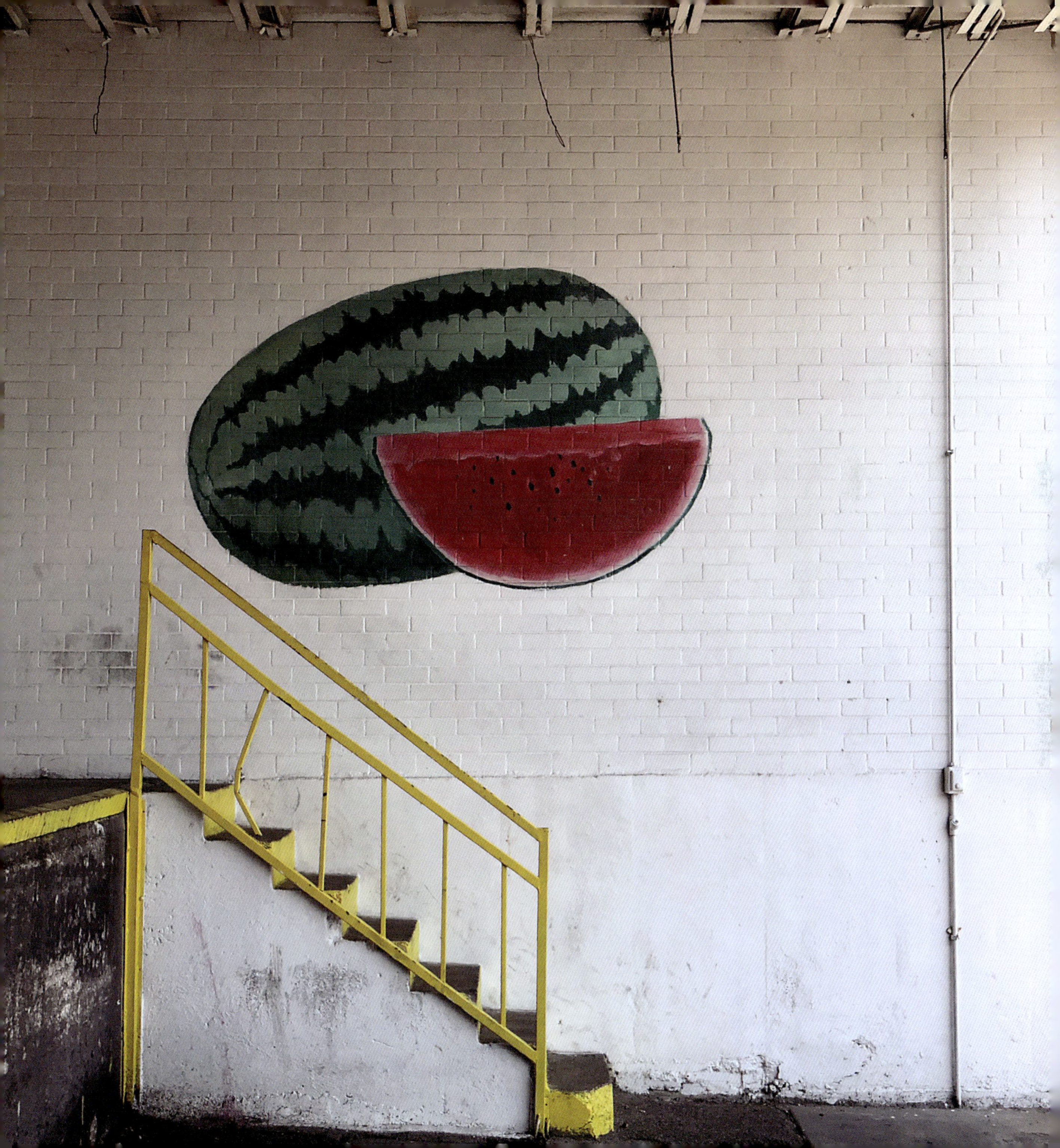

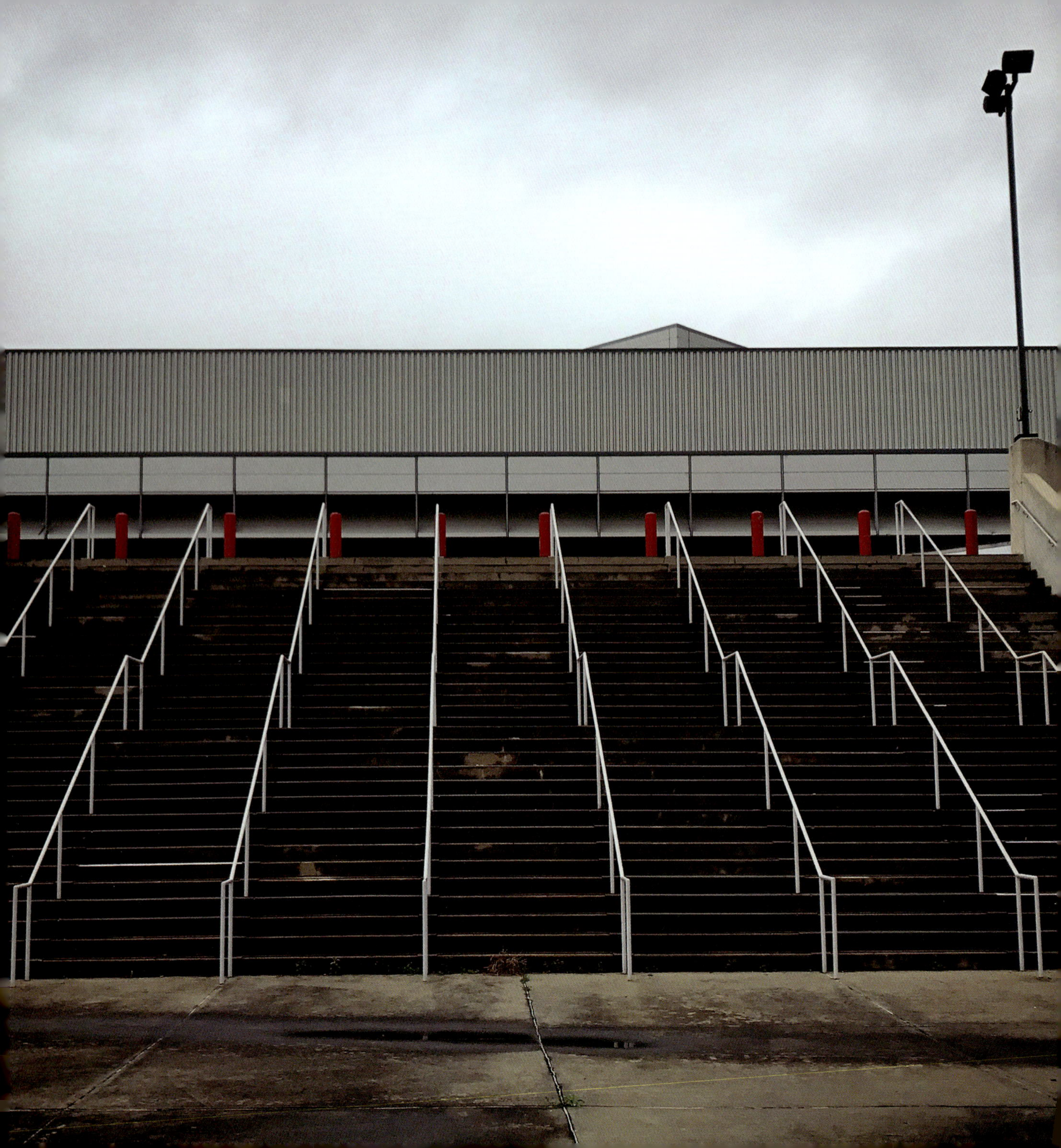

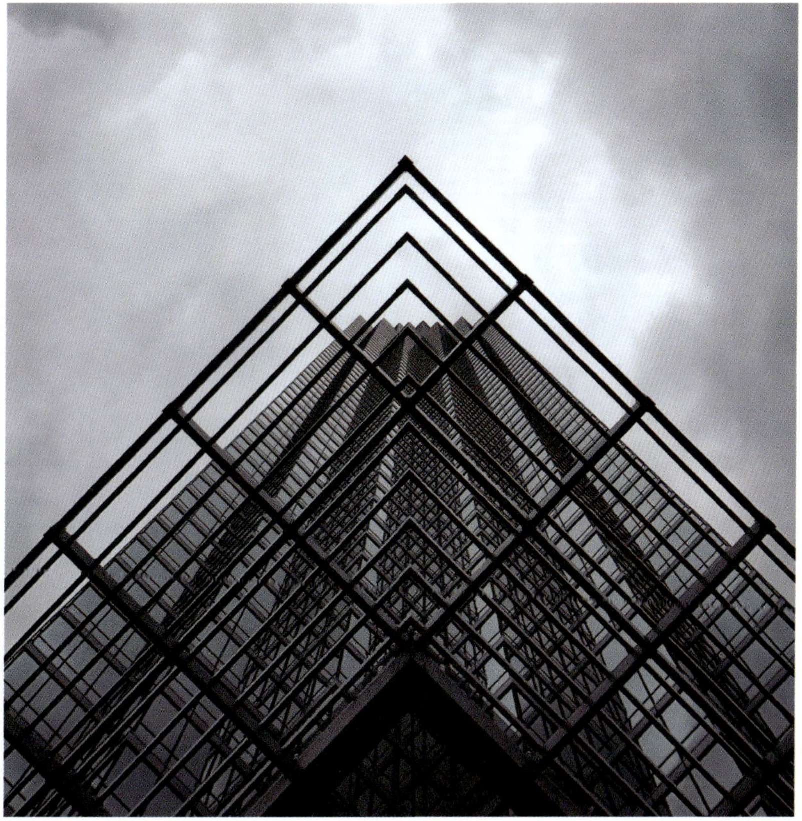

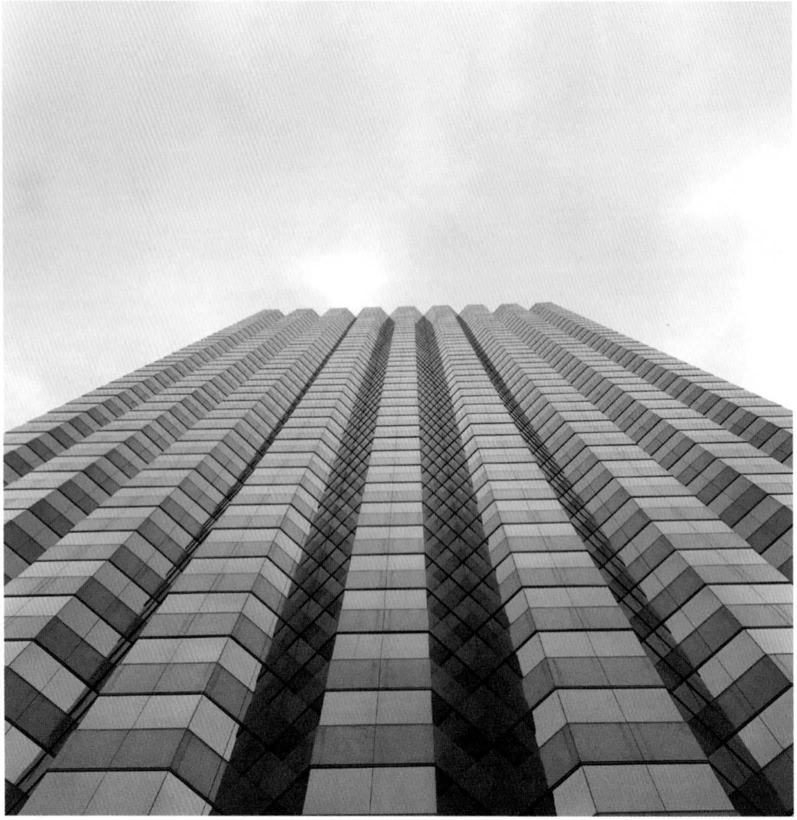

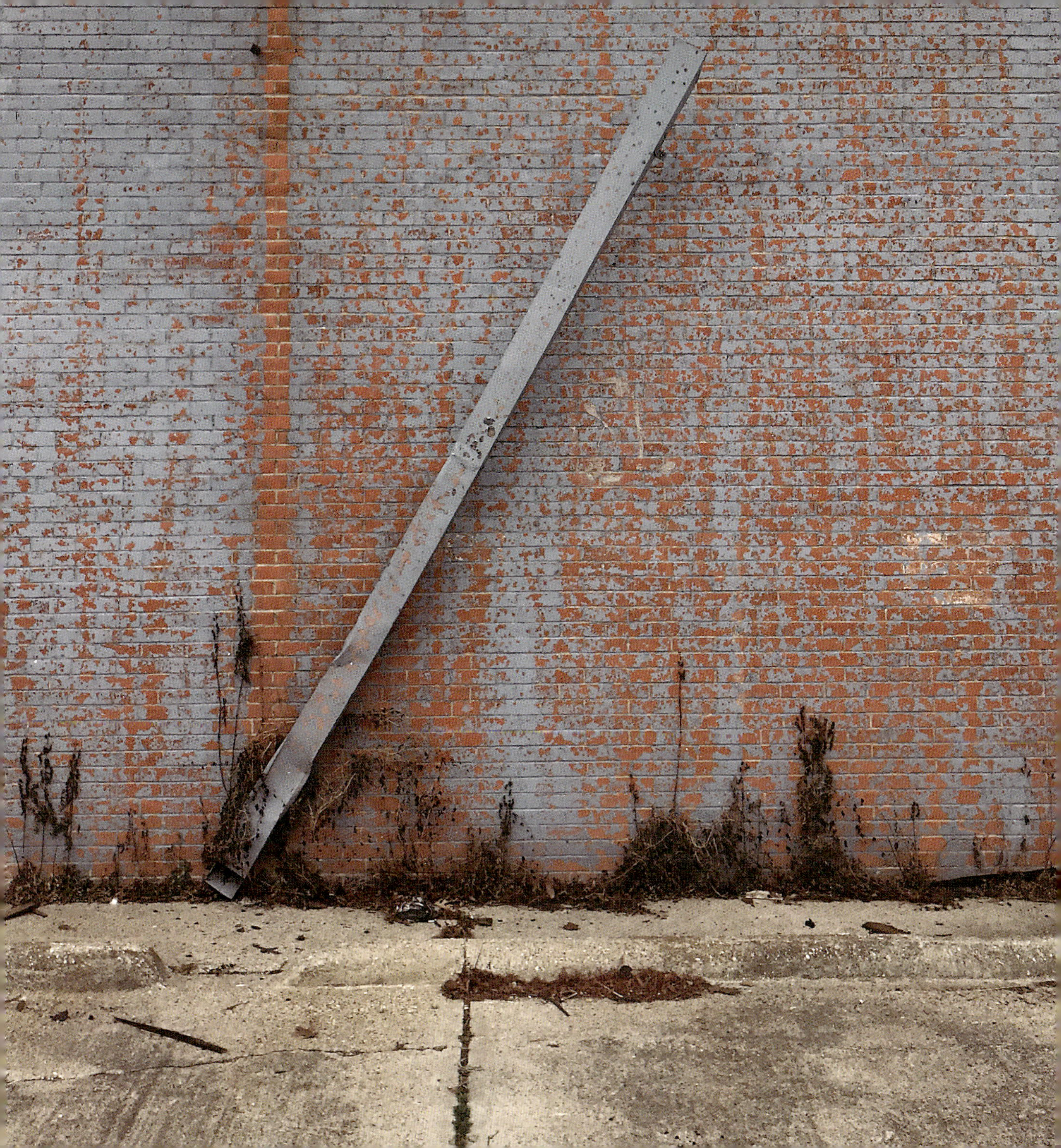

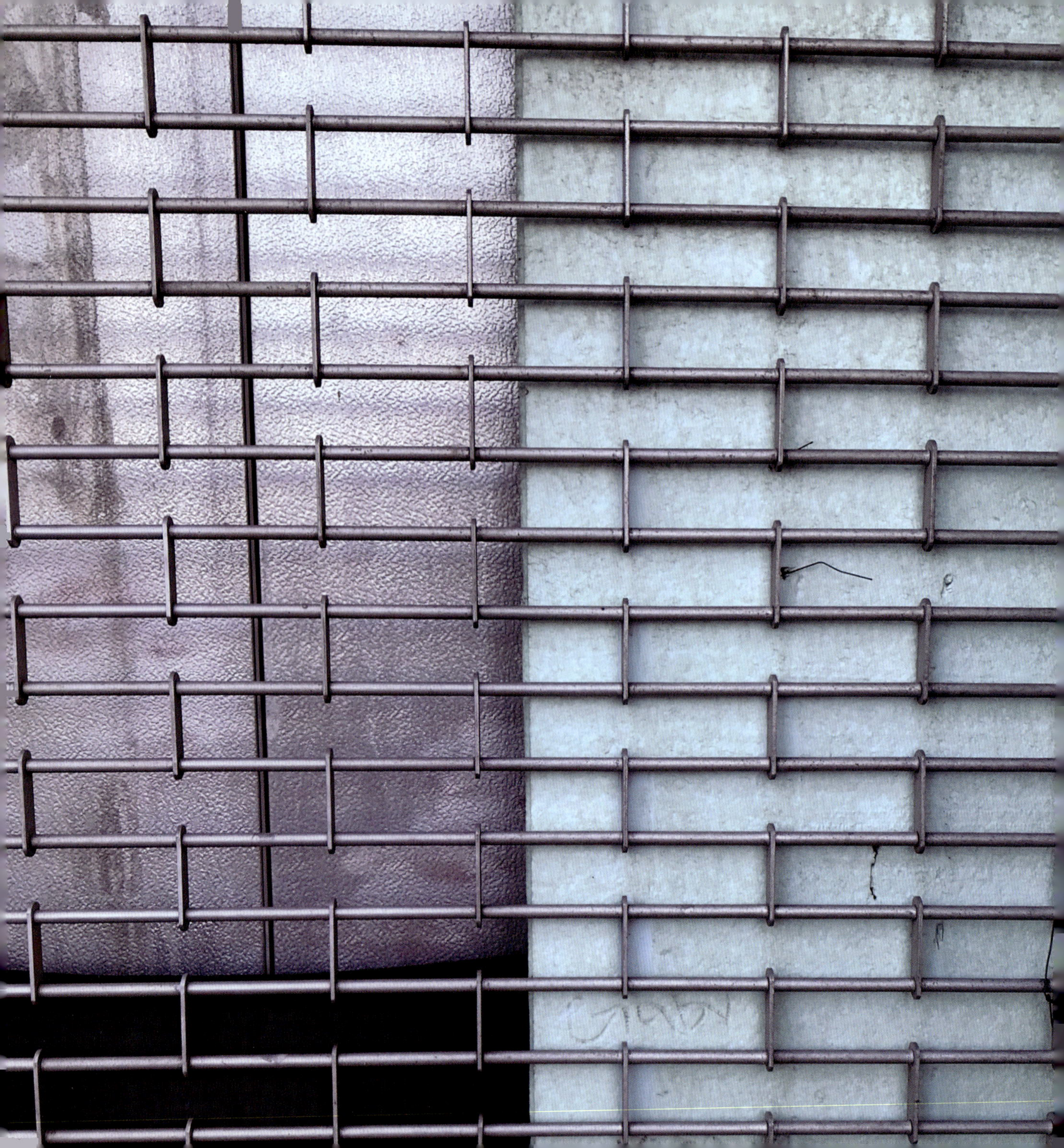

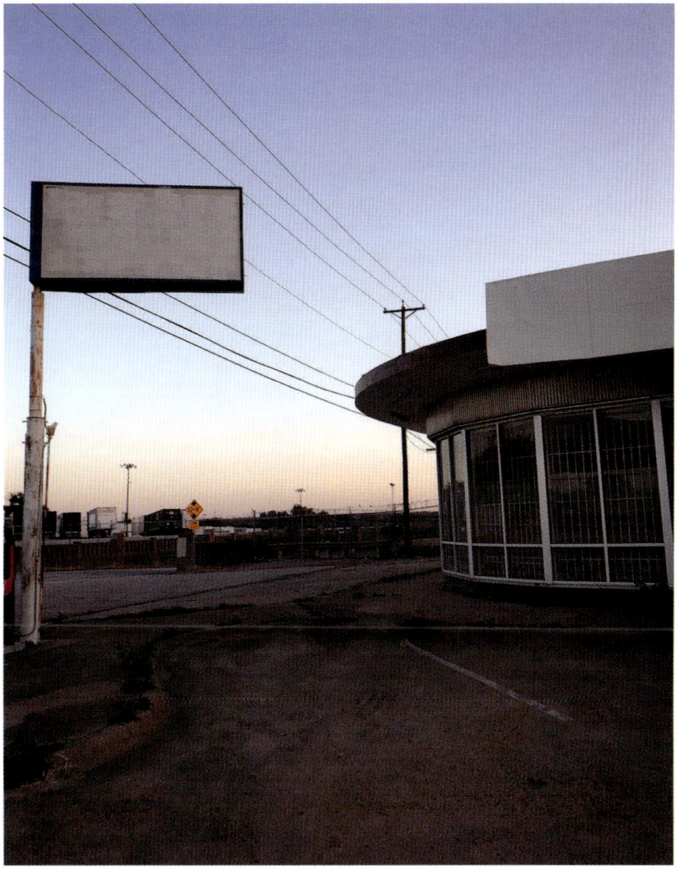

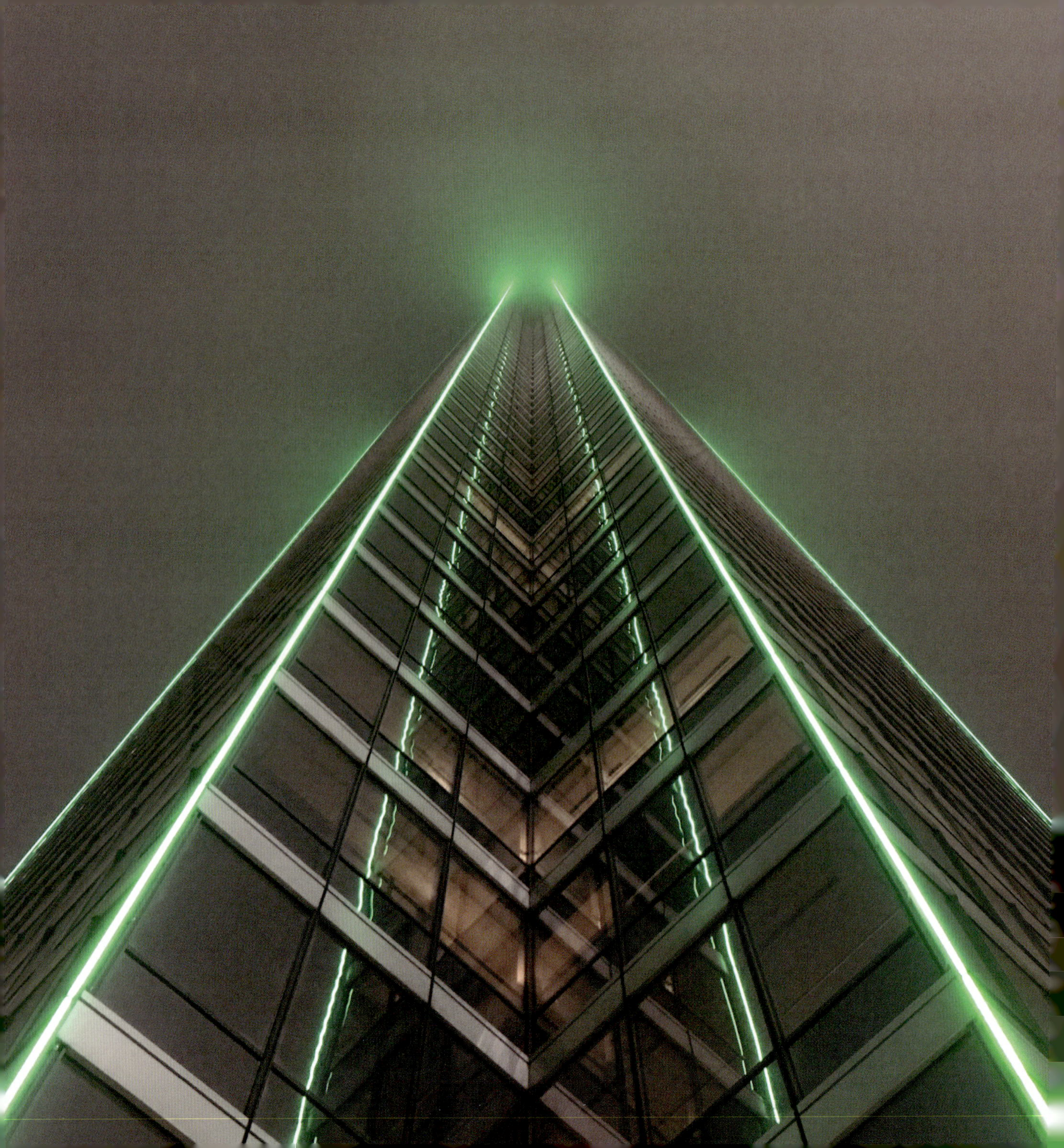

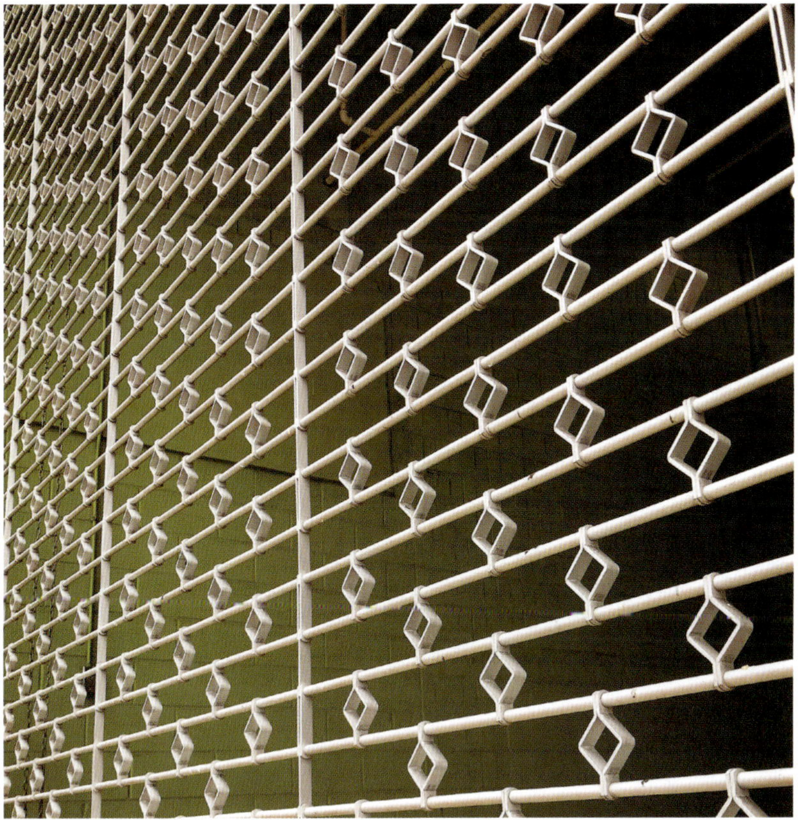

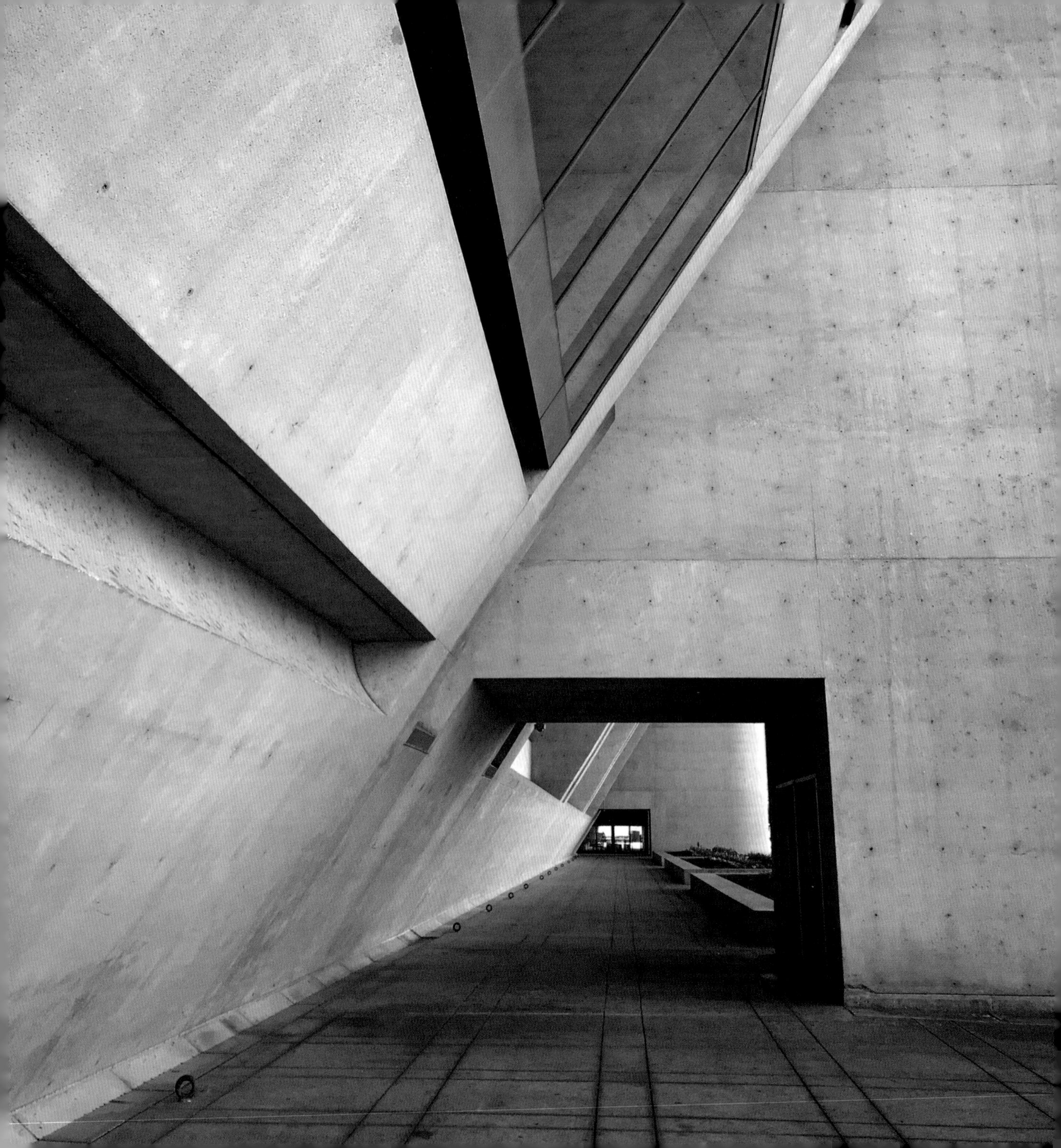

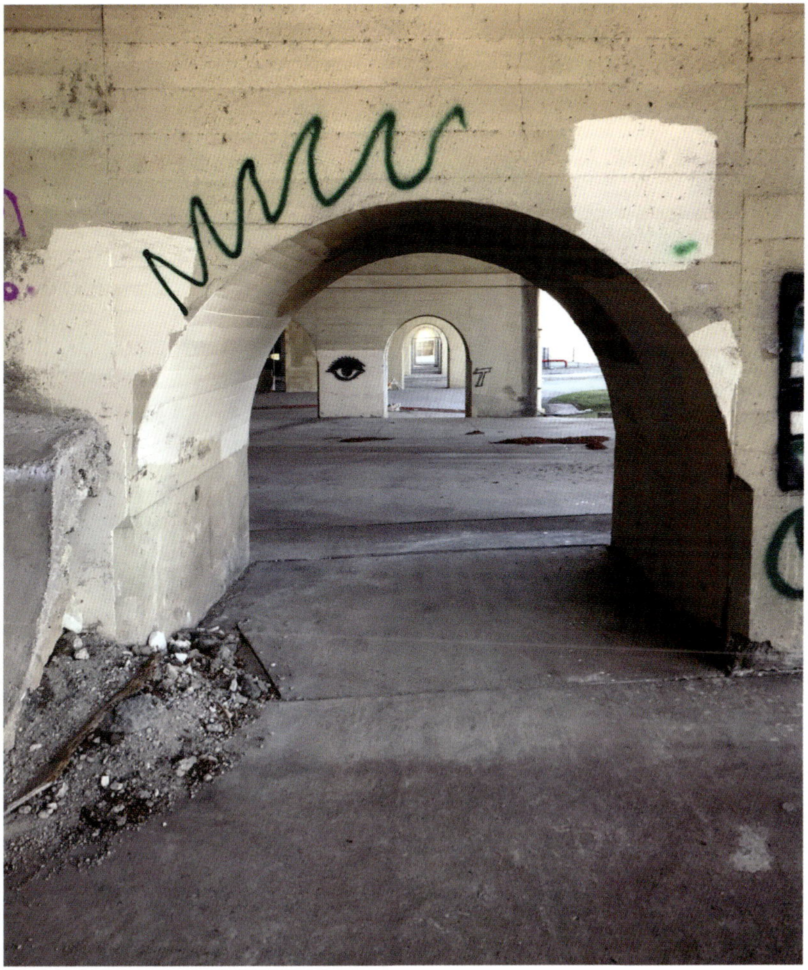

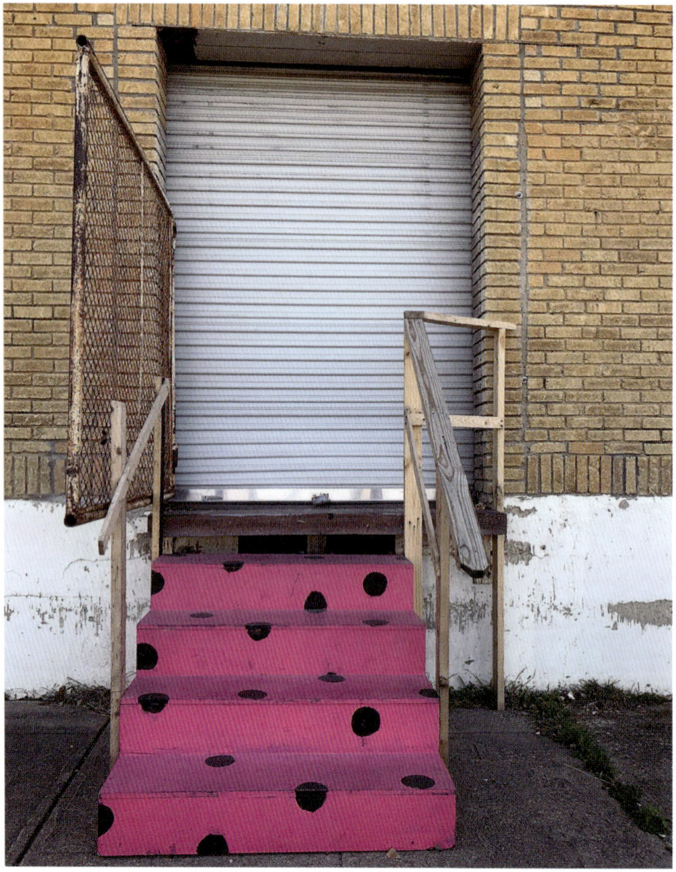

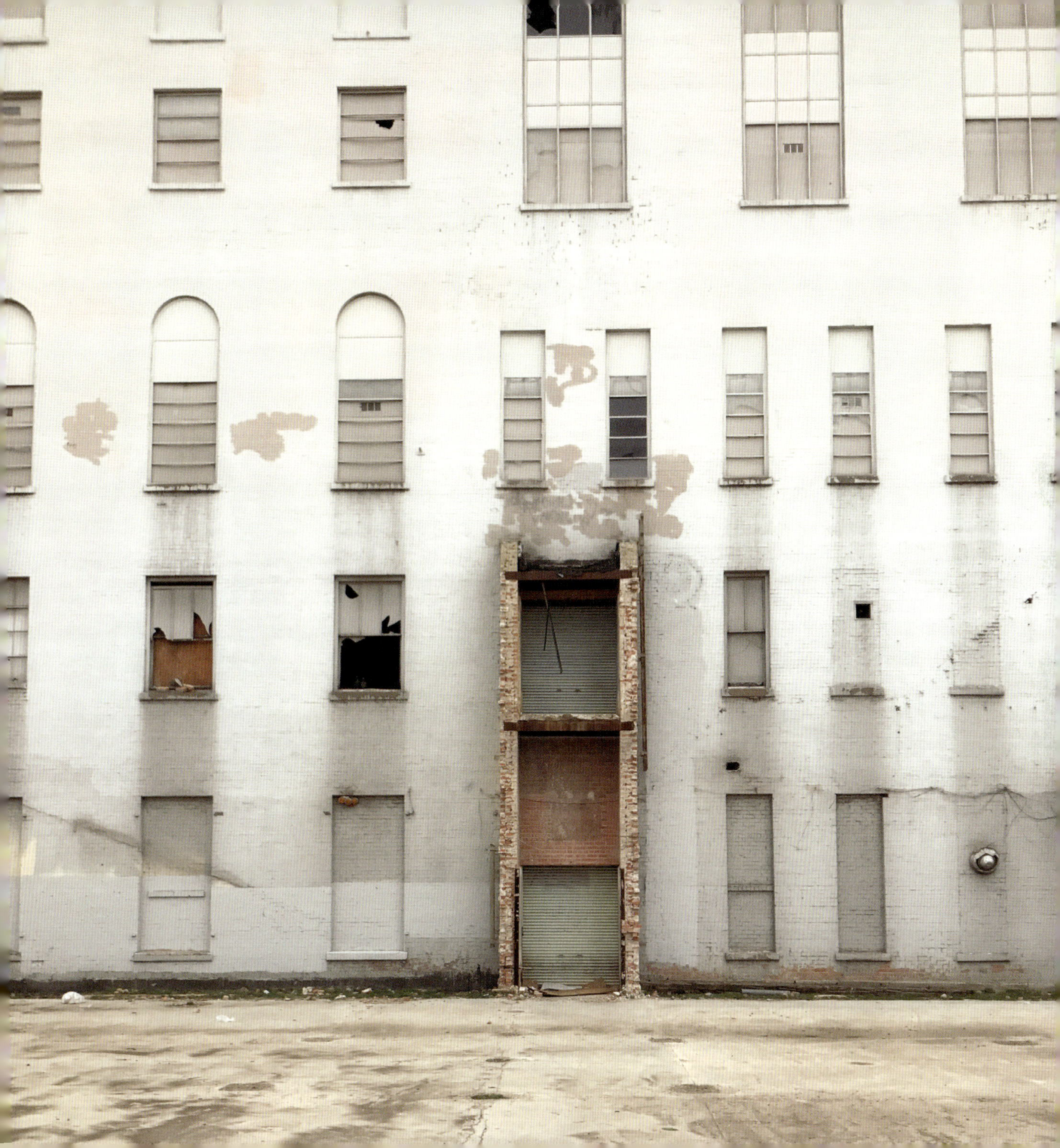

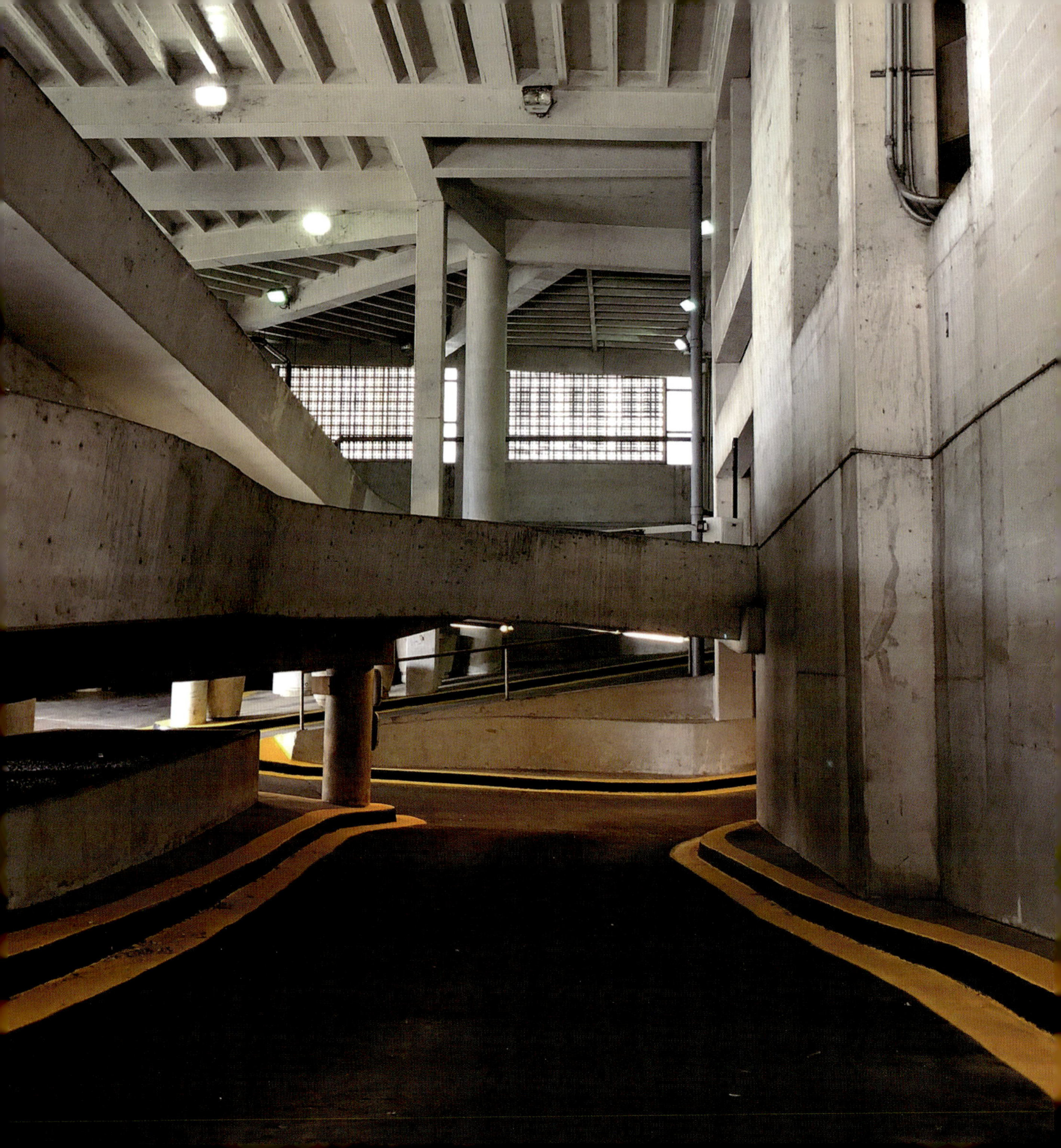

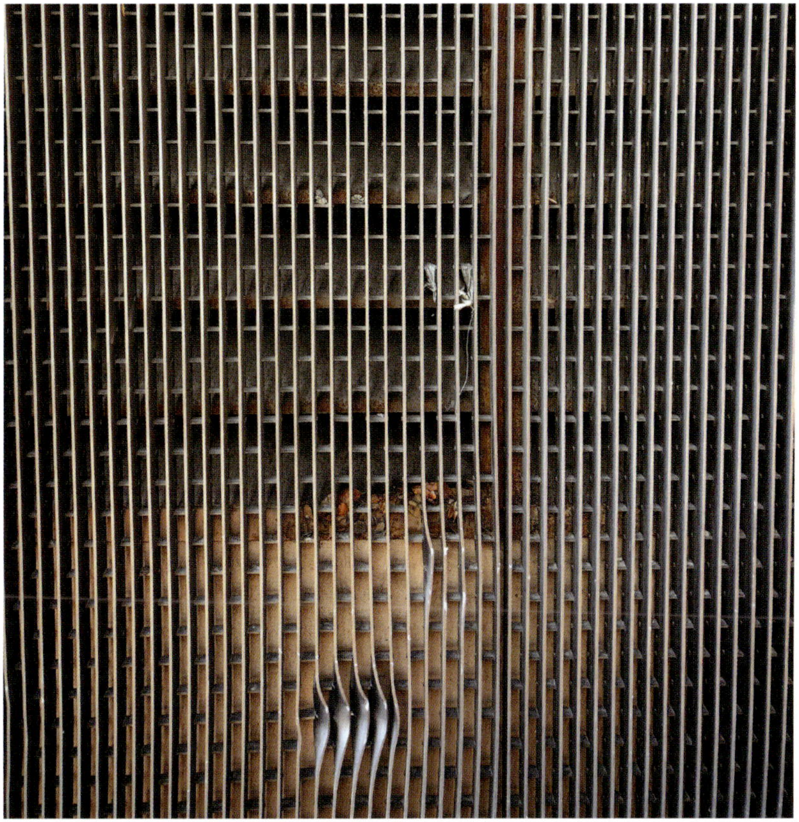

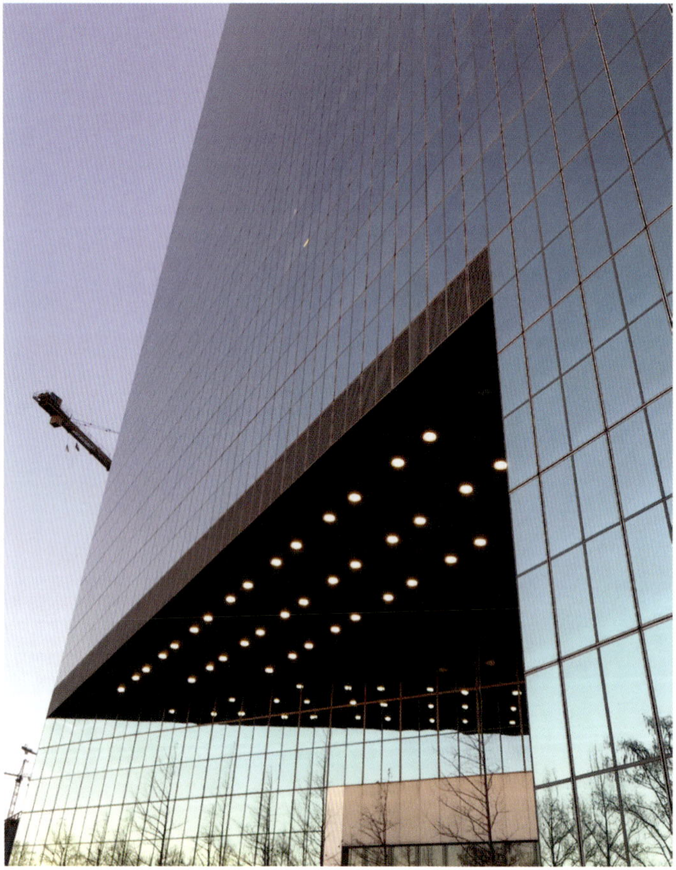

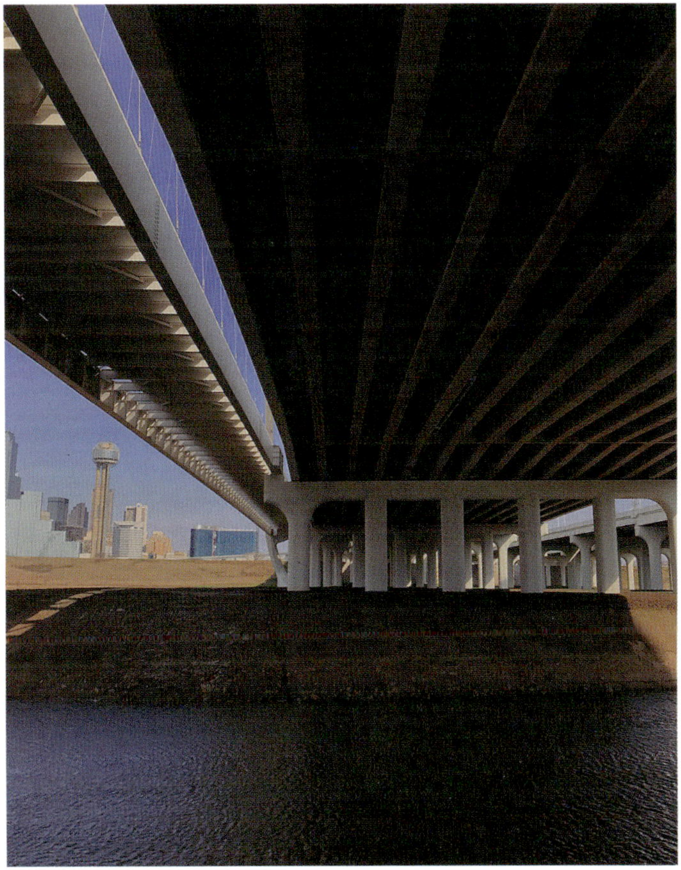

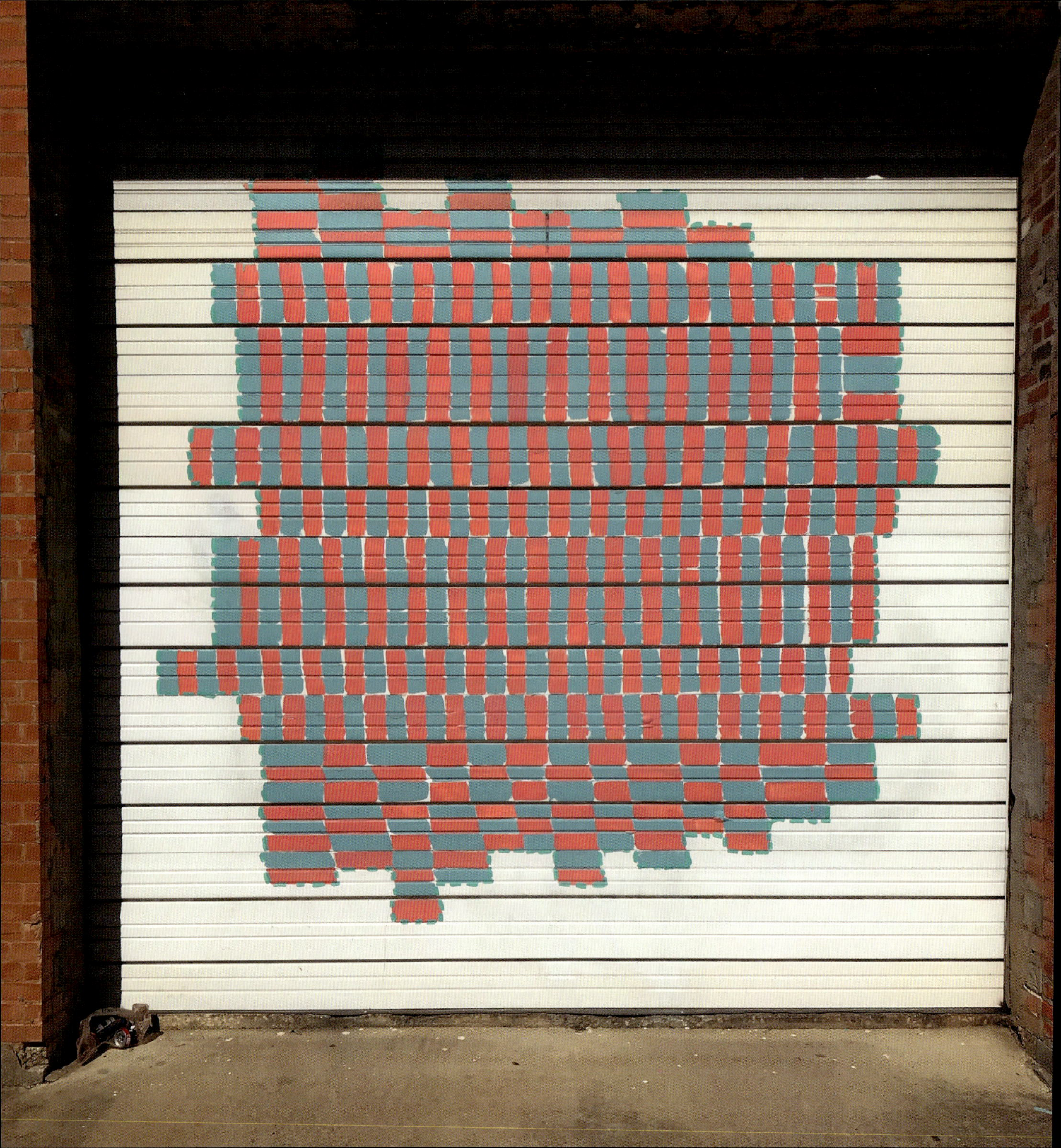

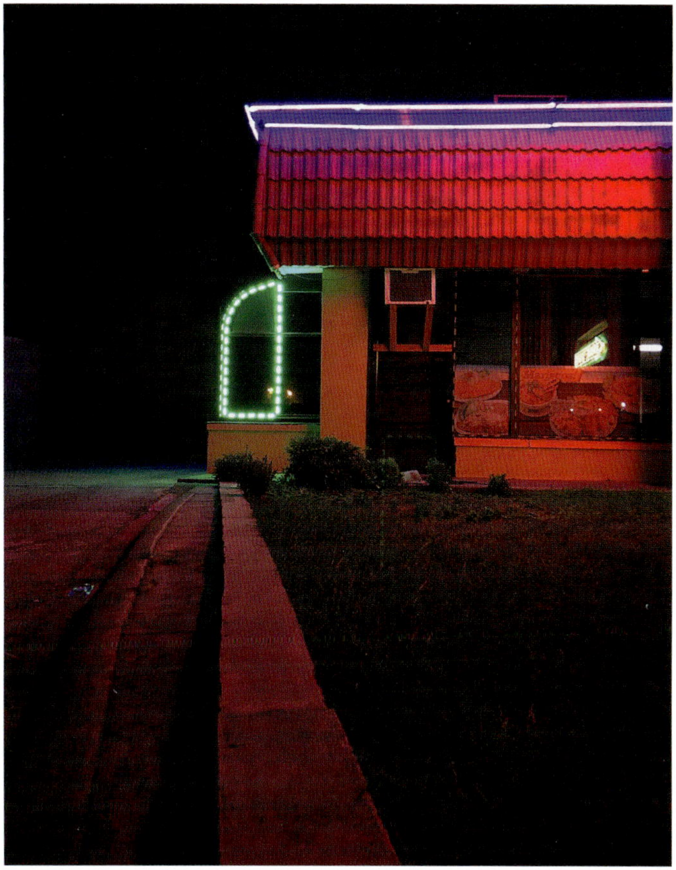

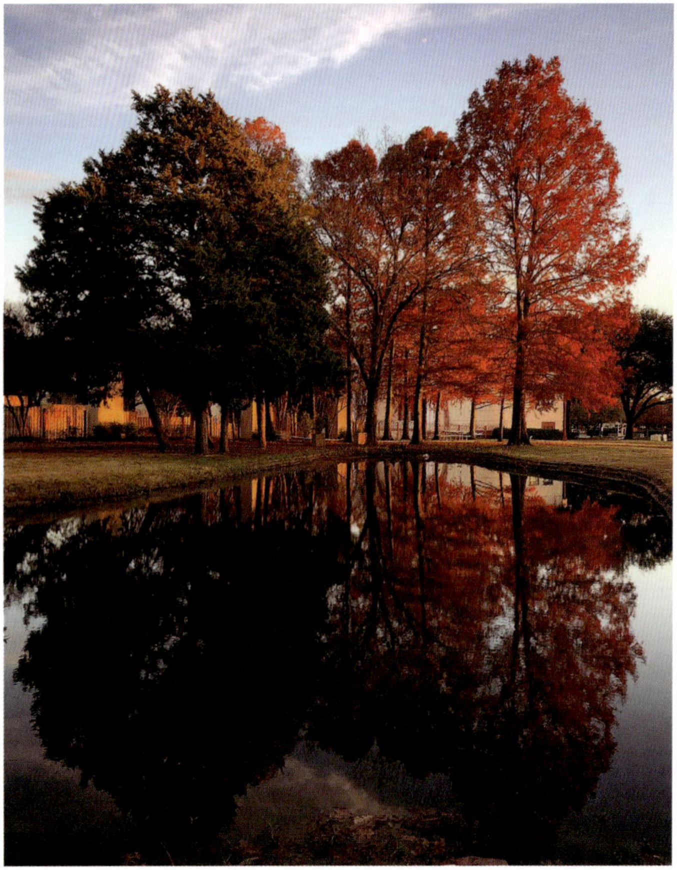

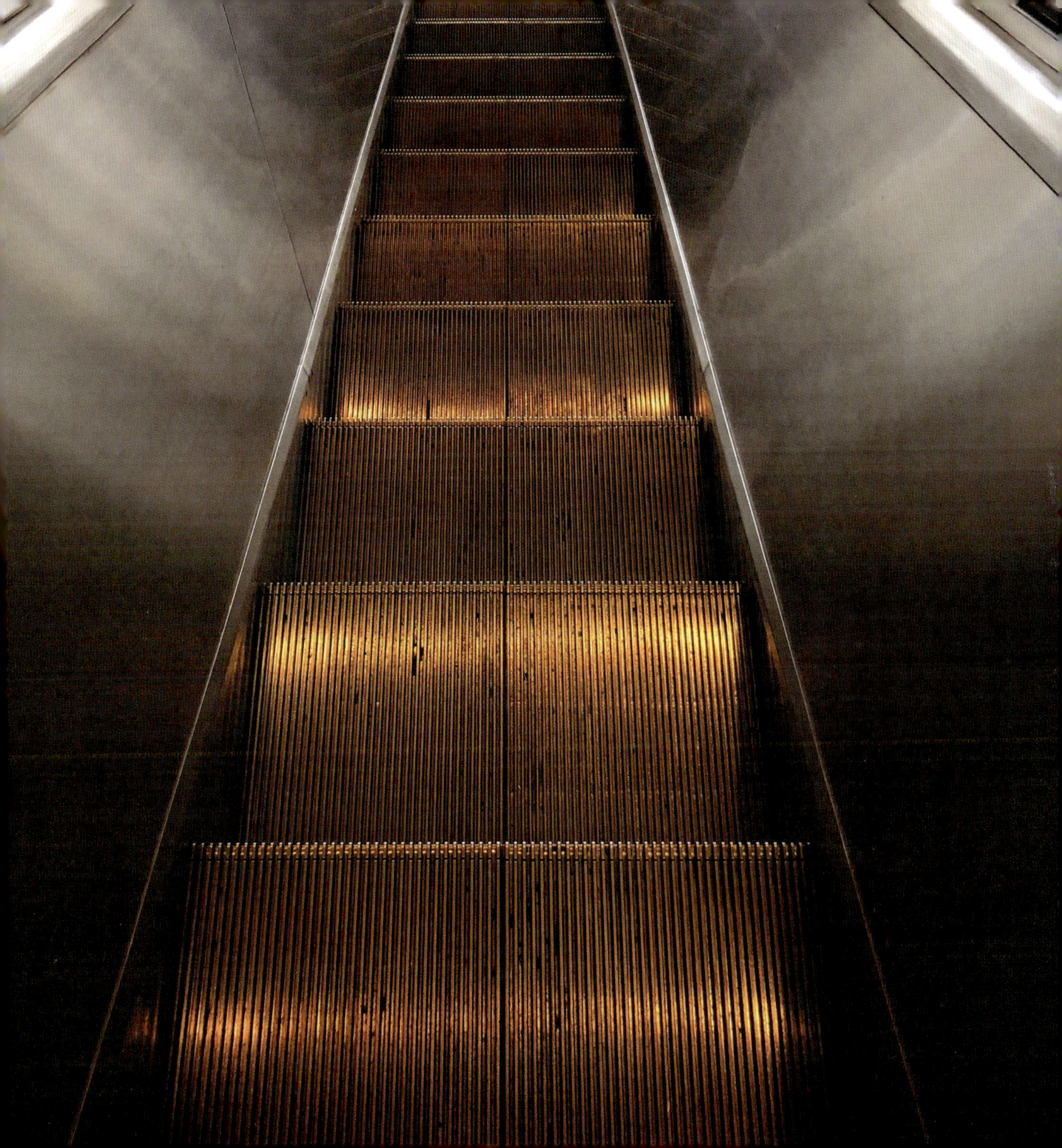

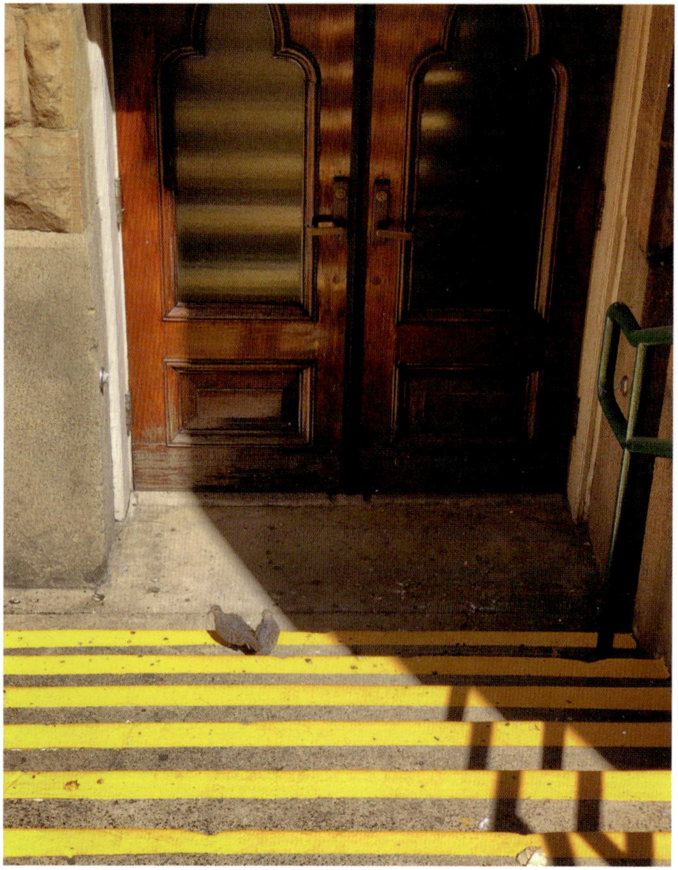

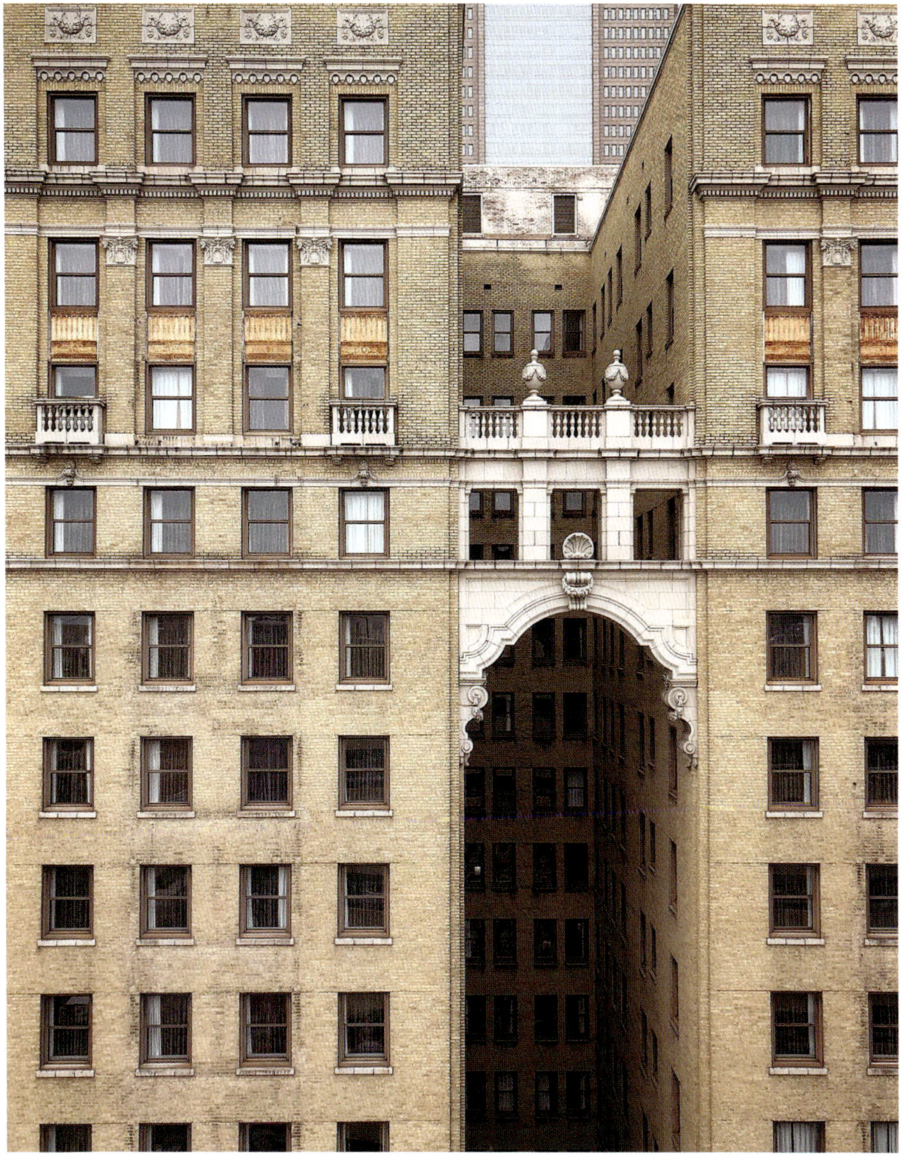

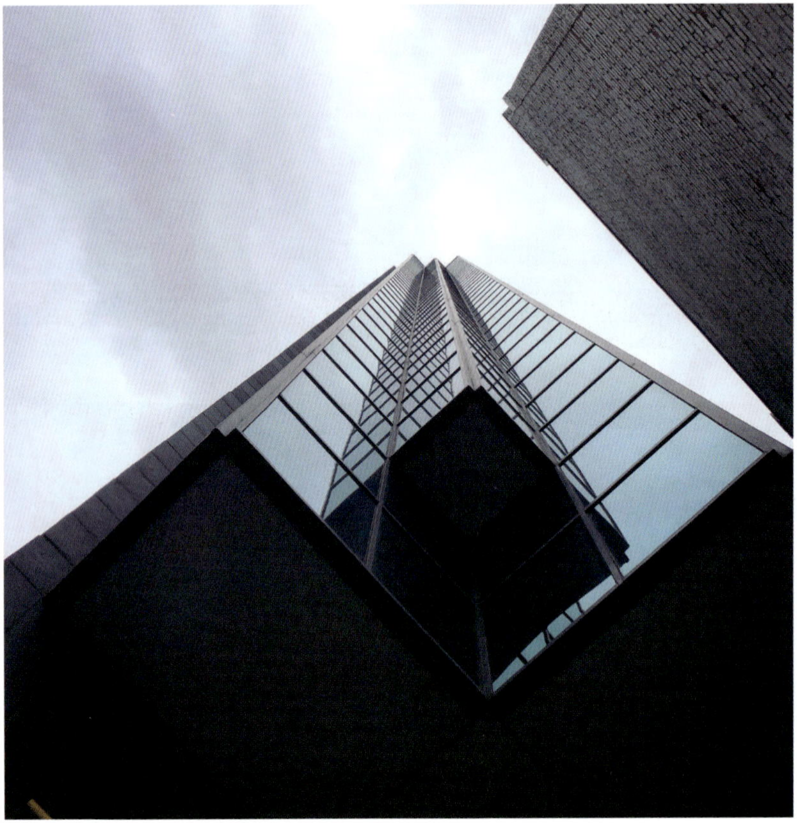

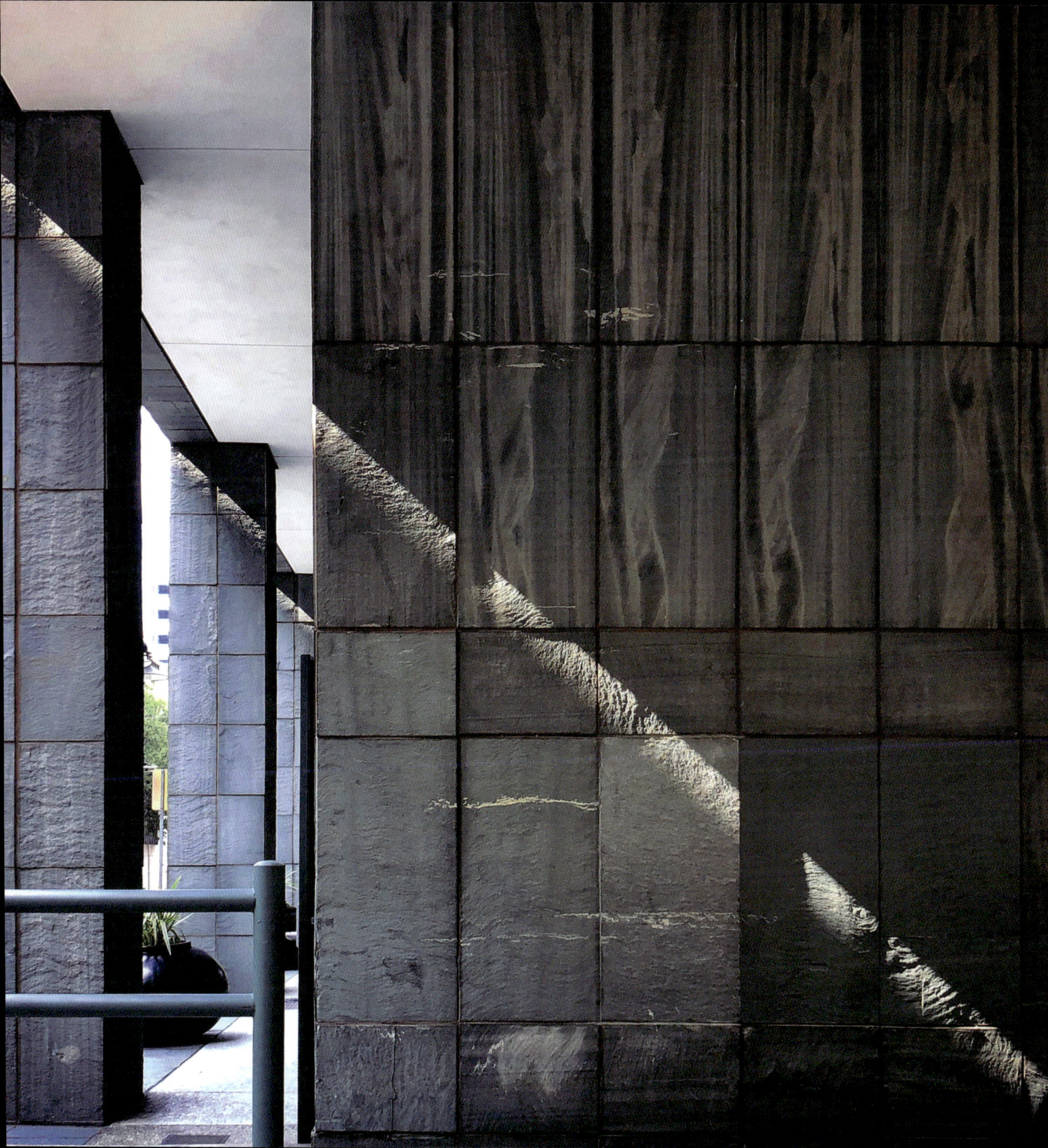

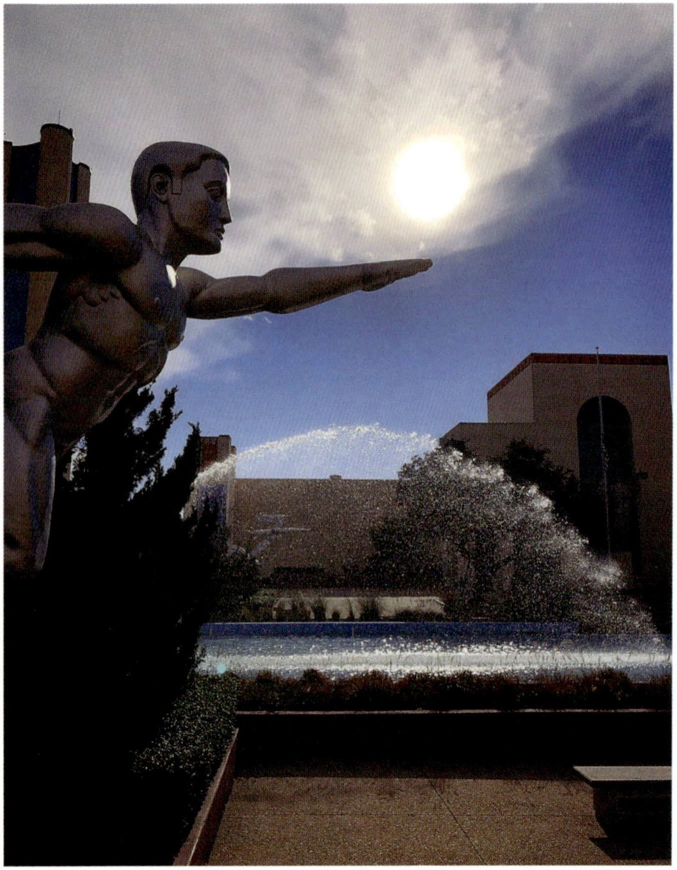

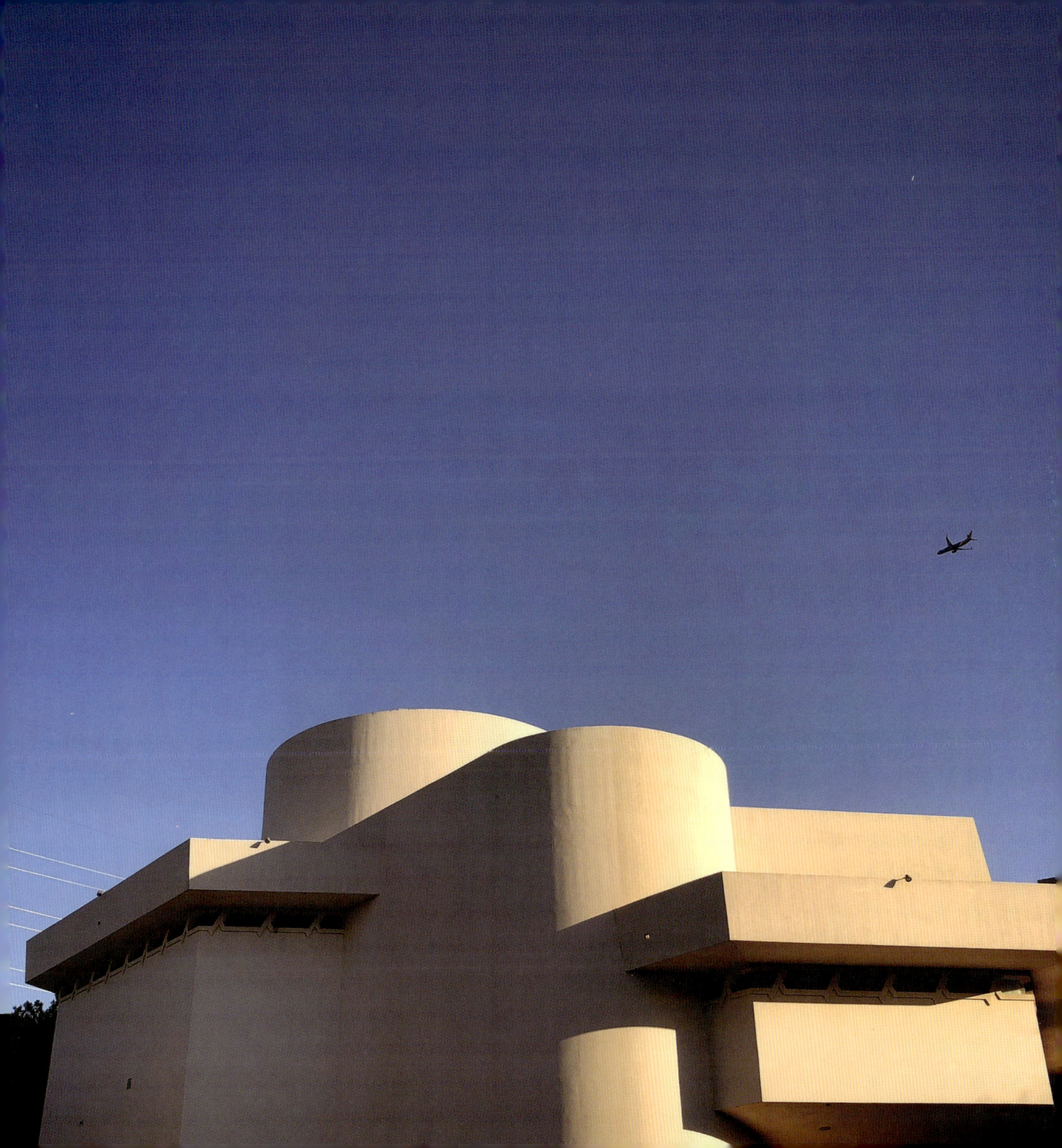

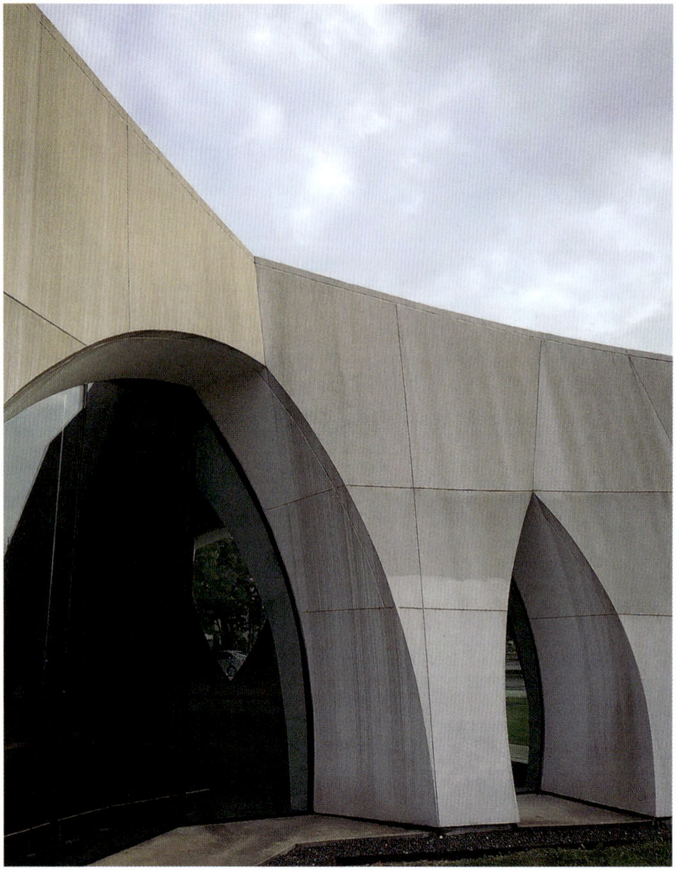

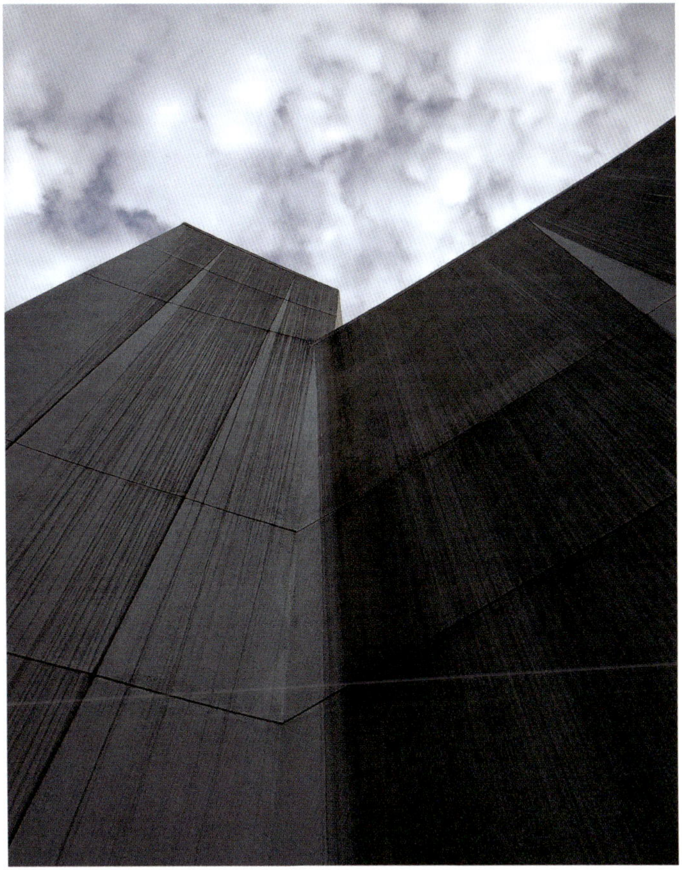

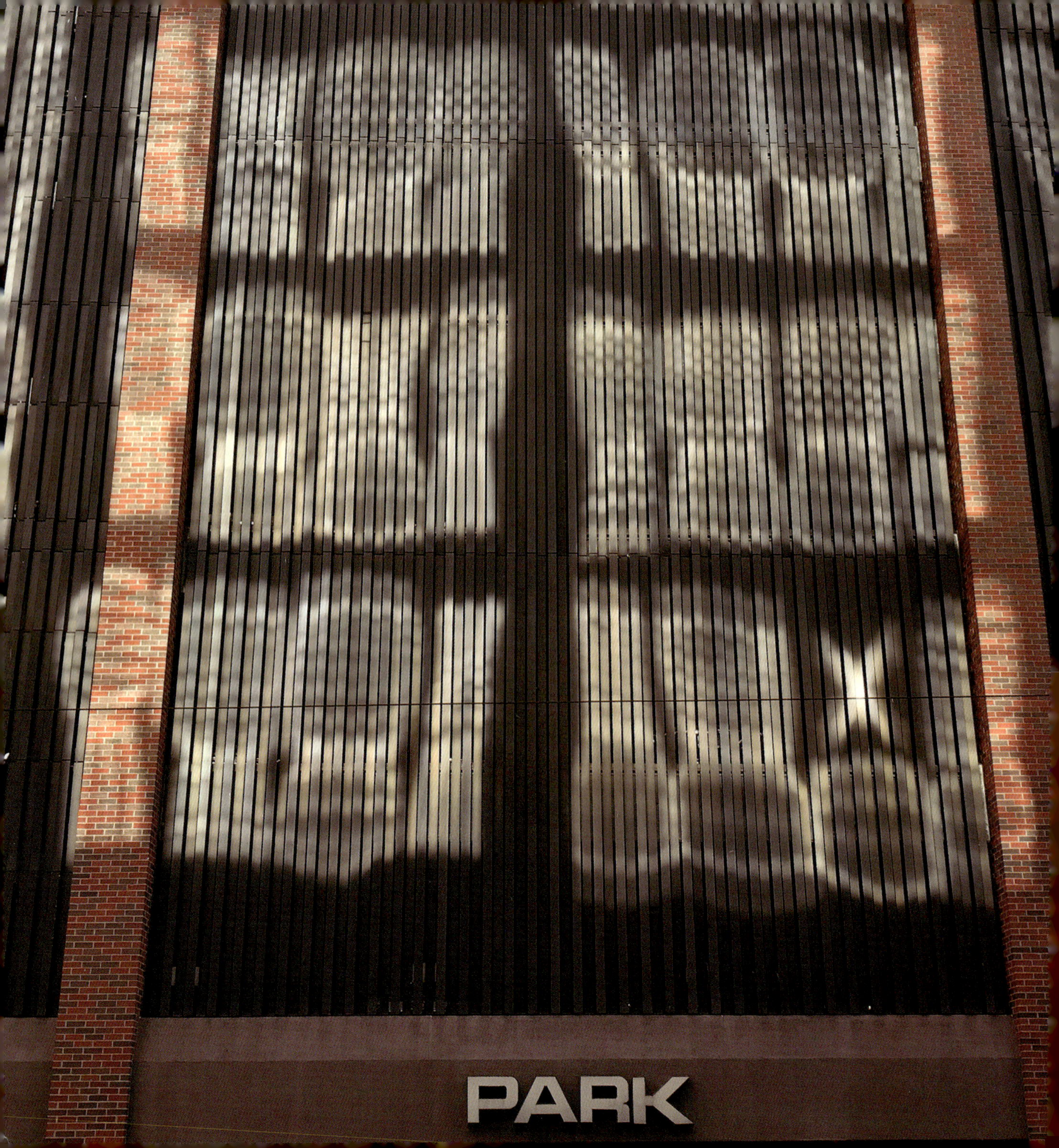
PARK

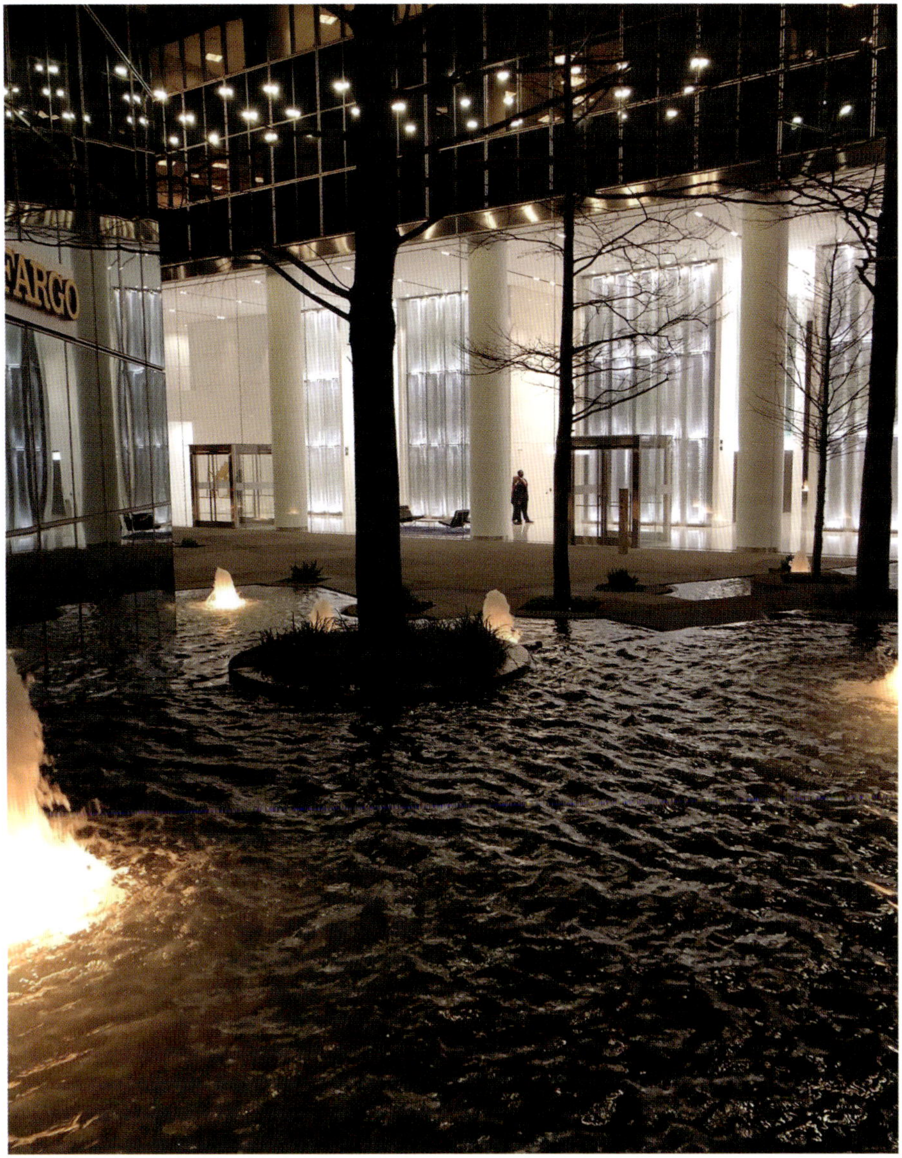
FARGO

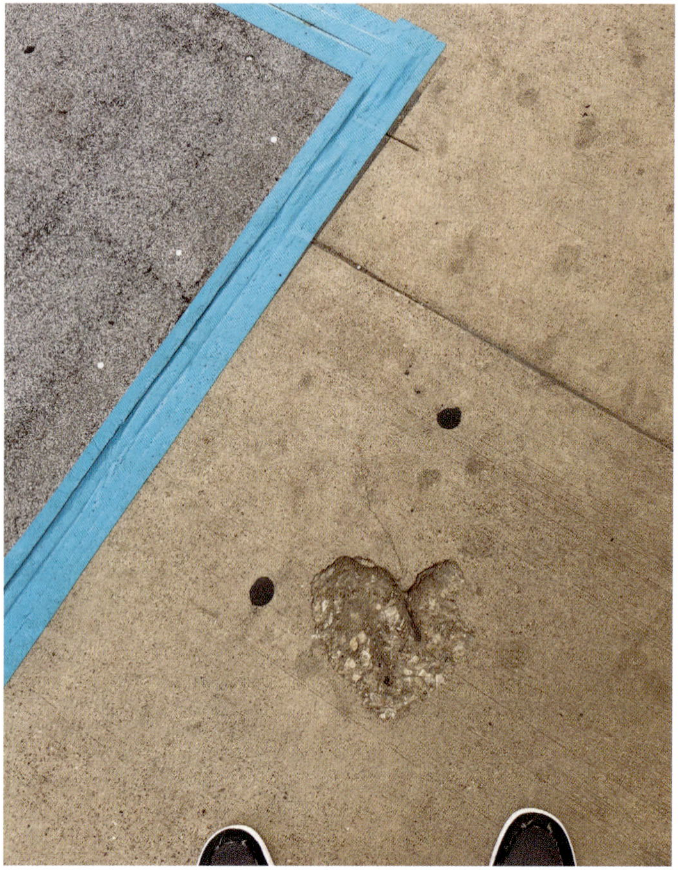

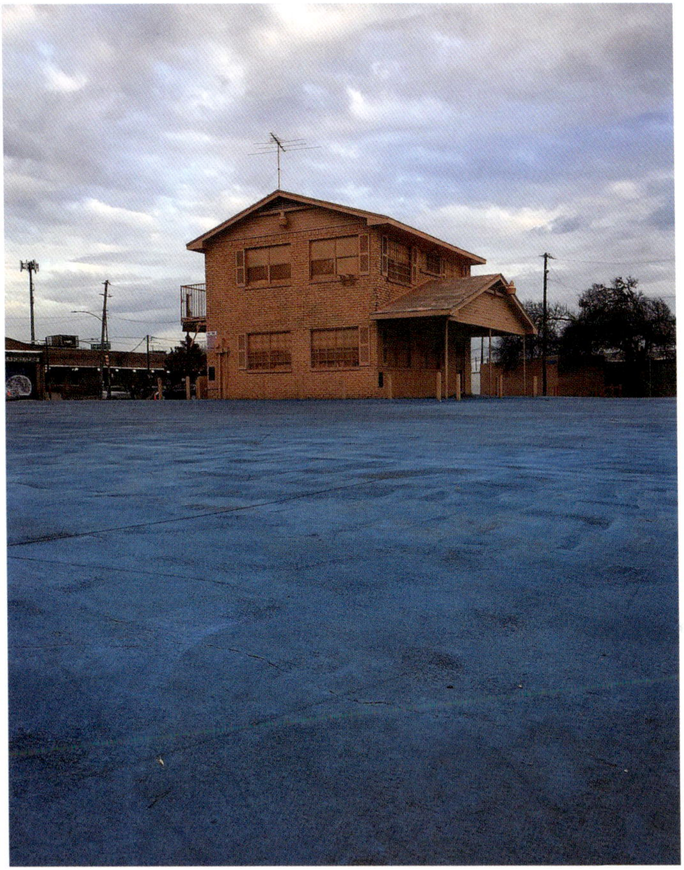

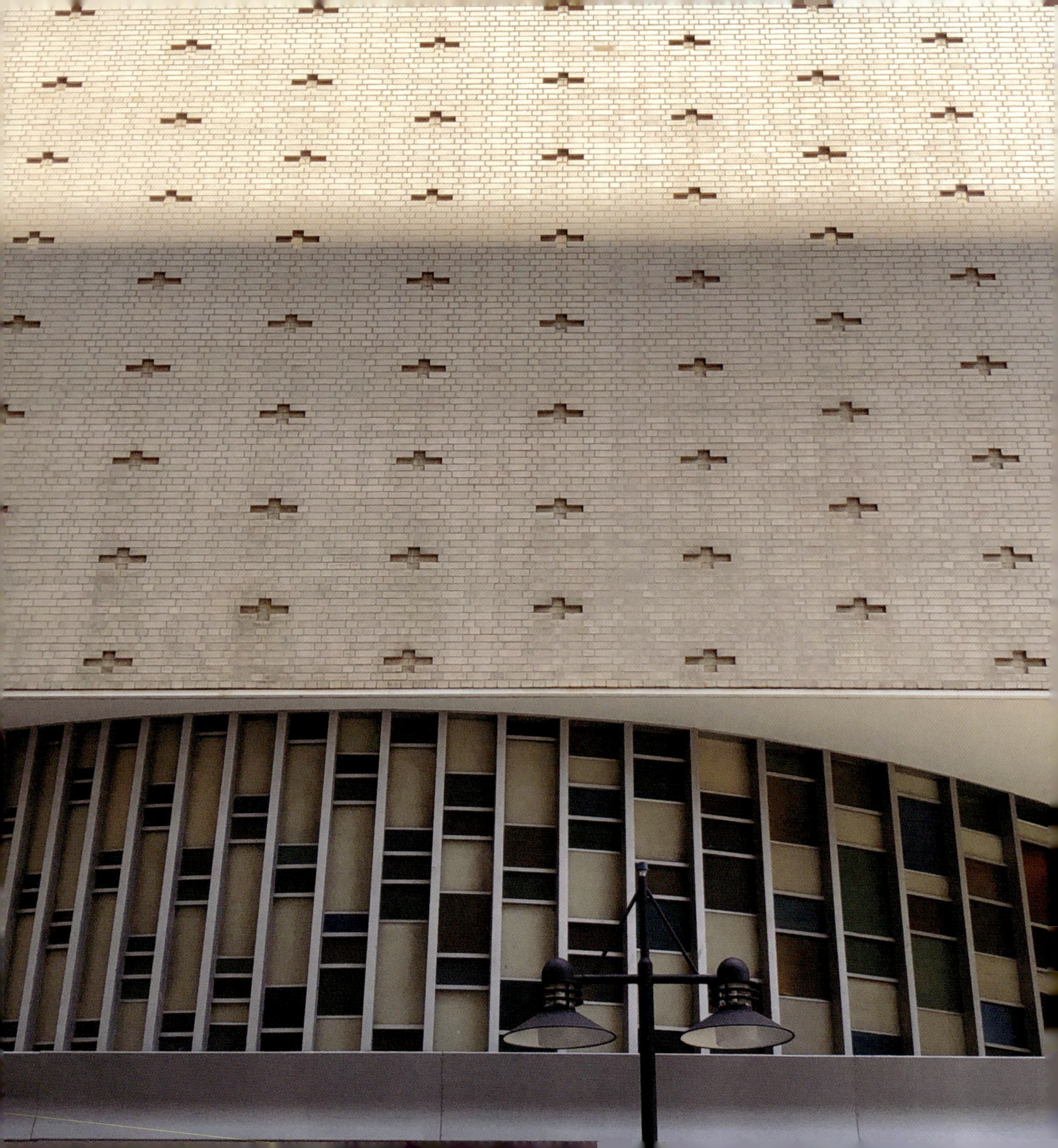

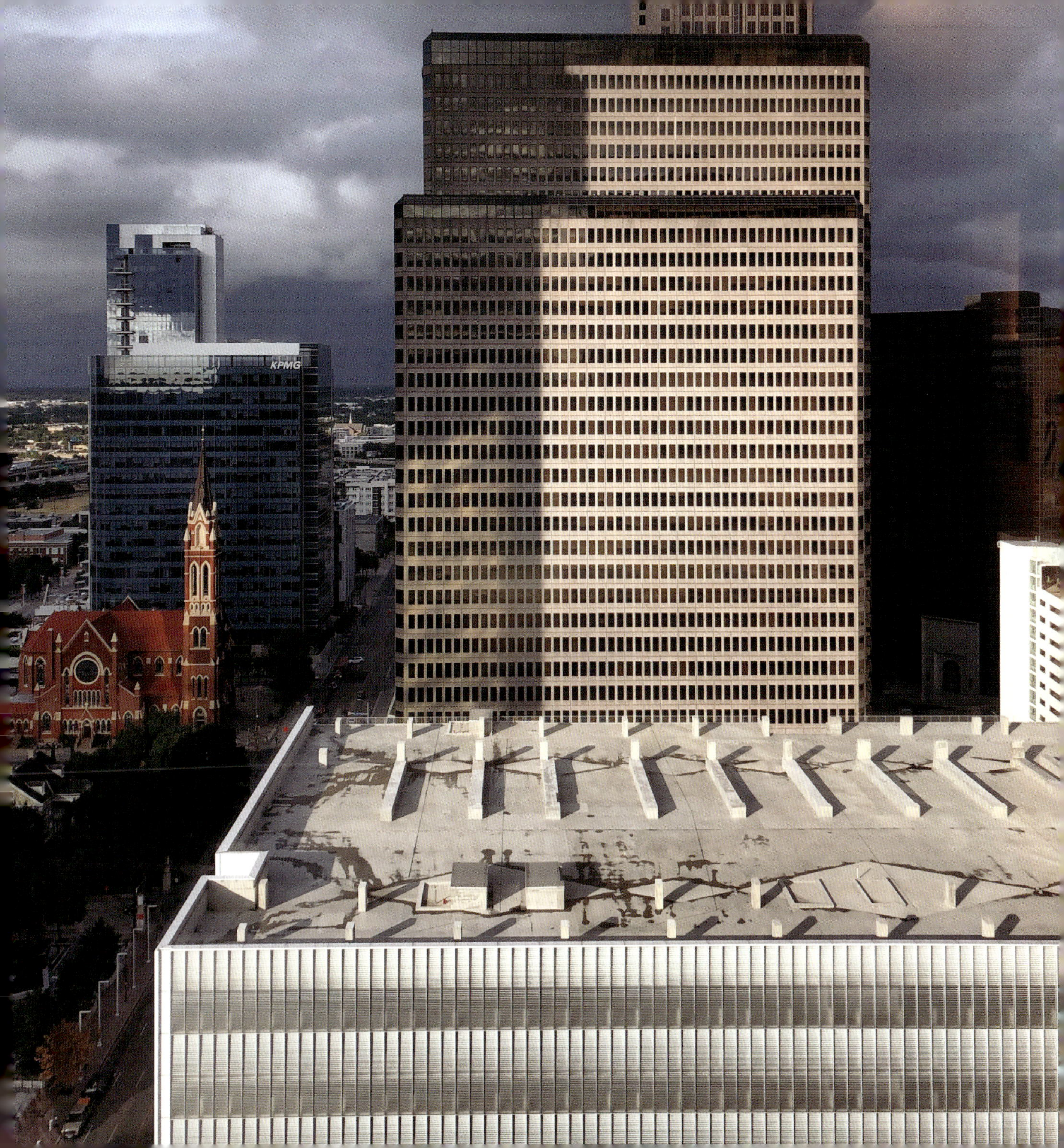
KPMG

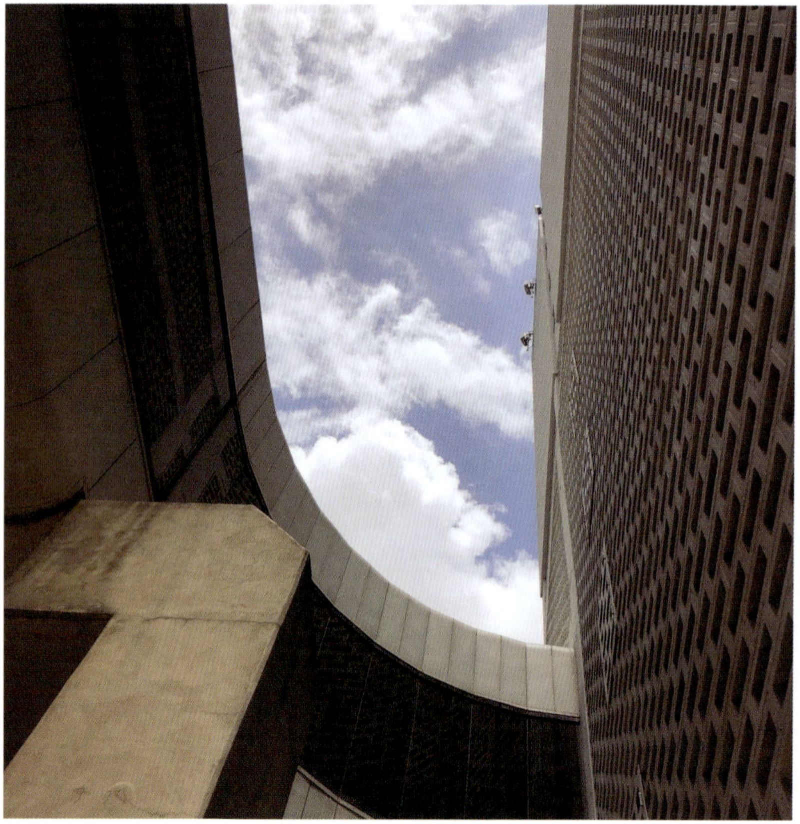

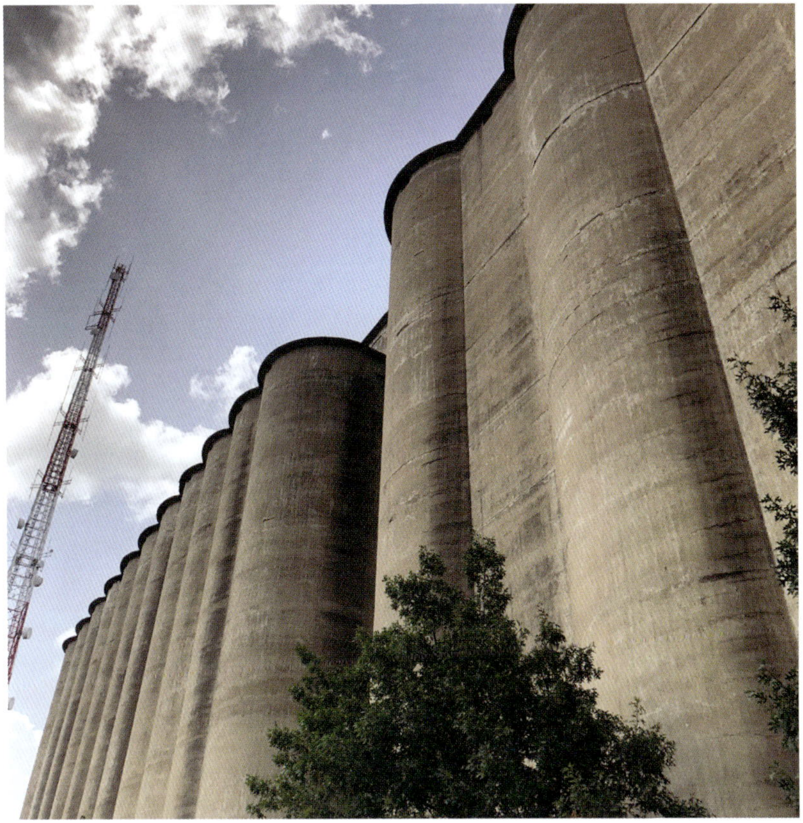

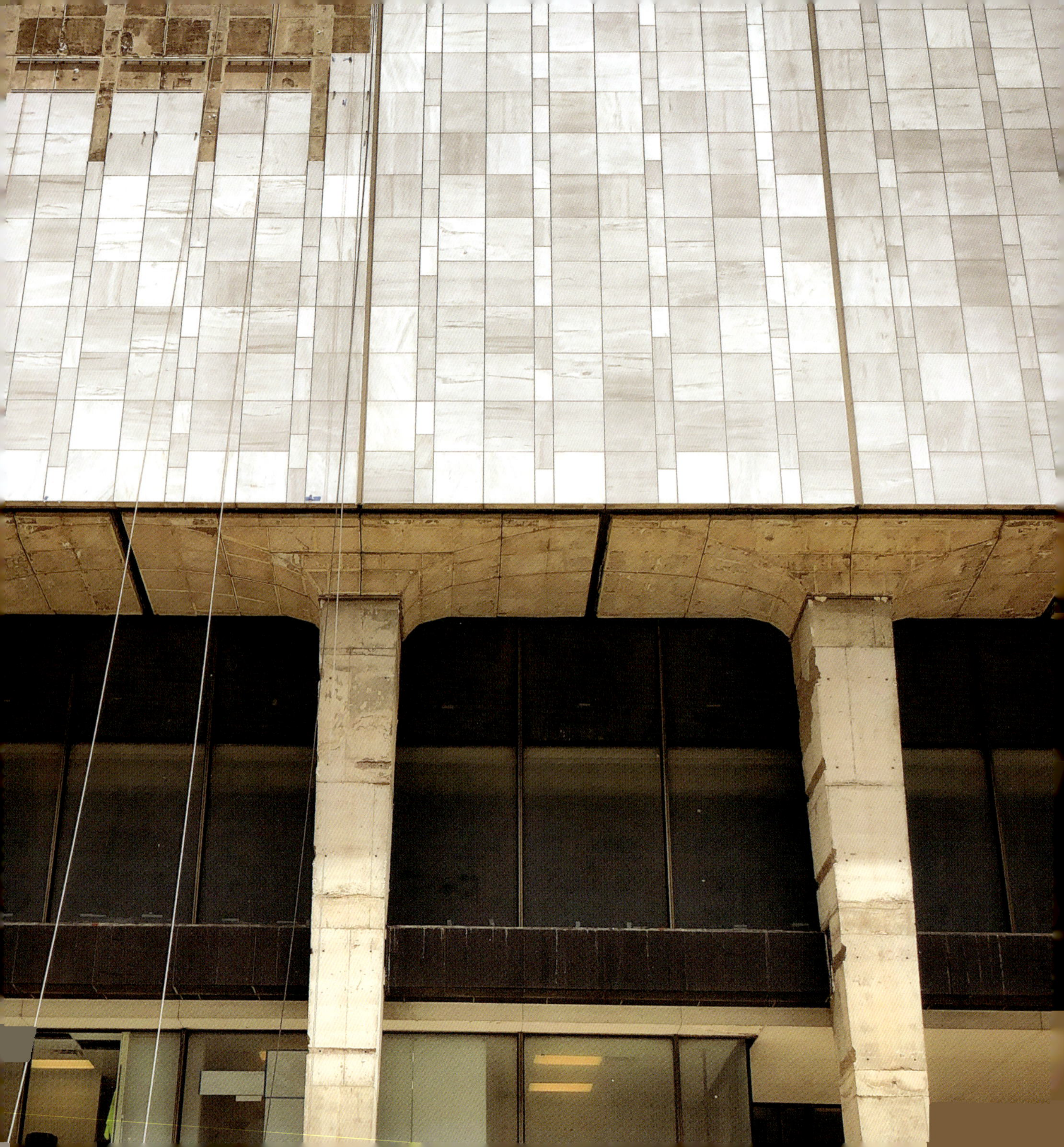

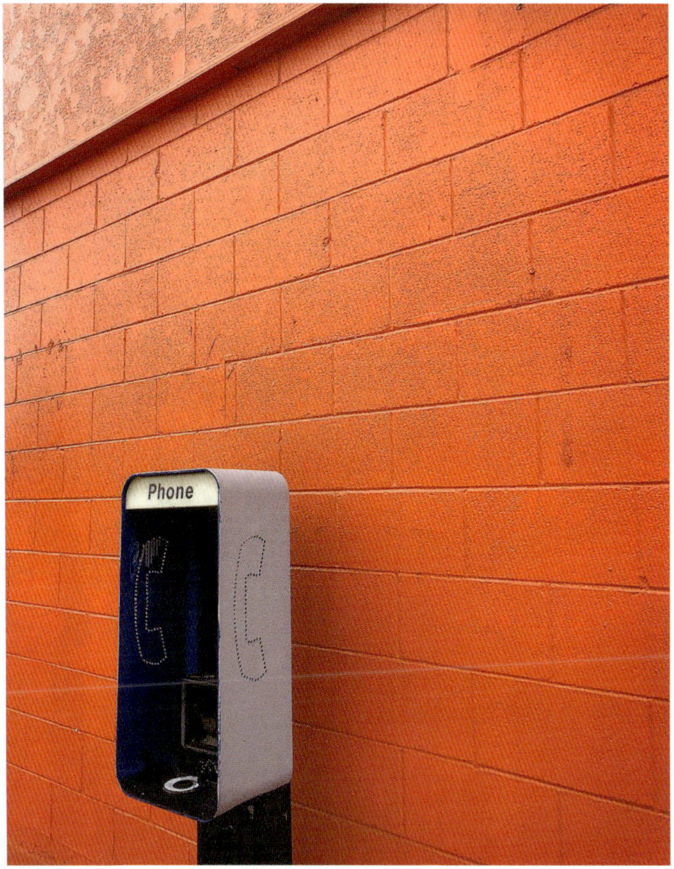
Phone

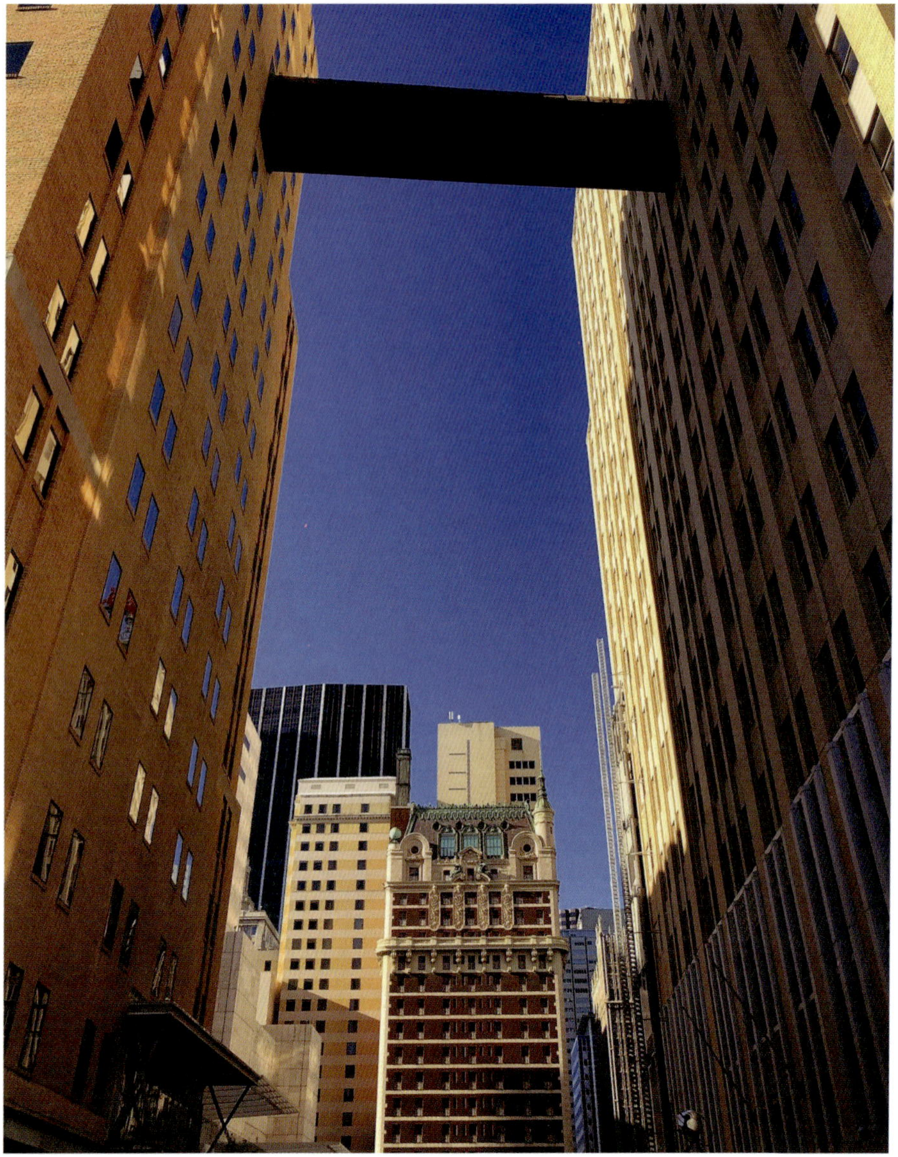

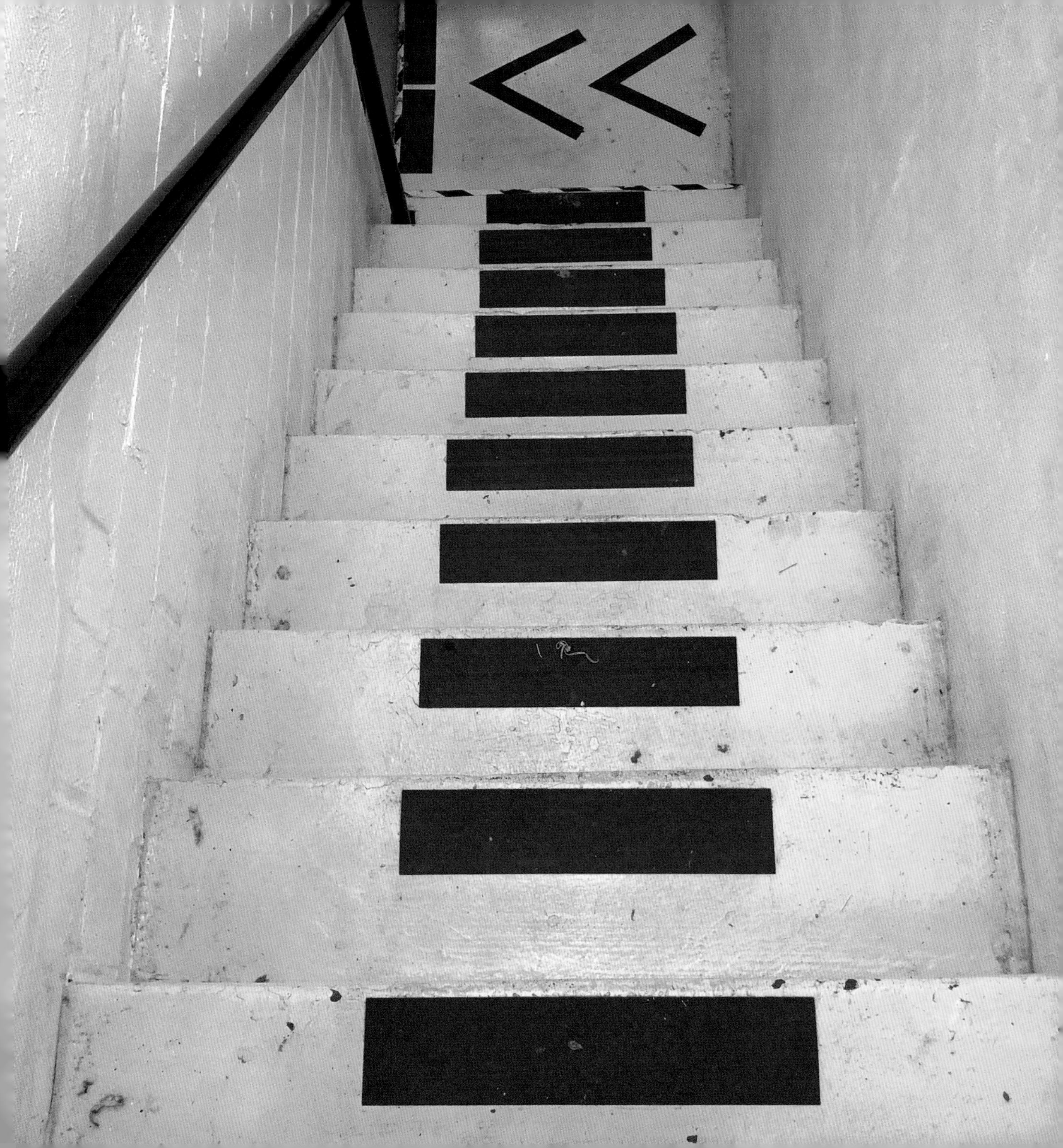

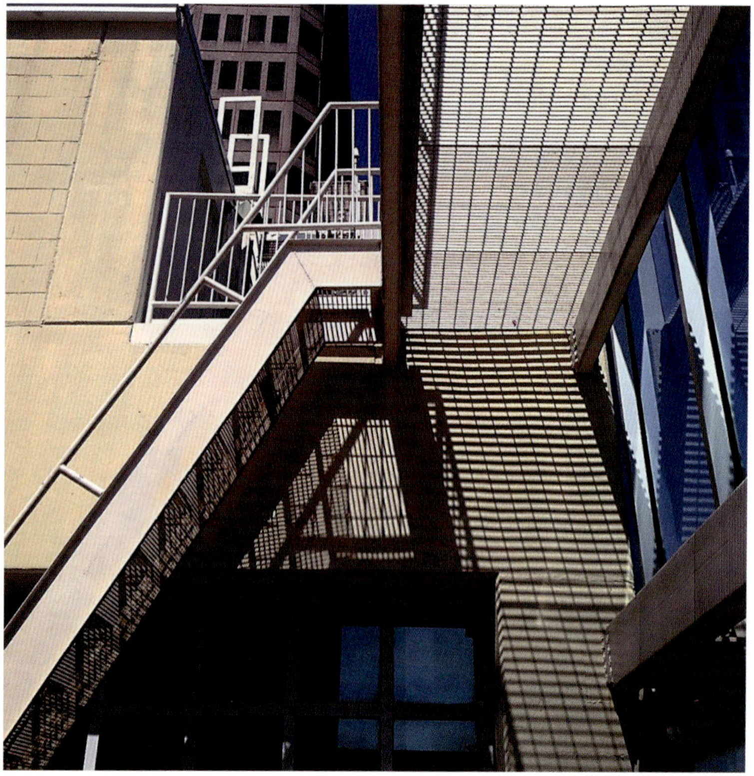

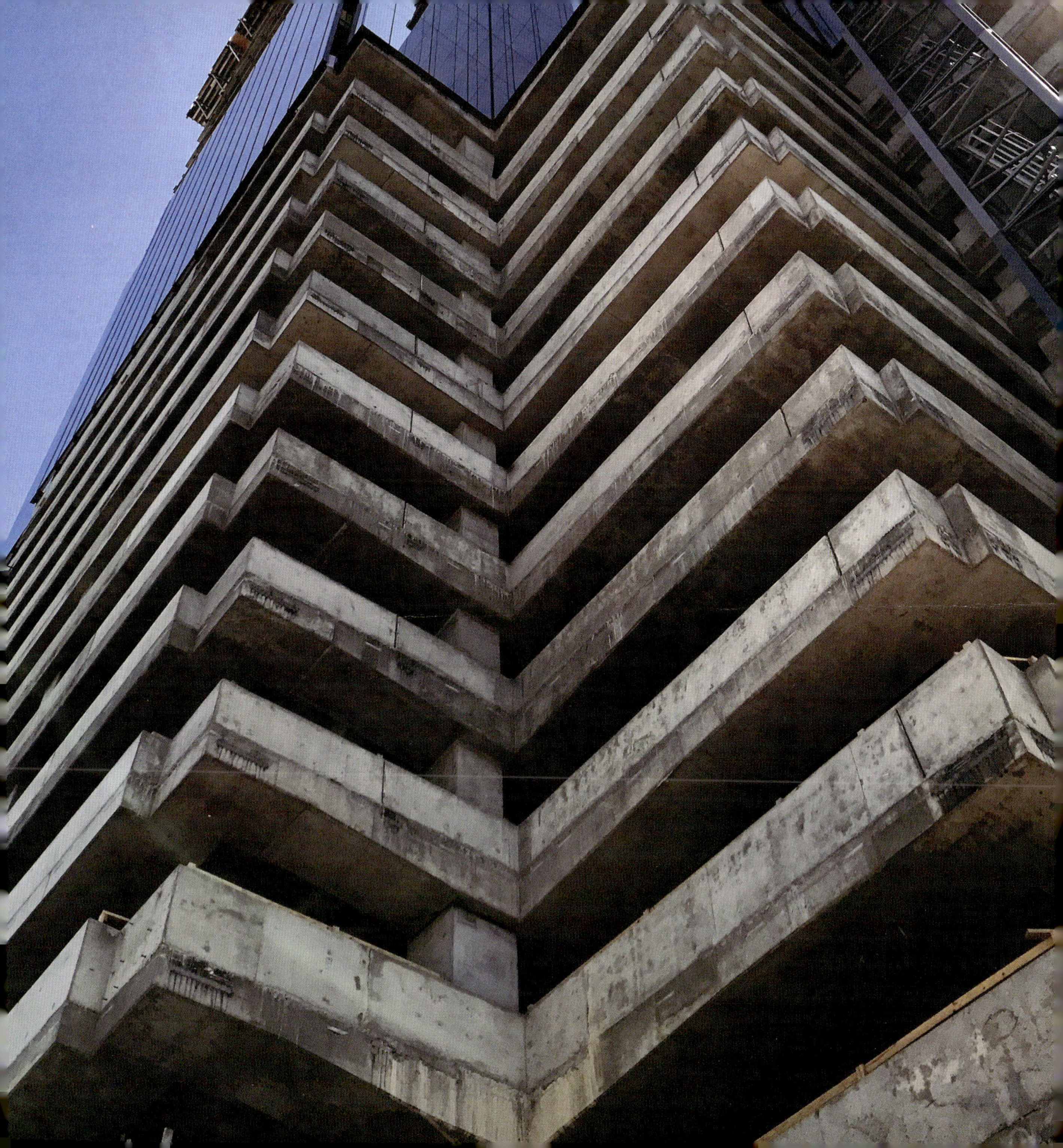

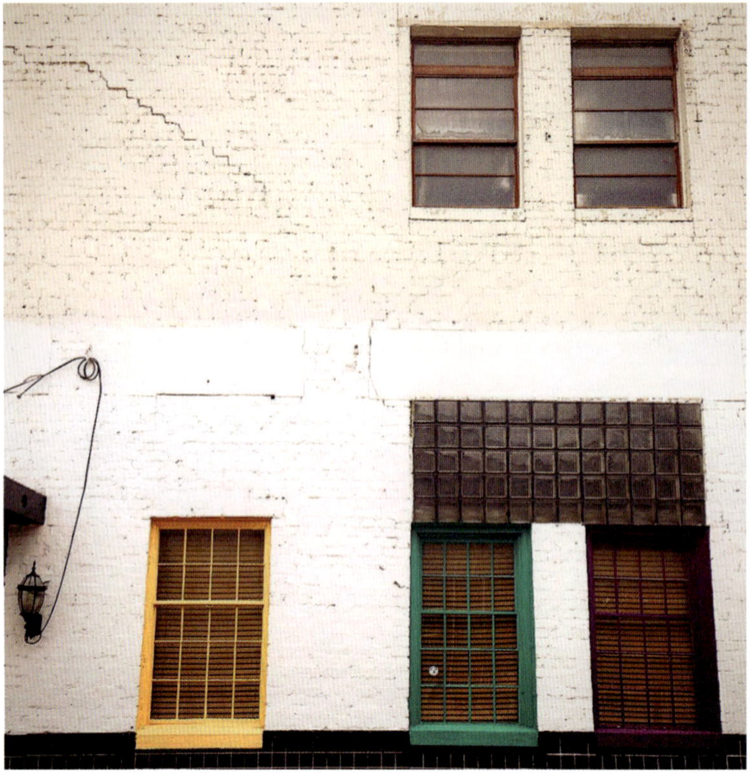

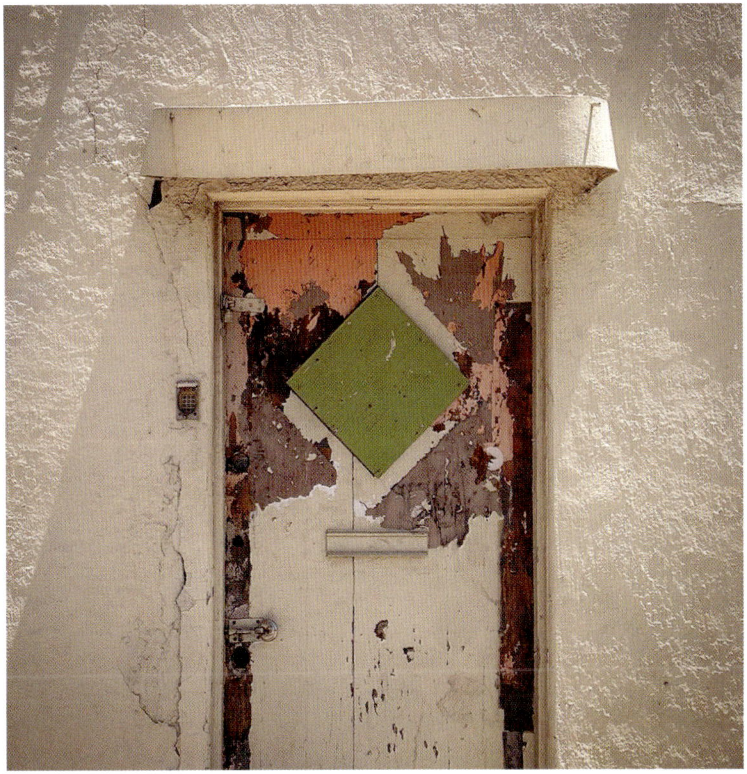

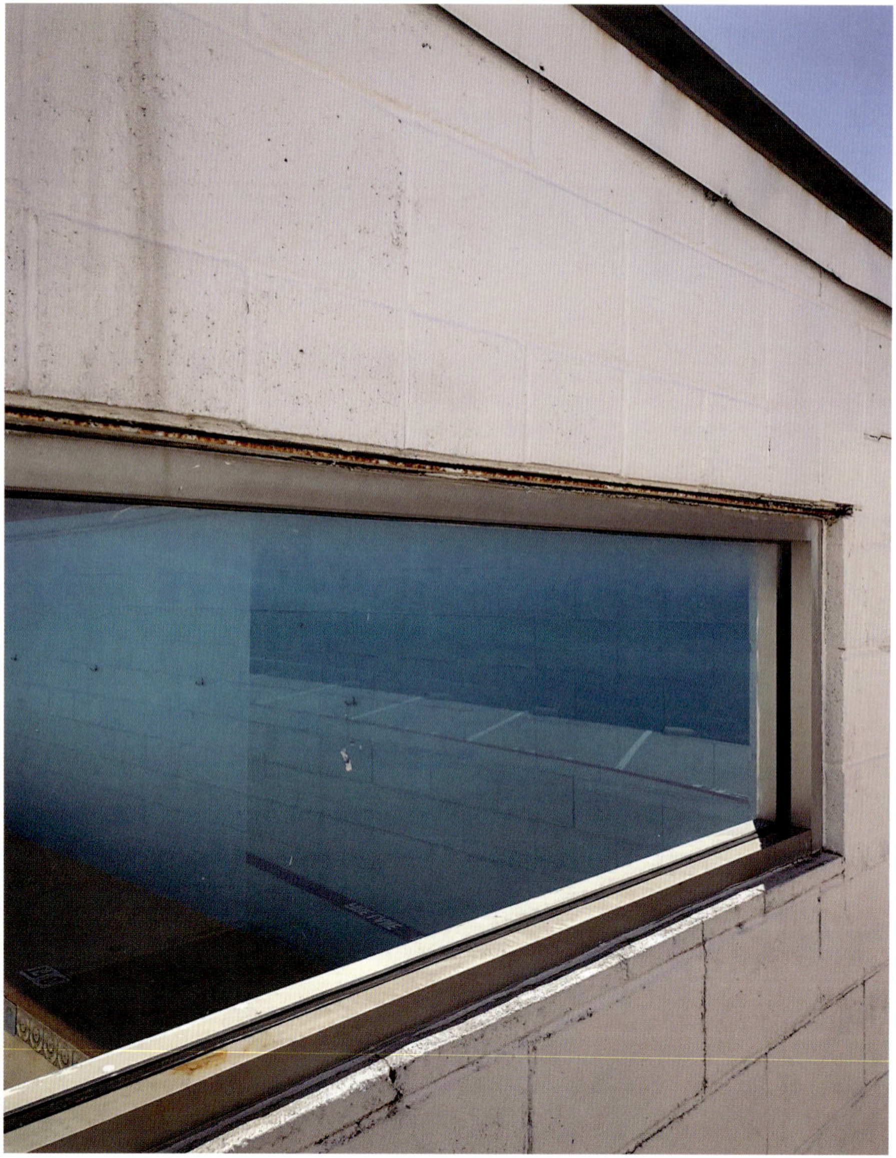

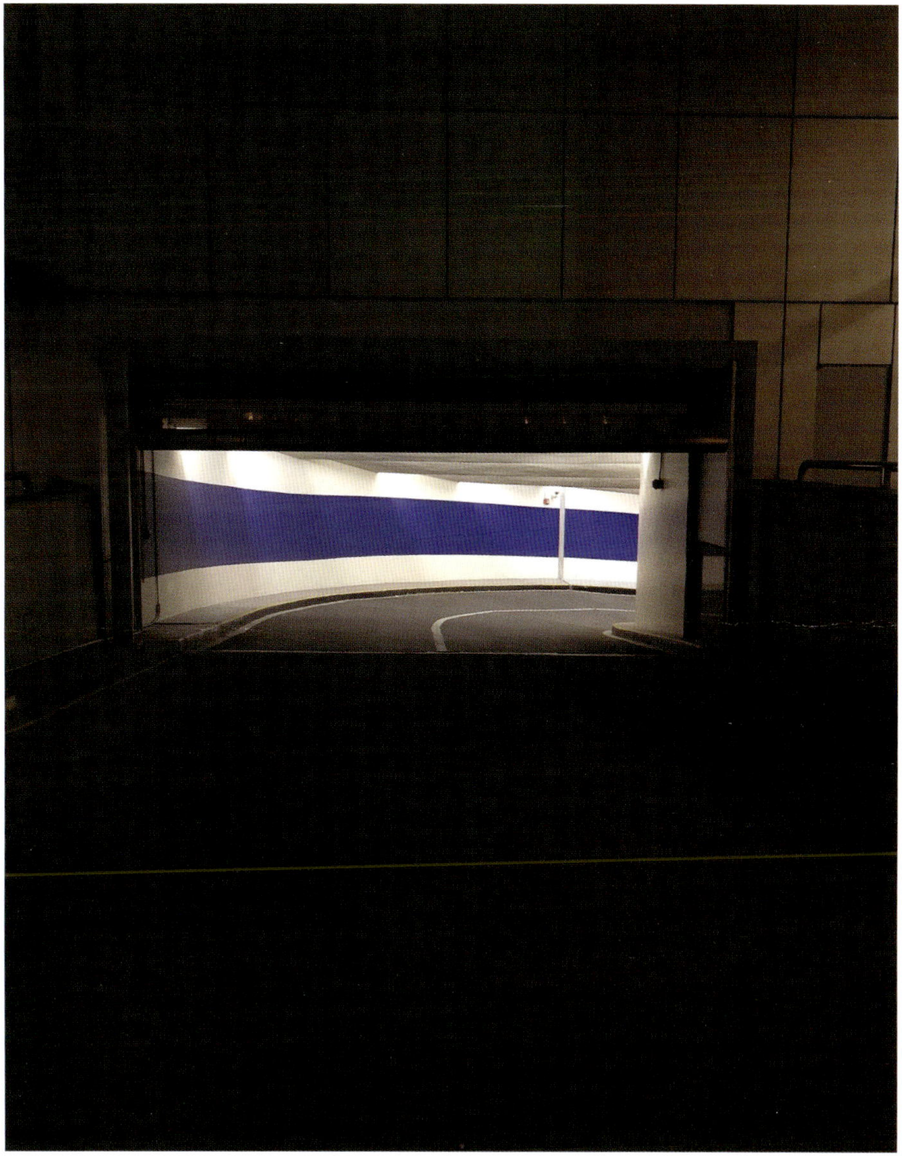

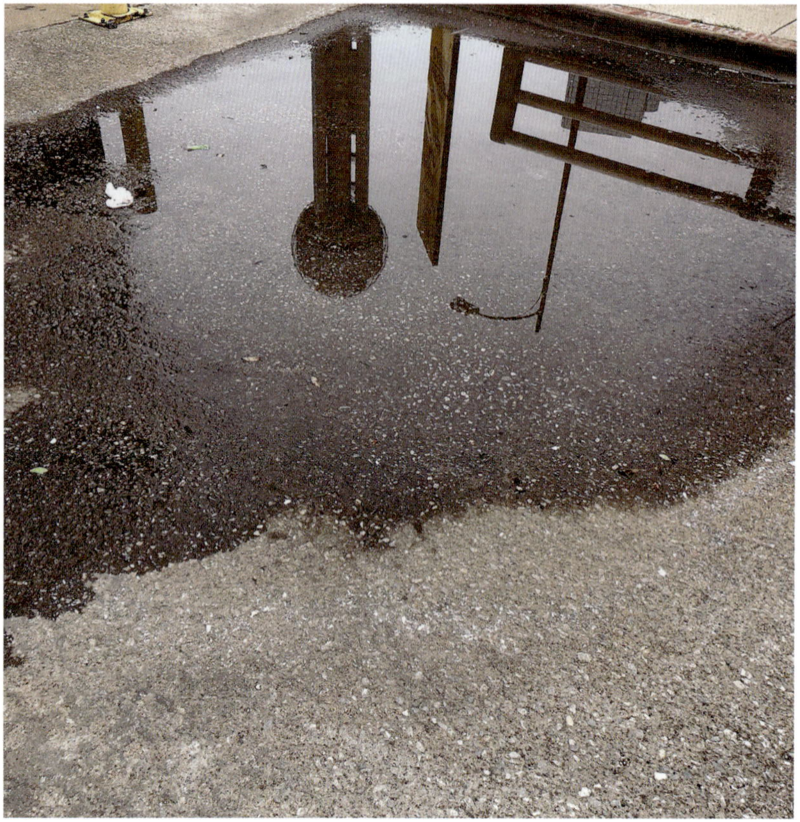

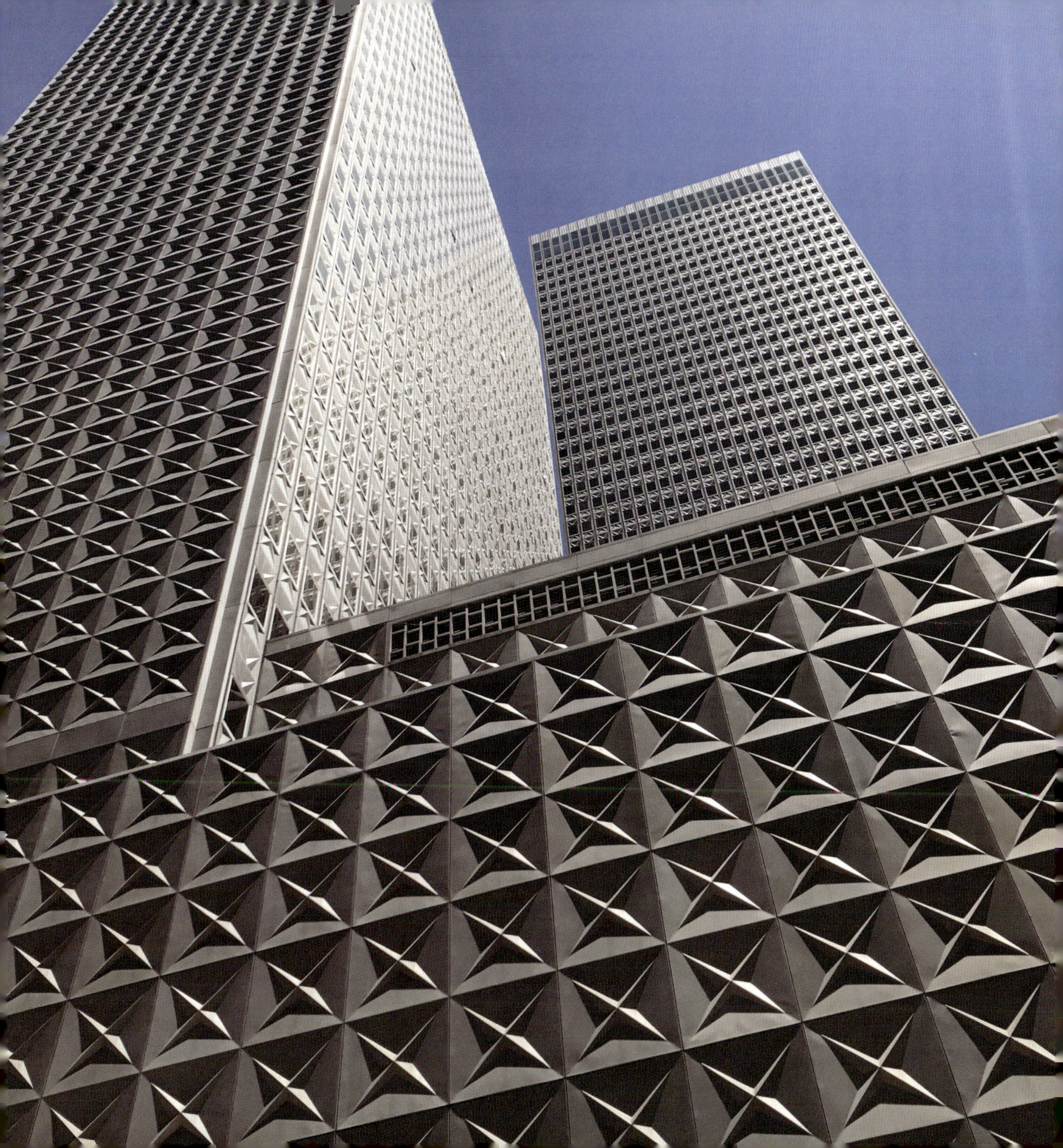

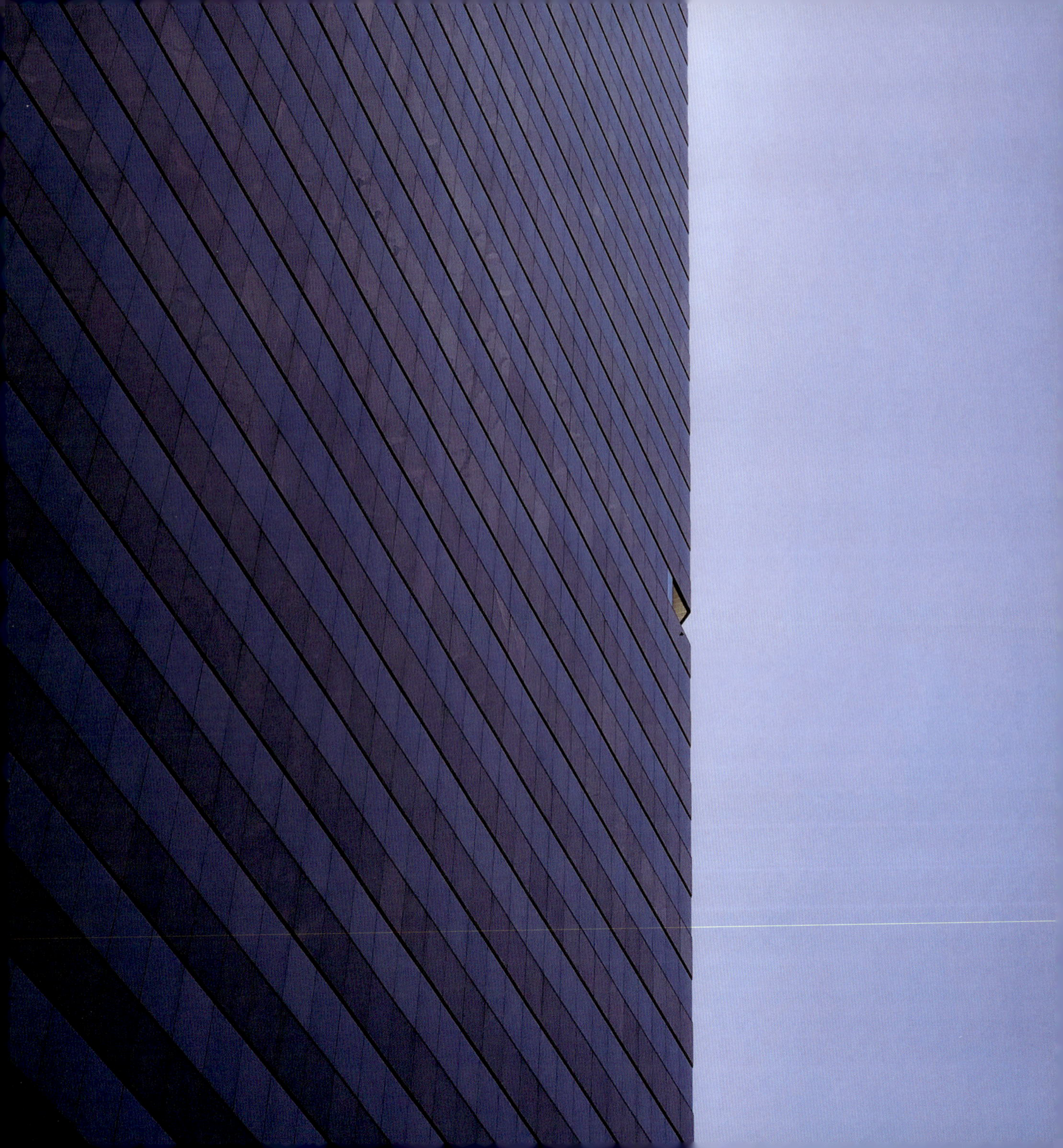

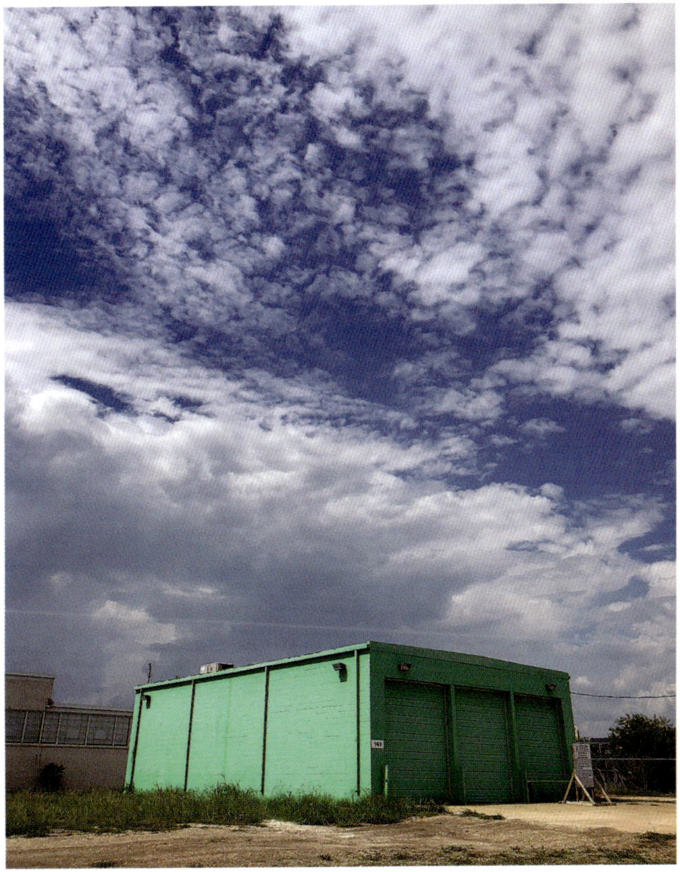

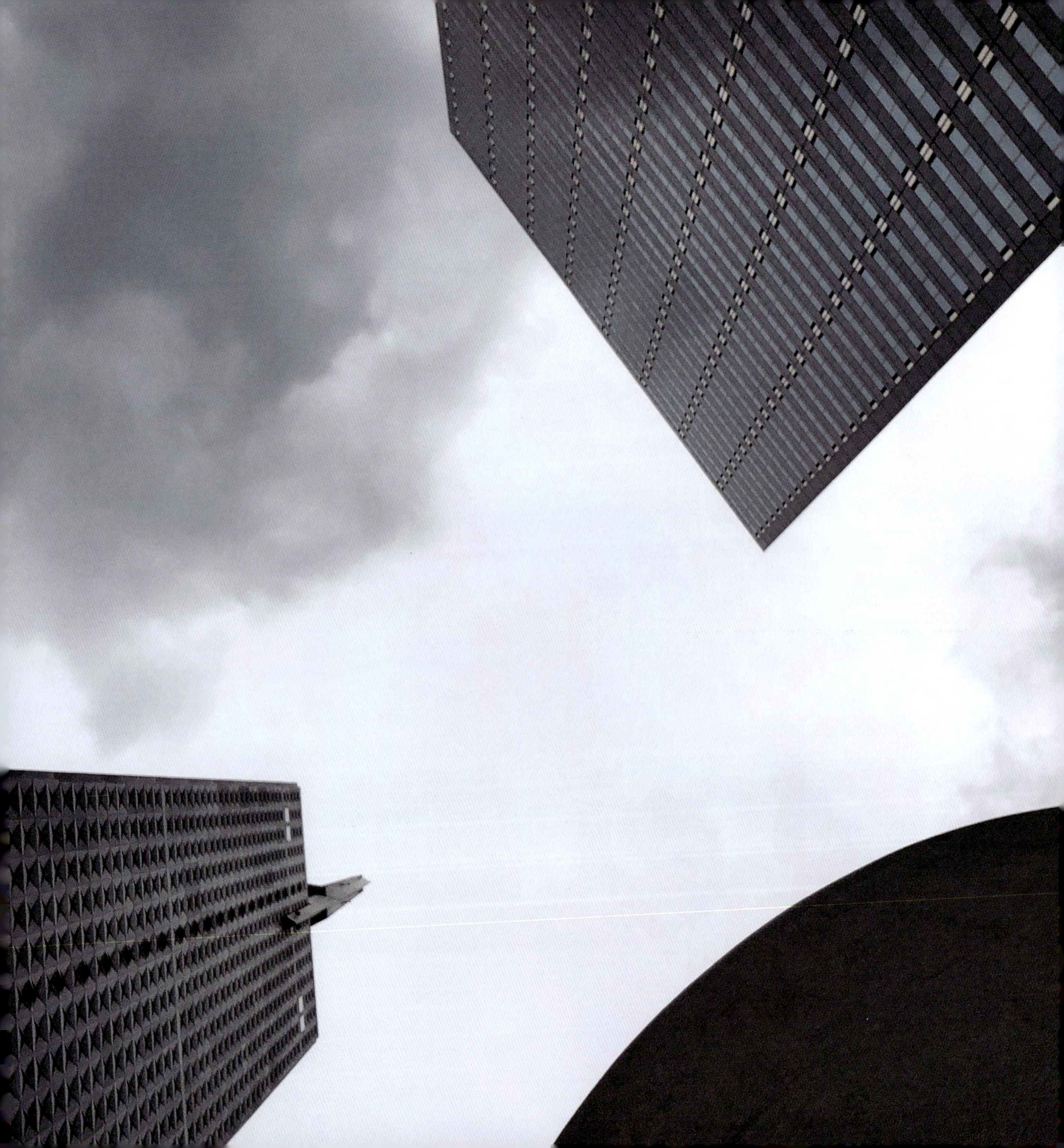

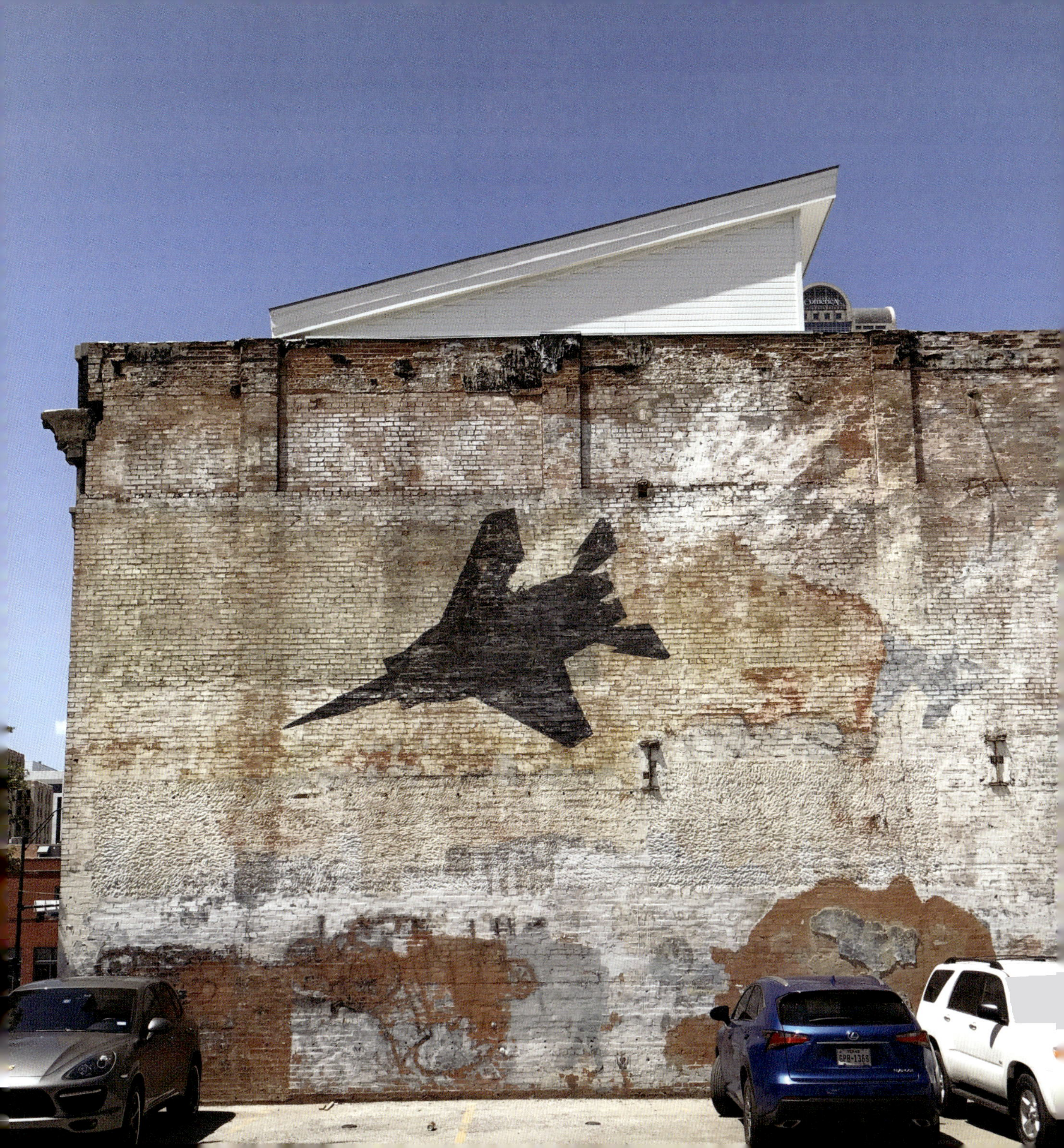

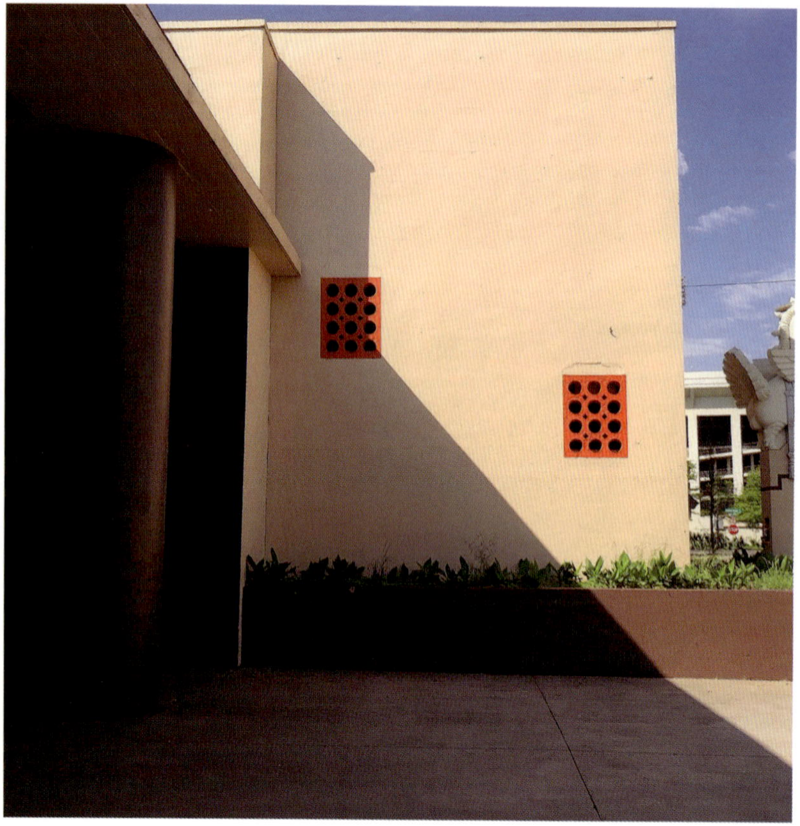

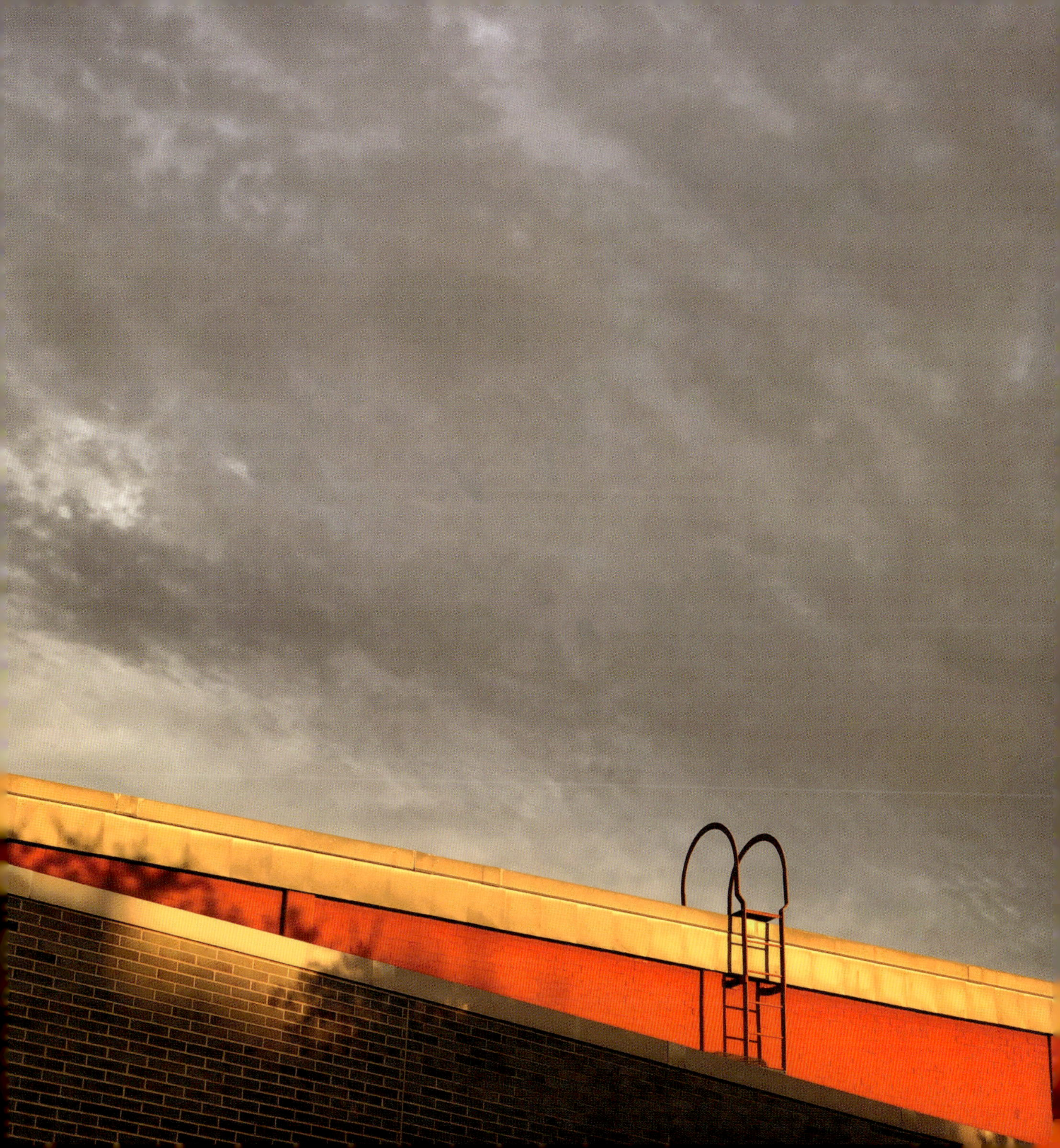

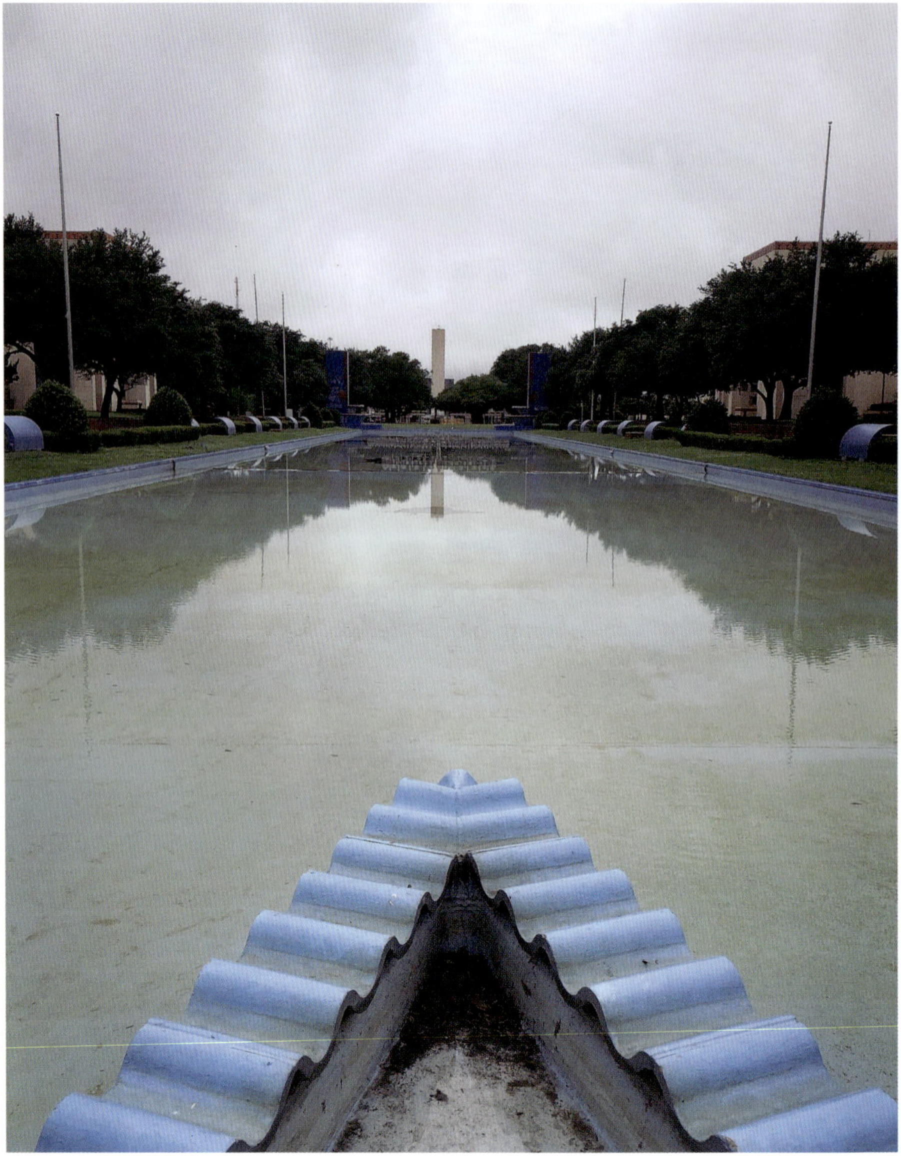

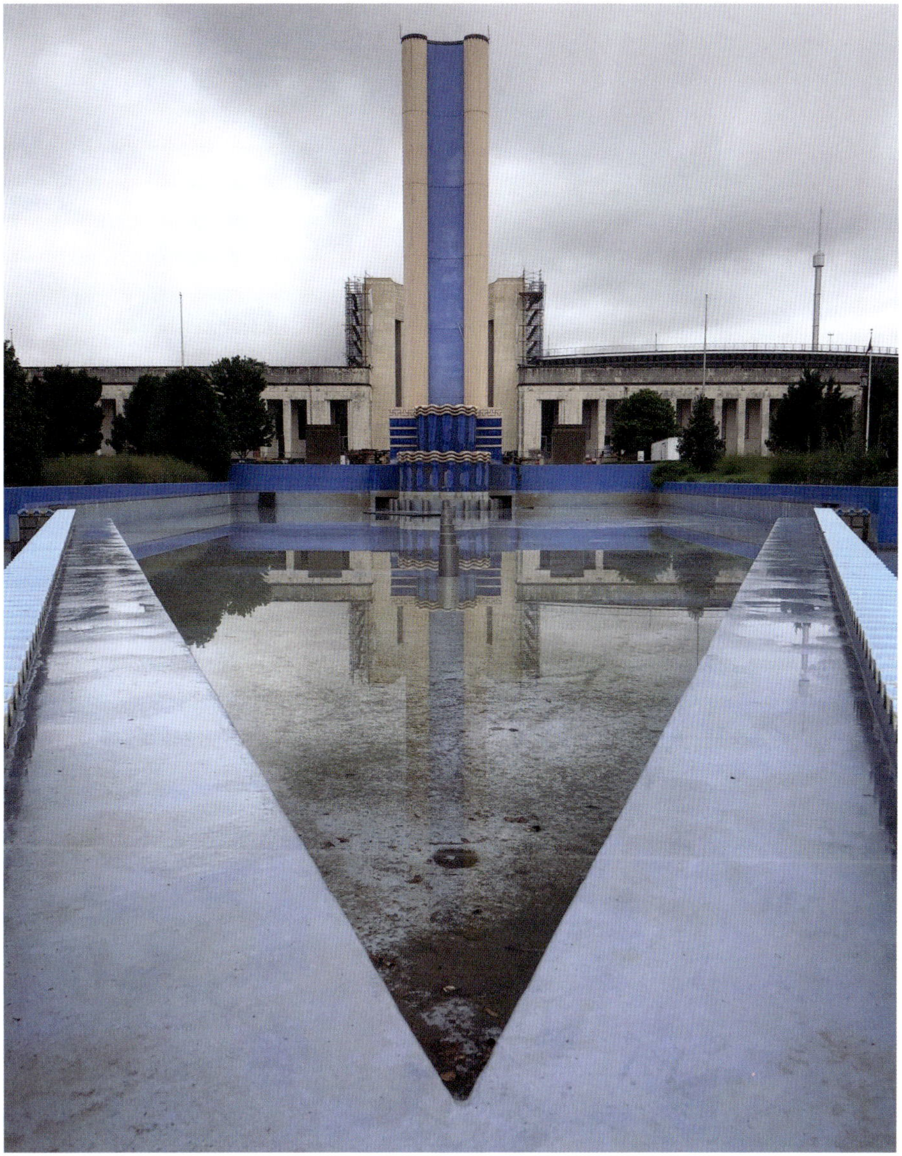

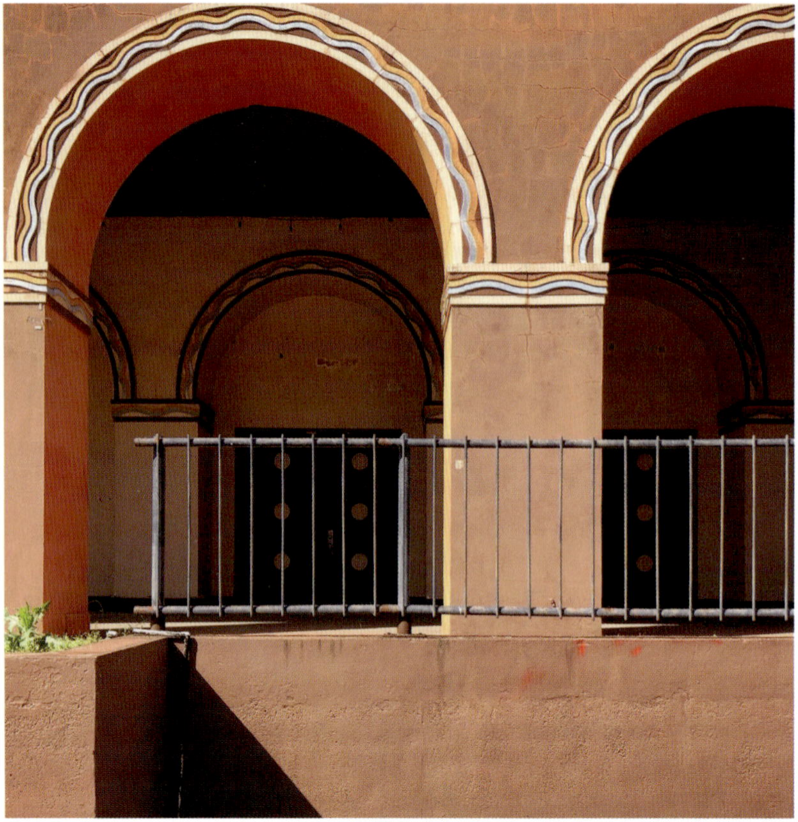

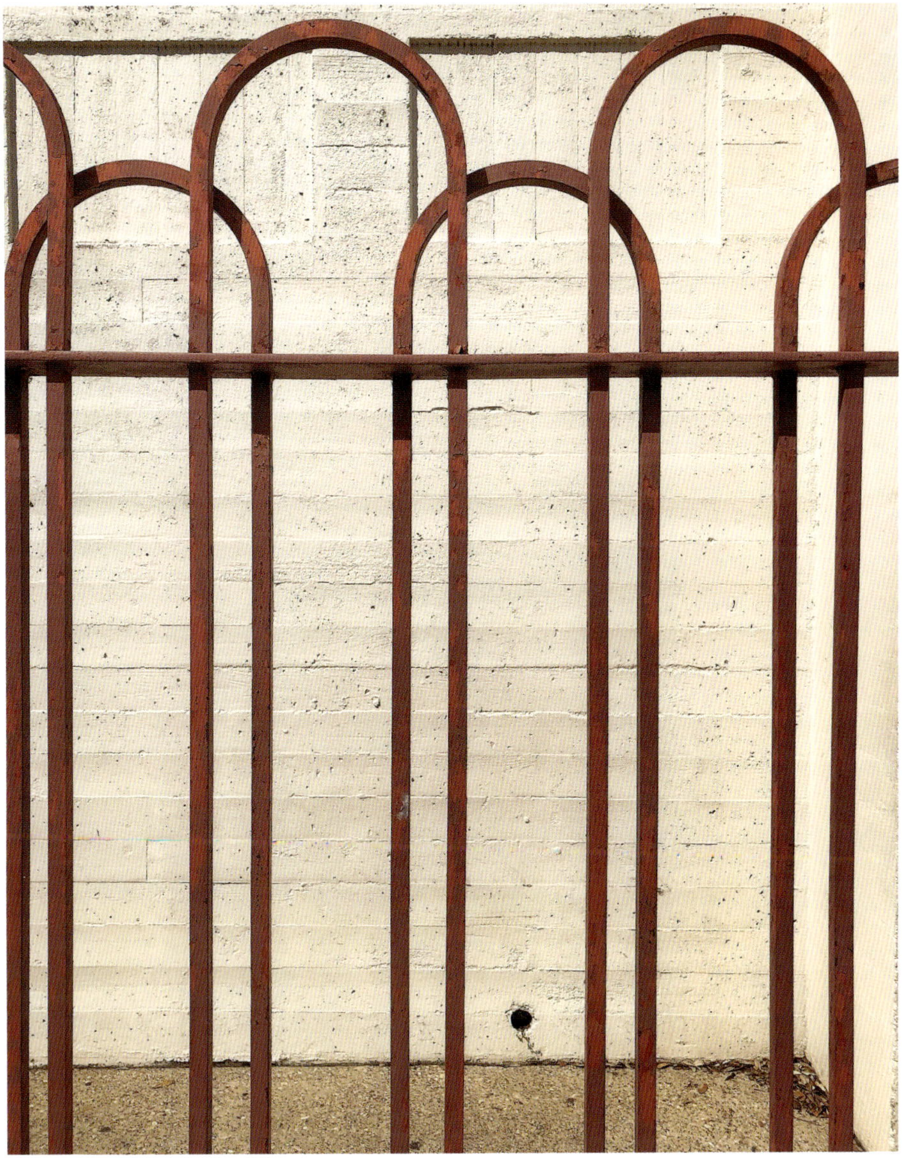

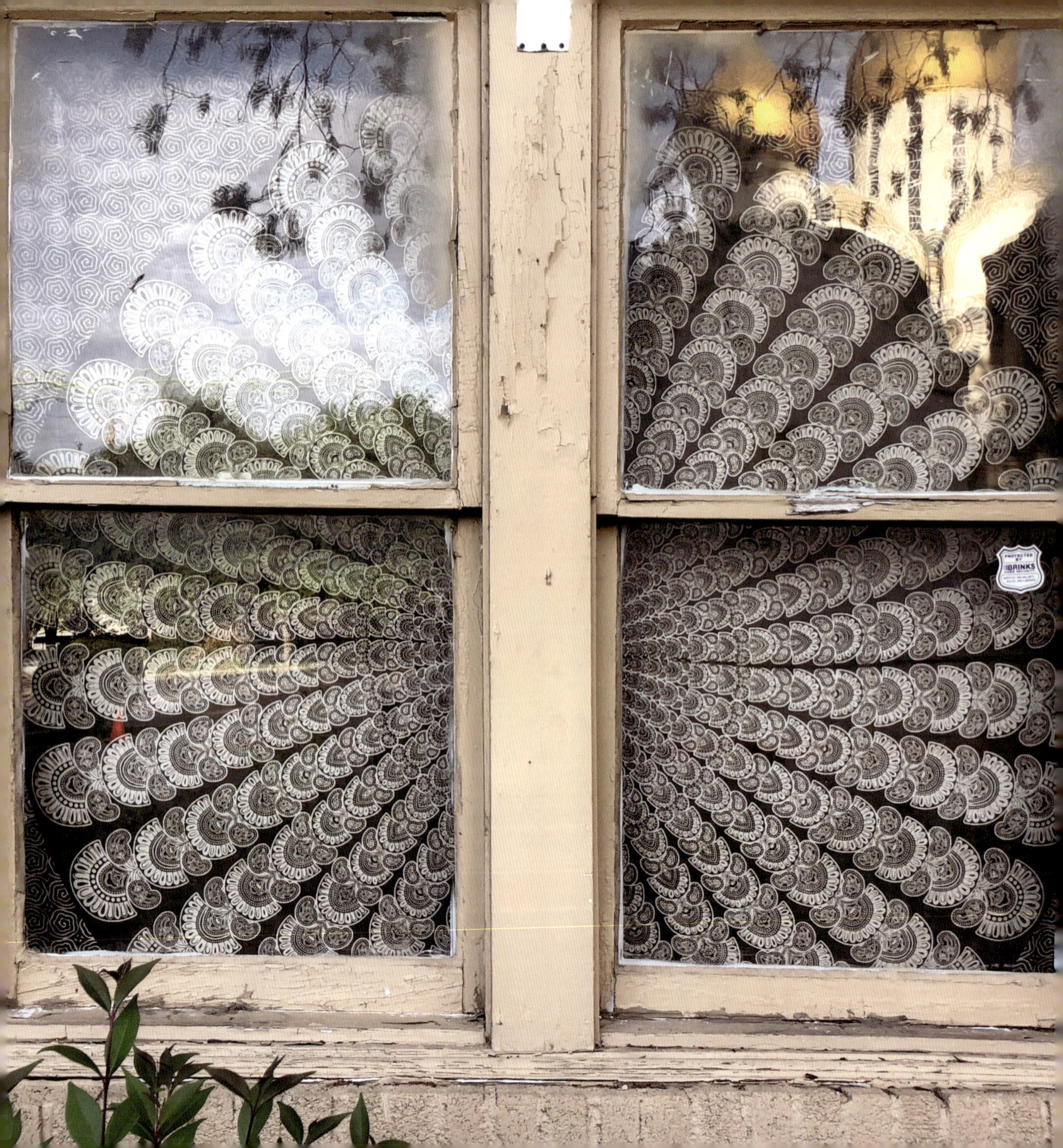
PROTECTED BY
BRINKS

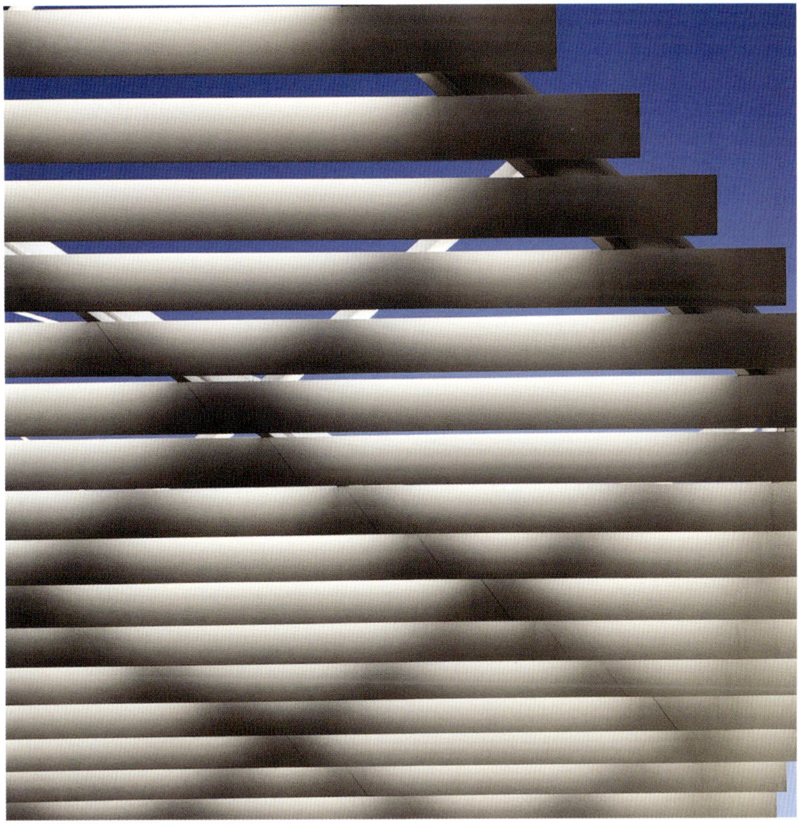

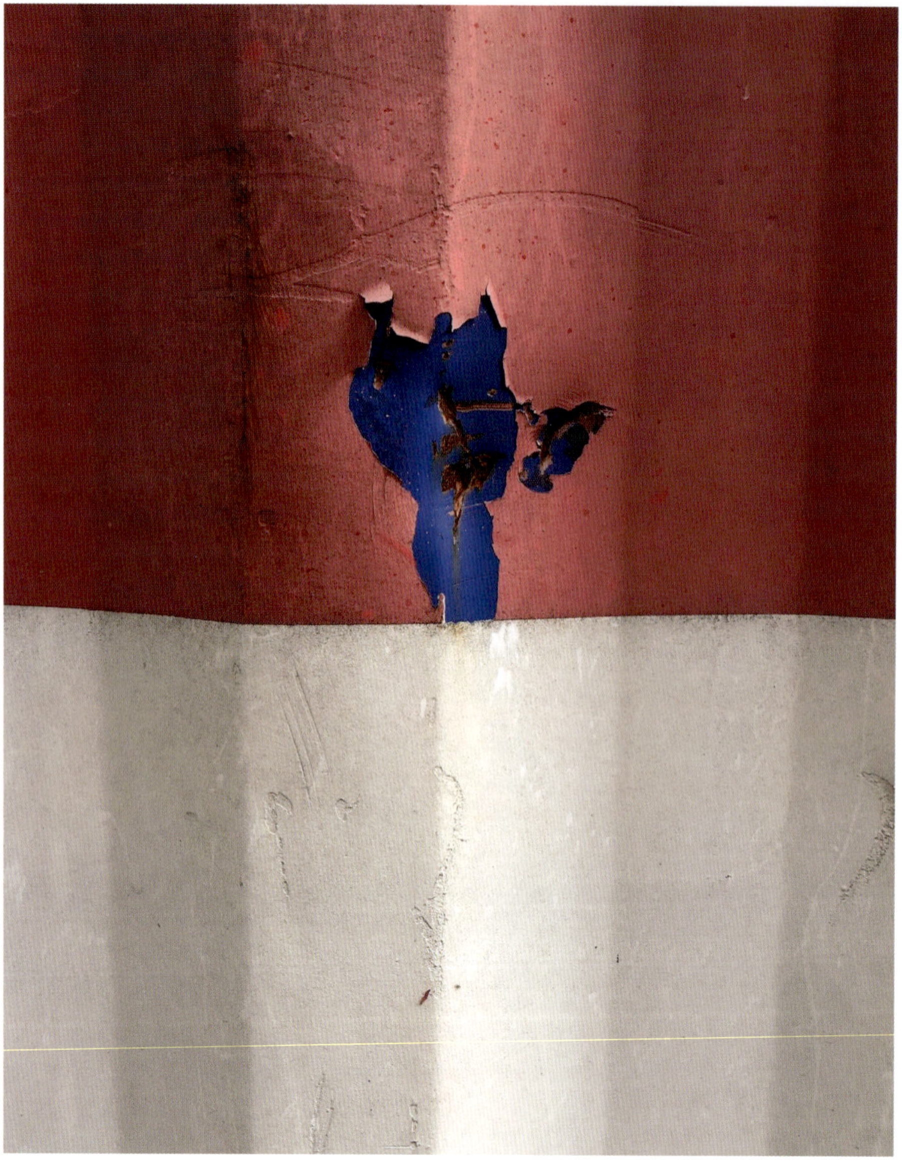

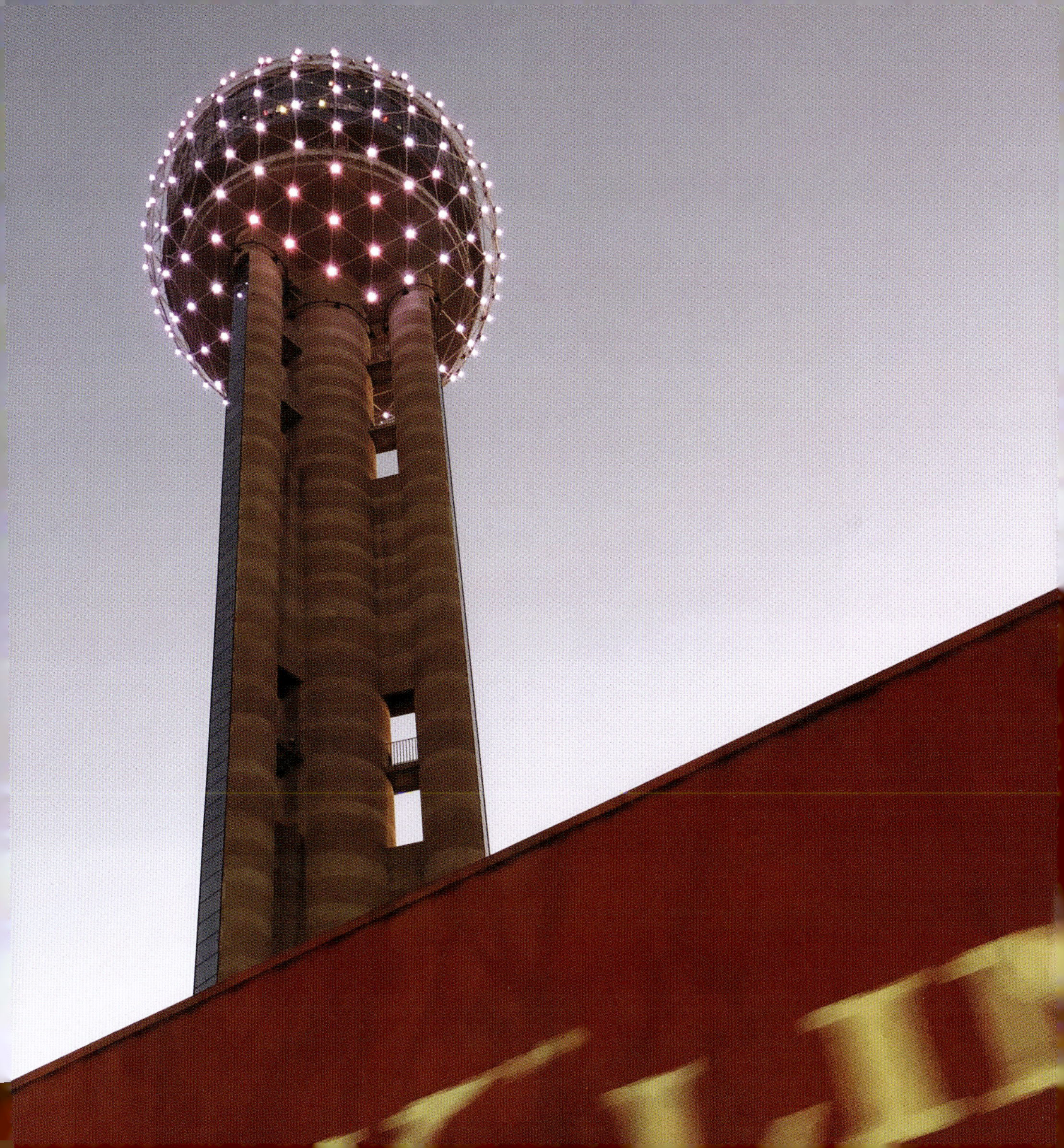

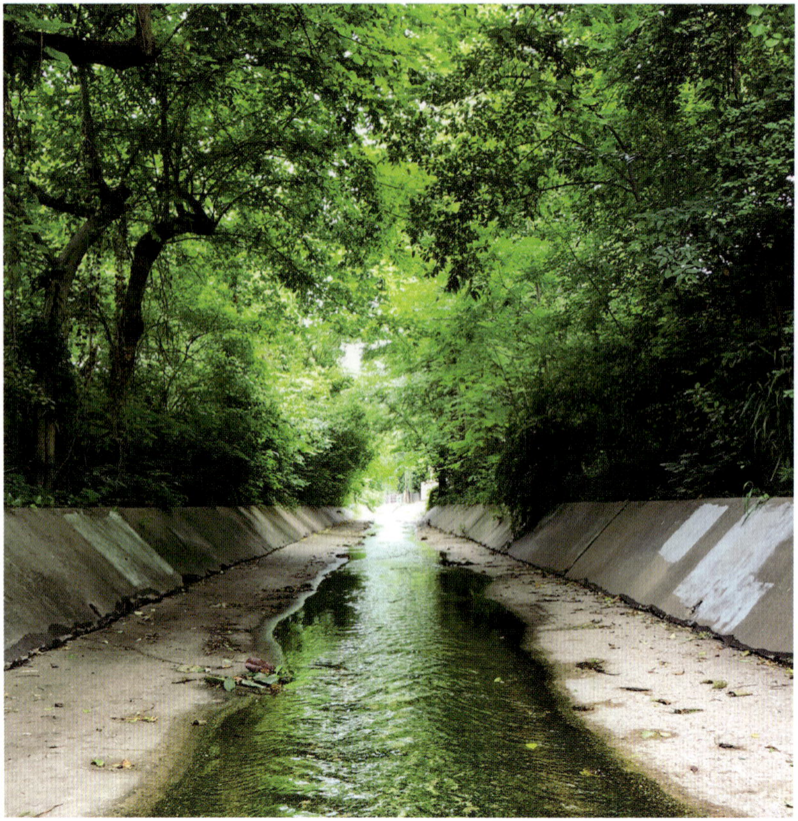

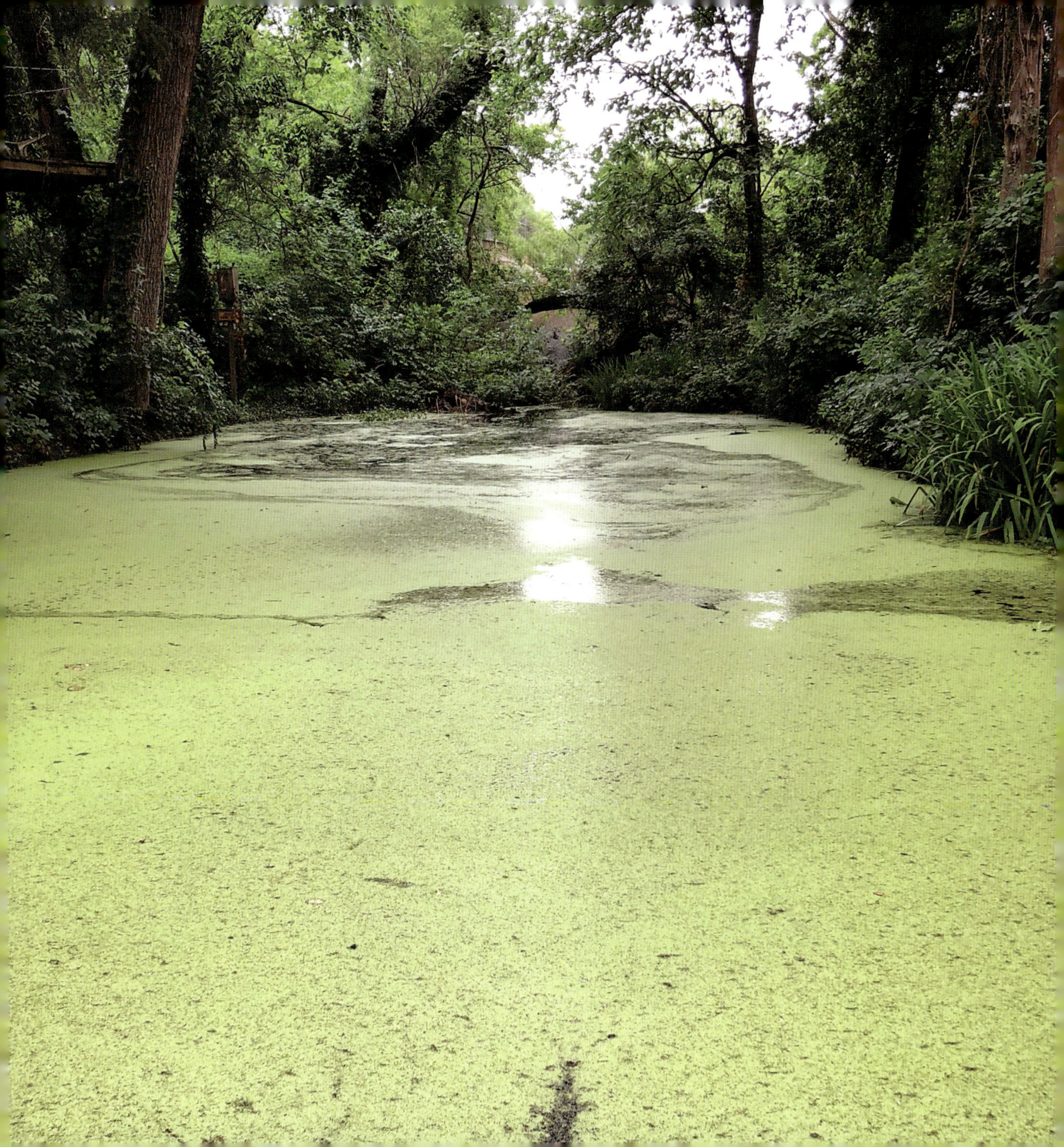

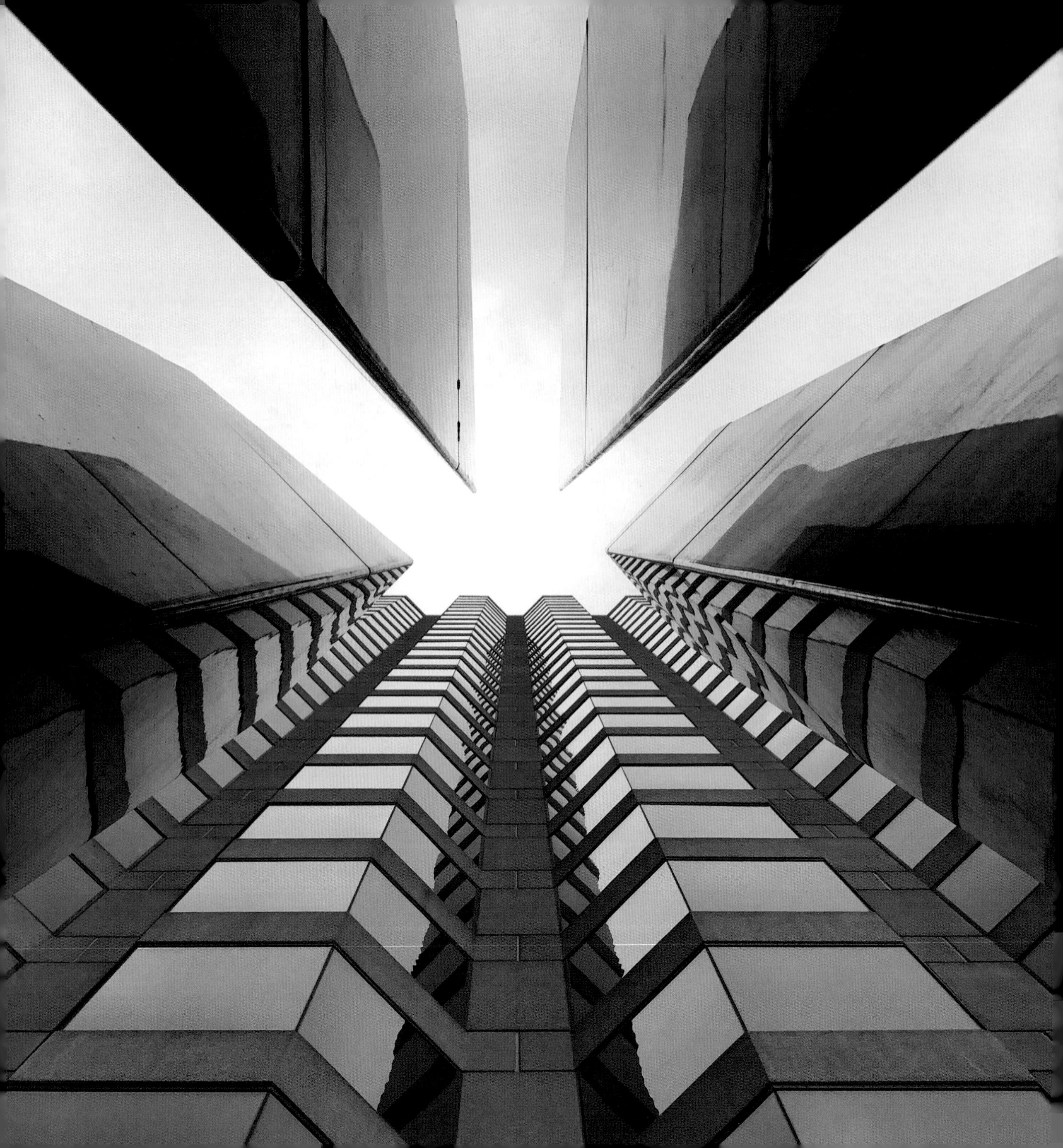

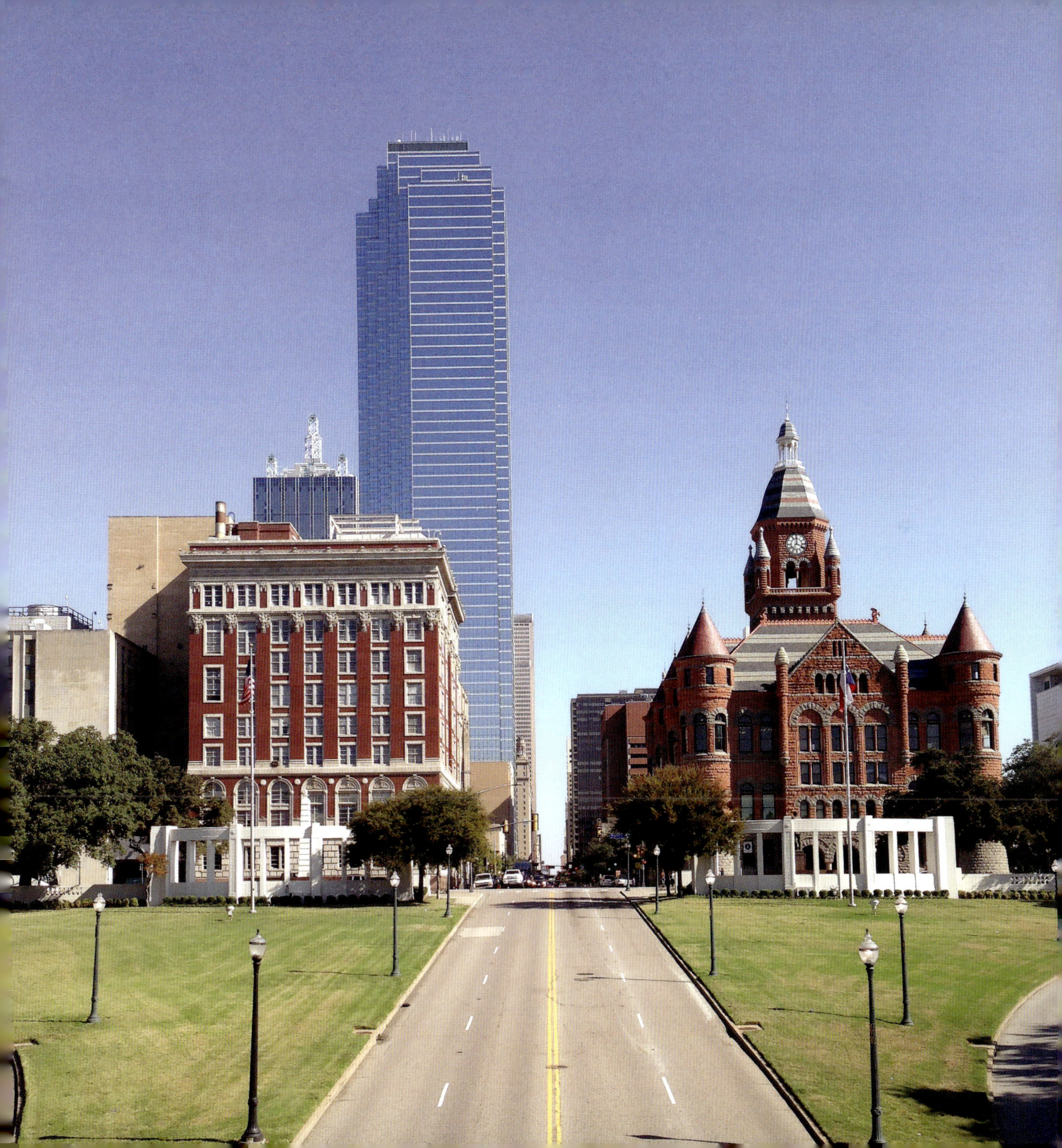

Formerly the music editor at the *Dallas Observer*—and, prior to that, a janitor at an elementary school in West, Texas—Zac Crain is senior editor of *D Magazine*. He has written about the explosion in West, Texas; legendary country singer Charley Pride; Tony Dorsett's struggle with life after football; and imaginary meetings with a mosquito and a Pegasus. He also popularized the phrase, "I see you, Big German!" Crain is the author of 2009's *Black Tooth Grin: The High Life, Good Times, and Tragic End of "Dimebag" Darrell Abbott*. He lives in Dallas.

ACKNOWLEDGMENTS

Thank you to Will Evans and Deep Vellum Publishing, without whom all of this would only exist as an Instagram page and the flicker of an idea that I hesitated to entertain, because I considered myself a writer not a photographer.

Thank you to Brandon Kennedy, Kirby Gann, everyone at *D Magazine*, all those who have patiently listened to me talk about walking with almost zero prompting, Sally, and Isaac Crain—the person I happily share a brain with, and who will one day do better things with it.

Finally, a special thank you to Stefania Morandi for the inspiration, encouragement, design assistance, love, and more than I could ever fully list in this space. This book is for you.

La Reunion

La Reunion Publishing is an imprint of Deep Vellum established in 2019 to share the stories of the people and places of Texas. La Reunion is named after the utopian socialist colony founded by Frenchman Victor Considerant on the west bank of the Trinity River across from the then-fledgling town of Dallas in 1855. Considerant considered Texas as the promised land: a land of unbridled and unparalleled opportunity, with its story yet to be written, and the La Reunion settlers added an international mindset and pioneering spirit that is still reflected in Dallas, and across Texas, today. La Reunion publishes books that explore the story of Texas from all sides, critically engaging with the myths, histories, and the untold stories that make Texas the land of literature come to life.